FARM
BUILDING
CONSTRUCTION

FARM
BUILDING
CONSTRUCTION

MAURICE BARNES

CLIVE MANDER

FARMING PRESS LIMITED
Wharfedale Road, Ipswich
Suffolk IP1 4LG

First published 1986
Second edition 1991
Reprinted 1995

A catalogue record for this book
is available from the British Library

631.2/

ISBN 0852 36234-X

Phototypeset by Galleon Photosetting, Ipswich
Printed in Great Britain by Butler & Tanner, Frome, Somerset

CONTENTS

Foreword to the Second Edition (1991)

More than 10,000 copies sold of Farm Building Construction produced four years ago by these two eminent authors is sufficient proof that farmers and landowners recognise the value of such practical information.

Their second edition is even more valuable and again acknowledges in a more uncertain world that every farming operation is different and the determining factor on investment must be based on business acumen and enterprise.

The farmer of today must be an entrepreneur first and a farmer second, and he cannot afford to invest in expensive buildings or equipment which will not show some cost benefit and improvement in business efficiency. He must also be conscious of the fact that we are moving into open competition in a European market after 1991 where people, goods, services and capital will move freely, through frontiers, and standards affecting the farming and construction industry will be harmonised. The real question is whether that competition will be fair, and only time will tell.

While the face of British agriculture has changed radically in recent years, structural changes at farmstead level have—in many instances—been based on the adaptation of existing buildings, not always ideally suited to modern practice, material handling and slurry removal.

The authors of this book are both practical men who have been associated with the farm building construction industry for many years and their advice is always based on common sense and their wide farming knowledge.

Murphy's law reminds us that when things get difficult we should read the instructions. Those of us who are contemplating DIY farm building have plenty of sound advice available and we can all learn from other people's mistakes. To avoid the risk of more expensive mistakes, this further book provides a very straightforward and simple guide to the basics of our requirements in planning and constructing new farm buildings, including the modification of old buildings, together with the tools and equipment for modern building methods. It sets out the instructions very clearly and concisely, and I am sure farmers and landowners alike will benefit from the collection of ideas for improvement put together in this volume.

There will be increasing pressure to improve and maintain the environment in the countryside and farm buildings feature prominently across the landscape. It is therefore essential that we plan for aesthetic values as well as economic reward.

The Lord Plumb of Coleshill, DL, MEP

Acknowledgments

The authors wish to acknowledge the encouragement, support and help they have had during the preparation of this book from numerous sources. In particular we wish to thank the British Cement Association, the Farm and Rural Buildings Centre, the Ministry of Agriculture, Fisheries and Food, the East of Scotland College of Agriculture and the West of Scotland College, the Centre for Rural Building, the Electricity Council, the Timber Research and Development Association, the Brick Development Association and the Severn Trent Water Company for allowing us to use information from their publications in the text. Some other sources of information are listed below and their co-operation has also been much appreciated.

Finally our thanks to Anne, Ros, Anne and Sally who personally helped during the preparation of the manuscript.

Acknowledgments for Photographs and Figures

George Armitage and Sons plc
Brick Development Association
Bamlett Ltd.
B.C.M. Ltd.
British Cement Association
Challow Agricultural Products Ltd.
Frank H. Dale
Electricity Council
Farm and Rural Buildings Centre
Farmers Weekly
Farmplan Construction Ltd.
Metaquip Ltd.
The Centre for Rural Building
Eternit Ltd.
TRADA
P. A. Turney Ltd.
West of Scotland College of Agriculture

Chapter 1

TO BUILD OR NOT TO BUILD

The Agricultural Need

DRAMATIC CHANGES in farming practice which might dictate a need for new farm buildings are very rare. The move from in-byre or cowshed milking to parlours, for instance, was one such change. But that was in the 1960s! The development of cow cubicles for dairy cows which followed in the 1970s did not result in the same spate of new buildings. Initially it led to alteration and modification rather than the wholesale replacement of buildings.

In the early and mid-1980s the move to winter housing of sheep certainly led to the construction of many buildings for this purpose, but the economics of the enterprise demanded that unsophisticated, simple, low-cost buildings were used, and again conversion of existing buildings has been common.

During the last ten years in the majority of cases, new buildings have been erected either as a result of changes in the balance of enterprises on a farm, an increase in grain acreage at the expense of the livestock enterprise for instance, or the expansion of one particular enterprise— more cows, more sows, more beef animals or more cereals, and in the latter case an increase in yield as well.

It is this aspect of the agricultural need rather than changes in farming practice that has produced the demand for more buildings. This type of change is much easier to budget for and the new buildings, often involving high capital expenditure, can be justified. Perhaps this can also be termed an agricultural need. In many instances, however, it is the financial implications of building that must really hold sway.

Financial Implications

All new buildings will involve high capital expenditure which must be fully justified. In the current economic climate of agriculture this may seem difficult, but farm building construction which thrived in the mid-1970s has continued. Twenty-five-year-old grain stores have become uneconomic to manage—grain handling systems have changed significantly, and the equipment has also increased in size. As grain yields have increased, to retain a flexible marketing strategy ('you can't sell everything off the combine') additional drying and storage facilities have been erected. The budgets for these buildings have not always revealed healthy returns but they have been built nonetheless—the management factors having overridden the budgetary ones.

Replacement or additional dairy buildings were particularly difficult to justify in the mid-1980s, but between 1980 and 1984 investment in new silos more than doubled. The move to silage production as a method of conserving grass continued and the pressure was on for lower milk production costs. Despite the difficult economic climate this type of building or structure could be justified.

Political and conservation pressures can sometimes override the solely economic ones too. In 1991 new measures were introduced to reduce the risk of streams, rivers and other water sources becoming polluted. This may influence the decision of some farmers to build, almost despite the budgeting. This could be termed the financial implication of not building—pollute and face a fine, build and there is no pollution.

In the UK climate it seems that it is not possible to farm efficiently without good buildings. The financial implications of the do-it-yourself building are mentioned briefly in Chapter 3. The biggest saving to be made is in the cost of labour, but it is important to realise that when going it alone you will have to be your own surveyor or architect, quantity surveyor or estimating department of the builder/contractor. You will also have to be foreman and ganger— one organises the labour and the other checks it, as well as accountant, in addition to your primary role as the farmer/customer. There is no doubt that one of the biggest financial implications of do-it-yourself building could be the loss of 'farming' time. Some enthusiasts have been known to let the 'hobby' take precedence over the 'business'. That may be fun but it may also be expensive!

Tenancies produce specific problems. On some occasions it is possible that tenants will be undertaking building work independently of their landlords. The financial implications of this type of work must be negotiated in advance with the landlord or his agents. They will be very different from the owner/occupier circumstances.

Sources of Advice

There are innumerable sources of advice to help but it would be quite unrealistic to contemplate seeking help from them all. As has already been implied the initial decision must be taken on the basis of the agricultural and management needs and the financial benefits. Advice in this area can be obtained from ADAS (the Agricultural Development and Advisory Service) as well as from the Department of Agriculture in Northern Ireland, Scotland and Wales and the Colleges of Agriculture in Scotland. Advice can also be sought from professional management consultants including, of course, your accountant and your bank.

Not least among the financial matters on which advice may be needed are the influence of taxation and the latest tax changes on investment. In 1984 the late autumn budget made vast inroads into the investment allowances on farm buildings. It became even more important to achieve value for money and DIY construction became even more attractive.

On building design matters, again ADAS, the Department of Agriculture and Colleges can be of assistance. In addition it would be advisable to consult the local planning officer, the Water or National Rivers Authorities as well as the special interest bodies. These include the various advisory agencies also listed on page 215.

This book is concerned with building techniques but even a volume of this size cannot cover every aspect in detail. Engineering and farm building construction overlap to a large extent. Welding, for example, has not been included here but the repair of gates is well within the scope of most DIY builders.

The appearance of farm buildings and other aspects of conservation are topics which must be considered at the design stage. These will be discussed in more detail in Chapter 2, but the limited planning control and the non-rating of farm buildings places the responsibility to do a good, tidy job on the farmer.

Legislation and Regulation

To many considering do-it-yourself construction, this is the aspect of the building operation that is most daunting. 'Prior approval' from the Government before the start of building a grant aidable scheme is not always necessary as such but it is a good idea to discuss any proposals with the government agency responsible. In the UK your application for grant must be 'acknowledged' by this agency before work commences. In most instances, Scotland being a notable exception, it is not necessary for farm buildings to comply with the Building Regulations either, so the local building control offices will not be involved in many cases. Again it is a good idea to consult them.

The local planning officers can be most helpful as well on the appearance and landscaping of buildings. In many parts of Great Britain, some form of planning approval, as distinct from Building Regulation approval, will be necessary. At the moment any building which exceeds 465 square metres separately or when combined with another building within 90 m erected in the last two years is subject to planning approval, as is a building exceeding 12 m in height or one that is nearer than 25 m to a classified road. The 'planners' are not the ogres it was once fashionable to imagine them to be.

From 1988 buildings for livestock including

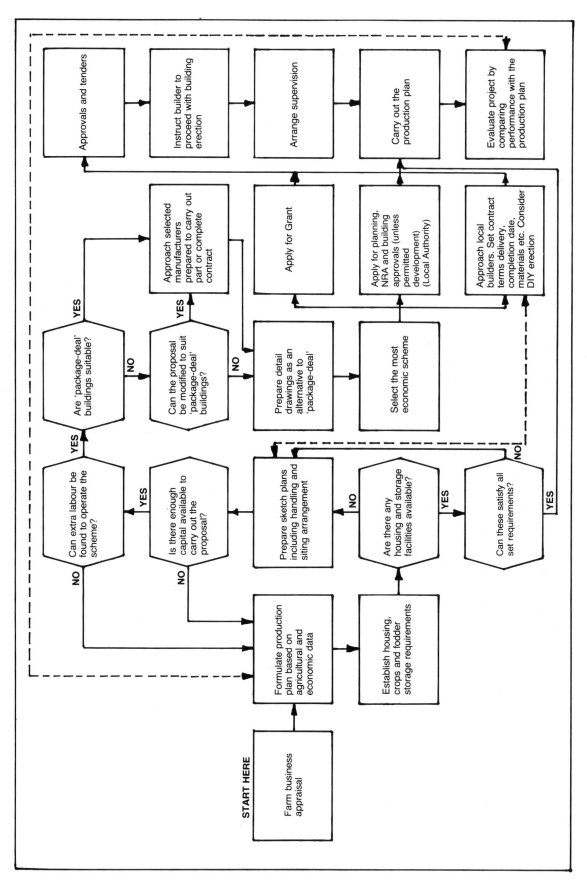

Figure 1.1 The Planning Process. Broken lines indicate comparisons, rectangles indicate action required and hexagons decision required.

extensions, and slurry stores of all forms, were subject to planning controls if located within 400 m of a protected building—generally dwellings and places of work occupied by non-farming people.

Buildings were being considered under what was termed the 'cordon sanitaire' and applications required full plans, elevations and other details for approval by the local planning authority. Smell, dust and noise were all considered but in particular the risk of pollution was paramount.

In 1991 new planning controls on farm and forestry buildings were introduced by the Government. Controls over the siting, design and external appearance of the buildings, which already operated in the National Parks, were extended to England and Wales.

Controls cover not only new buildings, but 'significant' extensions and alterations, farm and forestry roads, and certain excavations and engineering operations.

Planning authorities will take account not only of visual amenity but also specified nature conservation and heritage issues.

Controls over livestock units will be changed. Under the original 1988 amendment to the general development order, general farm buildings put up within 400 m (440 yds) of houses and other buildings could be used for livestock after five years. This rule will be abolished. This limitation is to be significantly extended.

Even more powerful legislation in relation to pollution was introduced in 1991 when the Pollution Control Regulations (slurry, silage and farm fuel oil) came into being. The approval of the National Rivers Authority must be sought for the use of all new structures covered by the Regulations. Perhaps the most critical of these regulations is that silos and slurry stores may not be built closer than 10 m to a water course and must be impermeable.

The Health & Safety Inspectorate are also much better as friends than enemies. Their demands are almost always 'reasonable'. Strange as it may seem they are as much concerned about your own health and welfare as they are about the health and welfare of your employees. They are there to protect you from yourself in some instances!

At present the Codes of Practice for animal welfare are not mandatory and are unlikely to be retrospective if they are made mandatory, but they have not been assembled by a 'load of cranks'. They represent the views of good, sound, practical farmers as well as those of veterinarians and others and should therefore be heeded. Your local ADAS office can give details of the relevant Codes for your project and where they can be purchased.

In 1991, in the United Kingdom most farm buildings are not subject to grant by the Government. For those that are the actual percentage of total costs that will be paid as grant changes quite frequently. In June 1991 under the Farm and Conservation Grant Scheme it was 50 per cent. It applied particularly to the installation and improvement of waste-handling facilities to avoid the risk of pollution. Information can be obtained at any local Ministry or Department of Agriculture office.

There are two bases for claiming a grant. One is termed *Actual Costs*, when all receipted invoices for labour and materials (including second-hand materials), supervisory or professional fees, as well as time sheets for your farm workers' labour, are submitted. The grant will then be paid as a percentage of the total 'Actual Cost'. The other basis is termed *Standard Costs*. In this instance there is a standard specification which should be referred to and used for materials and methods of construction – it is not permitted to use second-hand materials in this scheme with the exception of hardcore. When the work is complete the Ministry or Department of Agriculture should receive a list of quantities of the completed work, e.g. X square metres of concrete, 150 mm thick; Y cubic metres of excavation, etc. The Standard Cost has been set for all these items and grant is payable as a percentage of these Standard Costs.

The Planning Process

The Centre for Rural Building has produced an excellent chart* which takes in many of the processes we have already considered (Figure 1.1).

*CERMAK, J. P., *Farm Buildings, the Planning Approach*, SFBIU, March 1974.

Chapter 2

PLANNING THE BUILDING

Farmstead Layout

THERE ARE a few basic rules and objectives when planning and siting new buildings. Objectives such as disease control may conflict with the landscape designer's perspective of how buildings might be arranged. A great many factors need balancing and a compromise reached. Some important considerations are as follows, but the list is not necessarily comprehensive and certain aspects change with time, e.g. new methods, larger lorries, disease control precautions and more recent security problems of trespass, vandalism and theft. Appropriate landscaping is a craft in itself, and buildings should not just be hidden by leylandii. Historically farmsteads were probably built near a plentiful water supply but the fact that they were not always situated in a valley bottom suggests that farmers knew plenty of air movement gave healthier stock.

Clean Side—Dirty Side

Much as an airport will have strict zones either side of a customs barrier an ambition for any farmstead must be to have a reception area for visitors and delivery drivers clear of contamination from slurry, mud or straw. This clean area should allow for parking, the farm office, the farmhouse and rest rooms, etc. The only buildings opening onto this area might be for storage and perhaps for a grain store or farm workshop. All livestock and associated feeding and waste systems are contained on the 'dirty' side. A pig farm may best illustrate these points whereupon for reasons of hygiene the feed lorry is not allowed 'dirty' side but delivers food into hoppers placed at the perimeter. Pigs for market are walked along a race to a truck parked 'clean' side and employees approach through a shower/locker room with their clean clothes and work clothes placed accordingly.

In many situations a second entrance for tractors, cows and muck spreaders may be desirable because the advent of a clean area pre-supposes that it can easily be kept clean and tidy.

Uphill—Downhill

Much of the routine work on a farm is a simple materials-handling problem. It is always worth remembering that gravity will help. With a sloping site, place the feed uphill, the livestock in the middle and the waste system downhill.

With the requirement to control all dirty water run off, some collection system will always be necessary on the lower side of a livestock enterprise. It will be helpful if this can be properly planned and all the farm waste dealt with in one facility, being mindful that methods and legislation may produce yet more change. An example is that control of odour may become a stringent requirement and slurry stores may need covering or the contents aerating. Methane is a greenhouse gas and one may guess at future requirements to reduce its effect.

Neighbours

The advent of the 400 m rule within the planning regulations for livestock enterprises may produce difficulty on some established units (see also pages 10 and 12). Whilst the law does not apply in reverse, at least the farmer now has a strong case for objection if housing or other development is proposed within 400 m of his existing unit. Many who have sold a barn for conversion within an existing steading may now rue the day.

Neighbour troubles will become increasingly difficult to resolve because the environmental health officer now has increased powers to control noise and smell and such problems are best overcome by careful siting wherever possible.

Drainage

It should now be considered essential to keep storm water separate from dirty water to minimise slurry storage requirement. Ironically if a mechanical slurry separator is installed its throughput will be much greater working with a thin slurry than a thick one and a controlled degree of storm water dilution may be desirable.

Layout

Wherever possible buildings should be set out in straight parallel lines which enable machinery, particularly feeders, to operate in the most efficient manner. Buildings should always be planned with possible extension in mind and not hemmed in by a silo or slurry store wrongly situated. The width of a building may often be dictated by factors such as airflow considerations in an underfloor duct or the natural ventilation requirement of a cattle yard whereas length is immaterial. There are practical upper size limits for many units but these are more management considerations. 300 cows is about maximum for one UK unit because of grassland damage as they walk for grazing. 500 sows is a fair number for a pig unit before slurry and disease control factors suggest it may be better to start another unit on a fresh site. Poultry produce similar problems.

Cost

Electricity supply, water supply, roads, yards and aprons can be significant on cost to a building on any given site. All the above considerations may give little choice but to bear such cost. A certain site may be cheaper to develop in the short-term but the long-term effect of poor decisions may have repercussions for 25 to 50 years or even longer. Cost is a major factor but should be the last consideration if all the above is taken into account.

Site Selection

If money is unlimited it is unlikely that a do-it-yourself building is being planned! Therefore it is unlikely that the building will be erected on a green field site. That would be regarded by many as the height of luxury. If money is limited, and this must surely be the main reason for do-it-yourself construction, apart from the sheer pleasure and satisfaction of seeing your job well done, then extensions, adaptations and buildings close to or even within the existing farm building complex are much more likely.

The factors which influence the siting of the building are likely to be:

- Access to roads and other buildings related to the enterprise. Plenty of space should be left for vehicle movement (see Chapter 17)—10 m between buildings is desirable as the minimum.
- Aspect. Open-fronted stock buildings will normally face south or south-east.
- Services. These will be expensive to take long distances. Special provision may be necessary for the collection of silage effluent, isolation of excreta from diseased animals, etc.
- Falls and the amount of cut and/or fill—see Chapter 6. Both are expensive and fill is unsuitable for silos in particular because of the risk of pollution. Handling of materials must be worked out at this stage—the amount of uphill movement being kept to a minimum.
- Isolation of animals. New incoming stock may need special facilities.
- Bearing pressures of soils. Retaining walls need good ground for economic designs.
- Sites of special scientific interest, within a National Park or for other reasons of interest to conservationists will all need special consideration.
- Space requirements. See Appendix 1 for details.

Access

The arrival of five- and six-axle articulated vehicles onto farms and the increasing size of farm transport have revolutionised the demand for space in and around farm buildings. The three metres wide road and passageway between buildings is almost a thing of the past. It is a matter of pride to many truck and tractor drivers that they can negotiate the most difficult of alleyways and reverse their vehicles to pinpoint accuracy. But this pride could be at your expense. It is your job to protect your buildings—do not forget the effect of downpipes on widths of access. The driver's external rear-view mirrors may project 300 mm beyond his vehicle and the inner swept area (see Figure 2.1) of a big articulated lorry is very different from that of a rigid truck.

Big-bale handlers and forage waggons also need plenty of space, particularly to avoid the '3 point' or even 4, 5 and 6 point turns! (Figures 2.2 and 2.3).

Apart from the cost of the extra paved area, although this may be significant, an increase in space between buildings where vehicle access is the primary concern is unlikely to add greatly to material handling time. A loaded forklift truck will travel the extra few metres in a matter of seconds. The same is not true of animal movement however. Minimum distances not only reduce time but they also reduce stress and injury to the animals, and so this needs careful consideration.

If pigs and beef animals are to be weighed regularly, the races, crushes, treatment areas and other special requirements must be located carefully. Gates and fences must be properly designed and the equipment selected with care. The 'on and off' loading of animals must also be considered. Ramps and even weighbridges must not be ruled out.

Soil Types

The soil type will influence its bearing capacity; it will determine the amount of excavation necessary to achieve a reasonable bearing capacity, how much this changes with moisture content, the thickness of load-spreading subbase needed, the thickness of concrete foundations, how much 'heave' or lift with frost penetration, and so on. The chapter on foundations gives some realistic assessment of the differences and how they are recognised. Suffice to say at this stage that soil type is significant to the builder.

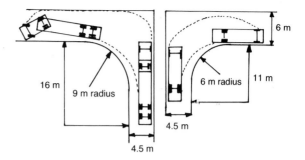

Figure 2.1 Typical swept areas of articulated lorries and rigid trucks.

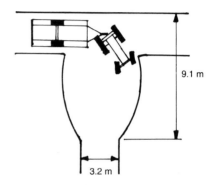

Figure 2.2 Big bale handler on front end loader.

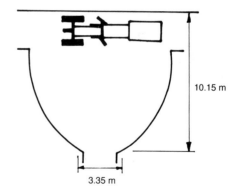

Figure 2.3 Reverse turn with large forage box.

It is important to know what the soil is on the site in question of course. Thorough investigation is essential. It would be unwise to assume either uniformity of soil or knowledge of soil type. Exploratory pits at least one metre deep should be dug. It is better to dig them on the perimeter of the proposed building area but some should be taken out within the building if retaining walls or column foundations are involved. It is essential to backfill these pits properly, in compacted layers, to ensure that subsequent settlement does not occur. Auger tests are a satisfactory alternative but in areas with high ground water levels these may be less conclusive than pits.

It has already been mentioned that the local building control officers can be helpful. This is particularly true with regard to soil types and the presence of sulphates in the soil. If these are known to be present in your area the additional cost of using a sulphate-resistant cement in the footings may pay handsome dividends. Sulphates will attack concrete, but high cement, low water content mixes with sulphate-resisting cement almost completely prevent this form of attack. It would be unwise to use a normal foundation quality concrete (GEN3 or ST4) in these circumstances.

Material Selection

When choosing materials the decision is mainly one of personal preference—influenced by price. The cheapest building is likely to have a steel frame, concrete block walls and fibre/cement sheeting for the roof. The floor will almost certainly be of concrete. Fortunately for the do-it-yourself builder these are also the easiest materials to deal with.

In Chapter 8 the relative merits of framed and traditional materials are outlined. But the *traditional* methods should not be forgotten; for small spanned structures they are very competitive and truly DIY. For spans over 8 m however, the portal frame comes into its own. For really large spans, 25 m and over, steel has no competitor. Such large dimensions are a real disadvantage in livestock buildings though, making ventilation extremely difficult. For grain and potato stores they have some appeal but even for these enterprises the length of lateral ducts for efficient ventilation is limited, and small parcels of different varieties of a crop are extremely difficult to separate in such large sheds. Careful thought is needed before any commitment to one of these very large span buildings. It might be a very big monument to your error.

Frames

The choice of material for the frames, as has been mentioned, is usually determined by personal preference and cost. Concrete may well be the most expensive but ought to be the most durable (Plate 2.1). Timber is likely to be more expensive than steel but may appeal on aesthetic grounds. Many people feel that a timber building fits well in the landscape (Plate 2.2). Steel is normally the cheapest material but may need some special protection in some environments (Plate 2.3). Concrete is said to have disadvantages because it is difficult to fix into but with modern percussion drills—these have a positive hammer action built in rather than just vibration (the technique employed on small household drills)—fixing into concrete is no longer a problem. The main reinforcing steel must be avoided though.

Fixing with timber or steel is not a problem, of course, but again the correct equipment is necessary, and for timber, nail plates and special

Plate 2.1   A farm buildings complex using concrete frames.

Plate 2.2   Timber framed buildings fitting well in the landscape.

Plate 2.3   A fine example of a steel framed building.

timber connectors are useful (Figure 2.4 and Plate 2.4). If saw cuts are made which reveal unprotected end grain, preservatives must be applied to the cuts before fixing the timber. Sawn ends are likely to deteriorate at a much faster rate than lateral wood surfaces. Moisture goes in through end grain at up to a thousand times the rate at which it penetrates lateral surfaces so end grain sealers must be used. Sawn surfaces are generally a much better background for paints than planed ones.

Unprotected steel surfaces must also be avoided in the normal farming environment. Once again sawn or drilled surfaces should be coated with a suitable protective paint. It is very unusual for the entire frame of the building to be re-painted but some maintenance may be required in some circumstances. To avoid this the additional cost of a fully galvanised frame should be considered.

Sheeting

The choice of roof sheeting and gable end sheeting must also be made. The range of coated steel sheets is increasing and more detail is given in Chapter 10. Undoubtedly profiles and colour ranges make the material a very attractive form of cladding. There are still a number of questions to be answered about the durability of some forms of steel sheeting however, particularly for livestock buildings where high humidity and condensation have caused problems over purlins.

Asbestos/cement sheeting is still available

Figure 2.4   A single-sided timber connector—timber to metal joint.

and if natural grey sheets fit the bill this form of roofing is well tried and tested, performs well in all environments and is the cheapest. Other fibre/cement sheets are available with a similar performance to the asbestos/cement products but are generally about 5 per cent more expensive although still cheaper than the coated steel alternatives. Coloured asbestos/cement or fibre/cement sheeting is also available in a range of profiles and colours. Aluminium sheeting is available but it is more expensive than asbestos/cement. It too is available coloured.

Walls

Chapter 11 contains much detail on the construction of brick and concrete block walls. The pros and cons of these materials are discussed in that chapter. Generally concrete blocks satisfy all needs in farm buildings and building with them is quicker, easier and cheaper than bricks. In farmsteads where brick is the traditional material blockwork needs to be used with care.

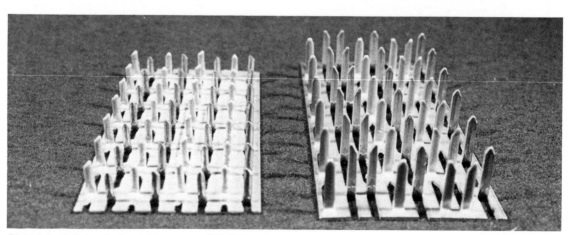

Plate 2.4   A timber 'nail plate' (*courtesy of TRADA*).

Table 2.1 Designated, Standard and other mixes for agricultural applications

Application	Designated mix	Standard mix	Slump mm	Comment	Site mix
Plain foundations in non-aggressive soils	GEN3	ST4	75	Use 125 mm slump for trench fill	Mix C
Reinforced foundations on non-aggressive soils	RC30	ST5	75	Use 125 mm slump for trench fill	Mix D
Plain or reinforced foundations in Class 2 sulphate conditions	FND2	NA	75	Classes of exposure are defined by a Building Research Establishment Digest —consult your local authority	NA
Plain or reinforced foundations in Class 3 sulphate conditions	FND3	NA	75		NA
Plain or reinforced foundations in Class 4 sulphate conditions	FND4	NA	75		NA
Oversite concrete (non-aggressive soil)	GEN2	ST3	75		Mix B
Blinding under slabs	GEN1	ST2	75		Mix A
Stanchion bases (non-aggressive soils)	RC30	ST5	75	These contain embedded metal	Mix D
Mass concrete (non-aggressive soils)	GEN2	ST3	75		Mix B
External paving	PAV1	NA	75	Contain an air entraining agent to give freeze/thaw resistance	NA
Heavy duty external paving	PAV2	NA	75		NA
Sugar beet storage areas	PAV1	NA	75		NA
Farmyard manure and slurry stores	RC40	NA	75	Equivalent to C35A	Mix E
Livestock building floors	RC35	ST5	75		Mix D
Crop store floors	RC35	ST5	75		Mix D
Workshop floors	RC40	NA	75	Good curing and finishing essential	Mix E
Floors and walls for silage	RC45	NA	75	High quality to resist acid attack	Mix F
Brewers' grains store	RC45	NA	75	High quality to resist sugar attack	Mix F
Parlours and dairies	RC45	NA	50	Low workability, high quality for abrasion resistance	NA
Floors used by small wheeled fork lift trucks	RC40	NA	75		Mix E
Mushroom sheds	RC40	NA	75		Mix E
Stabling floors	RC50	NA	50	High quality concrete to resist 'stamping' of shod horses	NA
Infill to cavities	RC40	NA	125	Use 10 mm aggregate	Mix F
Roads	PAV1	NA	75	Contains an air entraining agent to resist freeze/thaw (and salt)	NA
Reinforced concrete:					
mild exposure	RC30	NA	75	Exposure conditions will be determined by the engineer responsible for the design	NA
moderate exposure	RC35	NA	75		NA
severe exposure	RC40	NA	75		NA
very severe exposure	RC45	NA	75		NA
most severe exposure	RC50	NA	75		NA

Table 2.2   Site mixes for agricultural applications, and equivalent Standard mixes

	Mix A (ST2)	Mix B (ST3)	Mix C (ST4)	Mix D (ST5)	Mix E	Mix F
Site mixed by weight:						
Cement kg	50	50	50	50	50	50
Sand kg	160	140	115	95	90	80
20 mm aggregate kg	240	210	195	175	160	150
Yield m³	0.21	0.18	0.17	0.15	0.14	0.13*
Site mixed by volume:						
Cement	4 parts	3 parts	3 parts	3 parts	Do not use	
Damp sand	9 parts	6 parts	5 parts	4 parts	volume	
20 mm aggregate	15 parts	10 parts	9 parts	7 parts	batching	

NOTES

Mix C replaces C20P and 1:2:4 mixes. Its equivalent in Table 2.1 is ST4.
Mix F replaces C25P and 1:1½:3 mixes.
* Use 10 mm aggregate for in-fill to cavities.

Floors

If a floor is needed in a building, concrete will serve all your needs. Floors are discussed in Chapter 13. The mixes to use for various applications are set out below in Tables 2.1 and 2.2. The methods of specifying concrete and the 'names' given to concrete mixes are constantly changing. Those used in Table 2.1 are up to date as of May 1995. The table is a very much simplified version of tables published in British Standards. The use of admixtures to modify the properties of the concrete is also discussed in Chapter 13. For farm roads an admixture called an air-entraining agent is recommended to give added protection to concrete exposed, even occasionally, to de-icing salts carried by vehicles from the local highway — see Chapter 17.

For areas in the UK where sulphates may be found in the ground you would be wise to consult the Local Authority Building Control Officer for details. Mixes for use in these situations are shown in Table 2.3.

Concrete—the Material

The basic ingredients of concrete are cement, sand or crushed rock fines (called the fine aggregate) and stones, either gravel or crushed rock (called the coarse aggregate). Water is added to this mixture. In addition a range of

chemicals called admixtures may be used to modify the properties of the concrete in some way. In some concretes the cement may be partially replaced by additions, either fly ash or ground granulated blast furnace slag (ggbs).

The quantities of all these ingredients must be carefully controlled if a consistent quality concrete is to be produced. By modifying the proportions of the ingredients—cement, fine aggregate, coarse aggregate and water—so the primary qualities of the concrete, its strength, abrasion resistance and chemical resistance can be modified.

Cements

A number of different types of cements are available:

• Ordinary Portland cement (OPC)—used for the bulk of farm concrete.
• Rapid-hardening Portland cement—used when high early strength is required.
• Sulfate-resisting Portland cement — used when the ground surrounding the concrete contains sulfates.
• Masonry cement—used in mortars but not in concrete. It has admixtures included at the factory.
• Portland blast furnace cement—this cement

Table 2.3 Requirements for concrete exposed to sulfate attack

Class	Total SO₃	Concentrations of sulfates expressed as SO₃ In soil		Type of cement		Requirements for dense, full, compacted concrete made with aggregates meeting the requirements of BS 882 or 1049 (See also Table 2.1)	
		SO_3 in 2:1 water:soil extract g/l	In ground-water g/l			Minimum cement[1] content Kg/m^3	Maximum free water:cement[1] ratio
1	Less than 0.2	Less than 1.0	Less than 0.3	Ordinary Portland cement (OPC) Rapid Hardening Portland cement (RHPC) —or combinations of either cement with slag[3] or pfa[4] Portland blast furnace Cement (PBFC)	Plain concrete[2]	250	0.70
					Reinforced concrete	300	0.60
2	0.2 to 0.5	1.0 to 1.9	0.3 to 1.2	OPC or RHPC or combinations of either cement with slag or pfa (PBFC)		330	0.50
				OPC or RHPC combined with minimum 70% or maximum 90% slag[5] OPC or RHPC combined with minimum 25% or maximum 40% pfa[6]		310	0.55
				Sulfate Resisting Portland cement (SRPC)		290	0.55
3	0.5 to 1.0	1.9 to 3.1	1.2 to 2.5	OPC or RHPC combined with minimum 70% or maximum 90% slag OPC or RHPC combined with minimum 25% or maximum 40% pfa		380	0.45
				SRPC		330	0.50
4	1.0 to 2.0	3.1 to 5.6	2.5 to 5.0	SRPC		370	0.45
5	Over 2	Over 5.6	Over 5.0	SRPC + protective coating[7]		370	0.45

1. Inclusive of content of pfa or slag. These cement contents relate to 20 mm nominal maximum-size aggregate. In order to maintain the cement content of the mortar fraction at similar values, the minimum cement contents given should be increased by 50 kg/m³ for 10 mm nominal maximum-size aggregate and may be decreased by 40 kg/m³ for 40 mm nominal-size aggregate.
2. When using strip foundations and trench fill for low-rise buildings in Class 1 sulfate conditions further relaxation in the cement content and water : cement ratio is permissible.
3. Ground granulated blast furnace slag.
4. Selected or classified pulverised fuel ash.
5. Per cent by weight of slag : cement mixture.
6. Per cent by weight of pfa : cement mixture.
7. See BS CP 102: 1973: Protection of buildings against water from the ground.

has added sulfate resistance compared to OPC. Ground granulated blast furnace slag is ground in with the cement during manufacture.
• High alumina cement — a very rapid harden-ing cement useful in a few specific situations; not used now for structural concrete.

All cements are made to comply with British or other National Standards.

Cement/water reaction
When water is added to cement a chemical reaction takes place between the water and the cement called hydration. Heat is given out and the resultant new chemical binds the fine and coarse aggregate together. Only a small quantity of water is needed for this reaction to take place. The water in the atmosphere may be sufficient to cause the cement in a bag to become 'air set'.

If moisture can be excluded, for instance by storing the cement in its bag in an additional polythene bag, then the shelf life of cement can be considerably extended. Cement should always be stored off the floor and in a dry building if possible.

In theory only about 25 kg of water is needed for each 100 kg of cement to complete the chemical reaction. In practice, however, at least 40 kg and, in some circumstances, even 100 kg of water will be needed for each 100 kg of cement. The extra water is required to make the concrete workable so that it can be placed and compacted. However, the more water added over and above that needed to achieve good compaction, the weaker and less durable the concrete will be (Figure 2.5).

Compaction is necessary to drive out the air from the mix. If air is left in it will reduce the qualities of strength and durability in the concrete. Generally speaking vibration is the best form of compaction whether by beam or poker vibrator. With machine vibration it is possible to compact a lower workability concrete and thus achieve better durability. For every

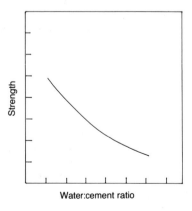

Figure 2.5   Relationship between water:cement ratio and strength of concrete.

1 per cent of air left in the concrete its strength and durability will be reduced by about 5 per cent.

The water used for making concrete must be clean—clean enough to drink. If dirty, contaminated water is used, this may also reduce the strength and durability of the concrete. Salty water—sea water—should only be used in unreinforced concrete in an emergency and must never be used in reinforced concrete as the salt will increase the rate of corrosion of the steel.

Aggregates
Whichever aggregate (sand and stone) is used, it should be obtained if possible from a recognised supplier, and must be clean and free from constituents which decompose or change significantly in volume (e.g. organic matter), or indeed which react with the cement (e.g. sulphates). If possible aggregates should be used which comply with the British Standard or other National Standards.

In addition to the normal range of dense aggregates—sands, gravels and crushed rocks—a range of man-made lightweight aggregates are also available. These are used in the manufacture of insulation blocks and, in agriculture, for insulated floors. They will be mentioned again in the chapters on walls and floors.

The grading of aggregates, the relative proportions of the different sizes of particles, is important to concrete technologists. For example, it affects the sand content of mixes used by the ready-mixed concrete suppliers. This will also be discussed on the chapters on renderings and floors.

From the economic viewpoint it is desirable to use the largest available size of coarse aggregate compatible with the dimensions of the work in hand. The rule of thumb is that the largest aggregate particle should not exceed a quarter of the smallest dimension of the work. In practice this is limited by the availability of aggregates in excess of 40 mm. In many instances a 20 mm aggregate may be the maximum size available.

Admixtures
As has already been mentioned, these materials or chemicals are added to the concrete mix to modify one or more of the properties of the fresh or the hardened concrete. They are referred to further in the chapters on rendering and floors.

Additions, usually fly ash, slag or microsilica, can also be discussed under this heading although they are not admixtures, as they are used to replace some of the cement in the mix. They are slower or 'later' to react with water than cement. They need the products of the reaction of cement and water to become reactive themselves in some instances. Although they make a useful contribution to the strength and impermeability of concrete, it is important that their use is carefully controlled to ensure that the resultant concrete produces the properties required both in the short and long term.

The need to compact concrete has already been mentioned. Compaction drives out the large bubbles of air which become trapped during mixing. Equally important is the process called curing which is designed to prevent evaporation of water from the concrete and thus enables the chemical reaction between the cement and water to take place. With concrete containing additions, curing is even more vital — it is imperative. If ready-mixed concrete is used with additions it may be wise to limit the percentage used as a replacement for cement to 30 per cent and increase the total weight of cement + fly ash by 10 per cent. In the case of slag up to 65 per cent replacement is permissible but this affects the concrete in such a way that it will mature more slowly. Both slag and fly ash are likely to increase the sulfate resistance of the resultant concrete.

Frames to British Standard 5502

When a building is being selected, in addition to deciding whether the main frame type is to be concrete, steel or timber, if the frame to be used is to comply with the British Standard for Farm Buildings (BS 5502), the class of building needed must also be determined. In BS 5502 buildings are classified in three main ways:

- *Design life*
  Class 1—50 years
  Class 2—20 years
  Class 3—10 years
  Class 4—2 years

- *Human occupancy*
  Class 1—unrestricted

Class 2—not normally to exceed 6 hours per day at a density not exceeding 2 persons per 50 m²
Class 3—not normally to exceed 2 hours per day at a density not exceeding 1 person per 50 m²
Class 4—not normally to exceed 1 hour per day at a density not exceeding 1 person per 50 m²

- *Location*
  Class 1—no restriction on location
  Class 2—not nearer than 10 m to a highway or human habitation not in the same occupancy.
  Class 3—not nearer than 20 m to the above in Class 2
  Class 4—not nearer than 30 m to the above in Class 2

Only the design life classification may lead to confusion. It does not mean that a building should be expected to fall down at the end of its design life. In fact probably 98 per cent of Class 2 buildings would survive for more than 20 years. A very small percentage, perhaps only 1 per cent, would not survive because the design loads (mainly the wind and snow loads which the building has been designed to withstand) had been exceeded before the 20-year period elapsed. Similarly about 1 per cent of Class 3 buildings will last less than 10 years.

Taken step by step the chart in Figure 2.6 leads to the correct class of building being selected for almost all farming operations.

To help decide which class of building should be used, a chart has been produced which, if taken step by step, leads to the correct class of building being selected for almost all farming operations (see Figure 2.6).

Preparing Plans and Specifications

It is not necessary to be a draughtsman to produce acceptable drawings. What is really needed is the ability to put your ideas onto paper. A roll of ceiling lining paper is a good cheap source for sketching on and dozens of sketches will probably be needed.

Tracing paper is essential too, because once the ideas start to take shape they can be added to

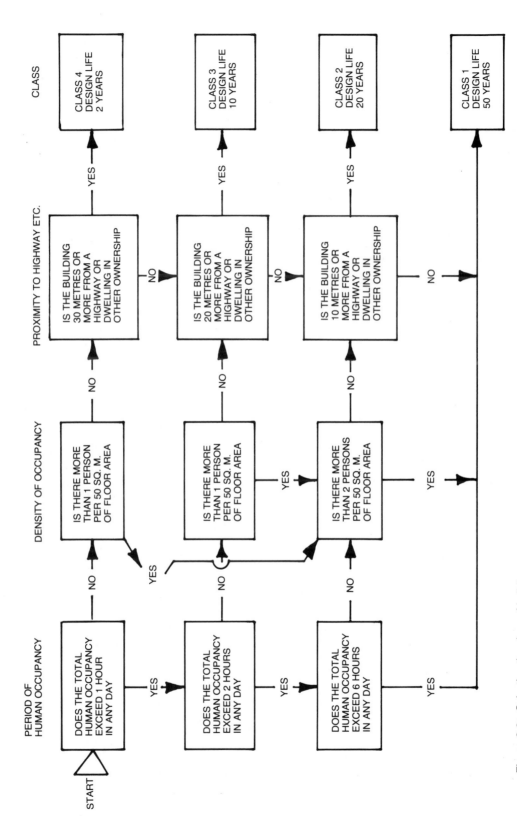

Figure 2.6 Selecting the class of building.

on tracings—re-doing everything to scale each time can be a very time-consuming business. A cheap drawing board and a set square is a good investment too. The drawings need not be elaborate as long as they can be understood, and at some stage the dimensions are correct. All sorts of variations can be tried, even the unlikely ones; these may turn out to be the ones chosen as the final version. It is very easy to change a building on a drawing—changing it during the building process itself is time-consuming, expensive, frustrating and sometimes impossible.

At this stage in the process it is a good idea to see what neighbouring farmers have done; visit other similar installations and borrow plans. Find out what 'standard details', 'standard drawings' and 'standard designs' are available. See if they suit your site, meet your requirements and how much you will lose if you 'lift' their ideas.

There is no reason at all why the building work should not be done personally, but a professional should be employed to help with the design. A surveyor, architect or even an engineer will be only too pleased to be consulted and he may take the whole job through all the 'regulation' stages for you too — for a fee of course.

Many of the framed building suppliers provide this sort of service as well. If the main frame of a building is to be erected by a reputable supplier the company will probably prefer to see the plans through the regulation stage anyway — that is a service to the customer that helps to secure the contract. When they have quoted the right price, encourage them to provide this service. They have the experience and the expertise; you may not have either.

If going it alone, ensure that plans, sections, elevations, location plans and block plans (local roads and neighbouring properties) are properly prepared. Also the movement plans for all materials and animals should be worked out — keeping the dirty side (muck and animals) away from the clean side (feed, milk, etc.) if possible.

If going it alone, ensure that plans, sections, elevations, location plans and block plans (local roads and neighbouring properties) are properly prepared. Also the movement plans for all materials and animals should be worked out—

keeping the dirty side (muck and animals) away from the clean side (feed, milk, etc.) if possible.

Obtaining Quotations

Even the most ardent do-it-yourself builder is unlikely to be able to tackle every last part of a building contract. In fact most fall at the first hurdle—the frame—and 'get up' to finish the job. So if a frame is needed quotations will also be necessary.

This may sound a relatively simple task. 'How much will a 20 m × 12 m shed cost?' Unfortunately, it is not quite as simple as that if the quotes are to mean anything and are to be really comparable. It is advisable that quotes are obtained for a framed building that has been designed and erected to comply with BS 5502, the British Standard for Farm Buildings and Structures—see Chapter 8.

In order to do this and to receive comparable quotes, the job should be discussed with the manufacturers, as specific information is required:

- Your name and address.
- The address of the site.
- The precise location of the building and its proximity to other buildings, etc., in, or not in, your occupation.
- The precise dimensions of the building—length, width, height to eaves, slope of roof, etc., and what Class of building or structure it is to BS 5502. The manufacturer's dimensions may be from centre of column to centre of column, or from outside of column to outside of column; you need to know which it is. See Chapter 4, Figure 4.10.
- What the main structural material is. What the purlins are made of?
- Are lean-to's required, now or in the future? Will the building be extended in the future? If so, how?
- What is the building to be used for?
- What is the altitude of the site?
- What is the estimate of 'ground roughness' factors—the manufacturer must explain this as it influences the designed wind speed his engineers use in their calculations.
- Whether the frame of the building is to withstand lateral loading from materials stored inside or not.
- What type of roof and gable end sheeting is

required. What profile is the sheeting to be and what colour?

- How far below eaves is the side sheeting, if any, to be taken? What profile and colour is it to be?

- What form of space boarding is required—what are its dimensions, method of preservation, etc?

- What sort of rainwater goods are to be supplied? Where are the down spouts and what are they made of?

- What form of ridge ventilation is to be provided, if any?

- How much roof lighting is required?

- What form of corrosion protection is to be provided to steel?

- What are the dimensions of the foundations? Who digs and fills them?

- Who provides gates and doors? How big are they? How are they made and what are they made of?

- Is there to be any roof insulation? What is its insulation value? How is it fixed and/or sealed?

- When is the contract to start?

- When will the building, or that part of it which is the manufacturer's responsibility, be completed?

- What, if any, are the stage payments? When are they to be made?

- What percentage of the total price will be held back by you and for how long after completion?

- Does the manufacturer carry insurances against 'failure to complete on time'?

- Who is to obtain planning approvals, etc.—you or the manufacturer? If he does it, he may save you many sleepless nights—assuming he gains approval of course!

- What other things will be included in his price and/or his drawings? Make sure that they are carefully specified by all the companies quoting or, again, the benefits of the comparability of the quotes will be lost.

- Are there any preliminary works to be undertaken? If so, by whom? For example, site clearance, cut and/or fill, drainage, etc. Will

drawings and specifications of these works be provided and if so by whom? (If the manufacturer cuts through an electricity cable or drain when excavating for foundations, he will not be happy if these have not been set out on the drawings of the site.)

The list on the previous page is not intended to be complete in every detail, but is a good guide to the sort of detail which should be discussed with the manufacturers quoting for the building.* Finally, enough quotes should be obtained, but do not necessarily accept the cheapest.

It would be unwise to pick the names of those asked to tender in too random a manner. Ask your neighbours who they have employed. The contractor and/or his men may be on site for several days—or even weeks, and you will need to get on with them.

They will need space for huts and storage of materials—and so indeed will you later on. They must have access for lorries and cranes. Access to toilets and even the telephone needs to be sorted out in advance. In view of this it is wise to prepare a list of suppliers and/or contractors in advance—big contractors for big jobs, small contractors for small ones is no bad maxim—to discuss the tendering period as well as the contract period. The influence of winter weather on the latter must be remembered, and enquire in advance as to whether the quotation from each company is to be fixed or fluctuating.

It will be necessary to discuss working hours with the supplier/contractor and what influence, if any, this or the restrictions to it, have on price. Also discuss what happens if you (or he) changes your/his mind on detail, as variations can be expensive.

Always ensure that instructions on variations are in writing, that way the extras can be negotiated. It is preferable to get quotations for variations before the work is done rather than haggle afterwards.

When a tender is accepted always do so in writing and include as much detail as possible—not least the price!

---

*See HIVES, J. K., *Think Before You Build*, MAFF leaflet 835 (1983).

Chapter 3

DIY COMMITMENT

IT MAY be satisfying to see one's ideas develop into a particular building project, having gone through all the planning stages, but it still requires a great deal of commitment to reach a successful conclusion. It is very much a question of scale. The degree of commitment involved for laying a new concrete apron is very different to that required for building a new dairy unit. But it requires very different skills to be able to interpret the elements of the design into a physical structure. The buying and ordering of materials is time-consuming and demands great attention to detail in a complex project, but the logistics of tying deliveries together in a sequence which does not leave the site cluttered with materials delivered too soon is a completely different skill.

The larger the project the more detailed the logistical planning must be to ensure the work is performed in a reasonable sequence. For example, storm drains would nearly always be laid as a priority on a new site to assist conditions in wet weather and to help ensure sufficient fall on concrete aprons when they are constructed. However, during a wet period care must be taken when excavating for drains if a concrete lorry subsequently has to pass nearby, since 'Murphy's Law' says it would be bound to get stuck in the backfilled trench.

Presumably, for most farmers, this work comes on top of the normal day-to-day running of the farm—milking, feeding, harvesting and administration, and does indeed require great reserves of determination and commitment. This chapter contains a few important points to be considered before attempting DIY farm buildings.

An important piece of advice given by a venerable farmer, himself a very accomplished builder, was 'see the end before the beginning'. In other words, do not start a project until you have visualised how it will look, and how you will build it in all its detail.

One of the greatest disciplines with agricultural buildings is the ability to complete projects on time. The management stresses are also great since a grain store must be completed and commissioned before harvest, whereas an over-run of a week or two on an industrial or domestic building is of little consequence. Any farm building and its associated fittings and equipment will take at least a year to plan and execute properly. Too often insufficient time is allowed and other events or the seasons take over. To attempt to build in a situation resembling a blind panic is simply ridiculous and to be avoided at all costs. Anyone who can heed this warning will be wise indeed because, in this situation, corners are cut, the standard of work deteriorates, parts are left unfinished—sometimes forever—and tempers become shorter as the frustration grows.

More seriously, costs can increase as a result of failure to find time to check prices with suppliers and contractors as the pressure mounts. At the same time the constructional standards can fall to the point where the life of the building is considerably reduced or it even fails in its first season. A simple example would be the failure to properly fill the voids of hollow concrete blocks where necessary. This is a slow and tedious job, yet vital if the wall is to stand any lateral forces. The better DIY farm builder will certainly derive much satisfaction from a well designed and constructed building, but there is little pleasure in a poorly constructed, ill conceived building, built in a rush.

Labour

Invariably with any building work there is a considerable amount of semi-skilled hand labour involved. Also, because of the most recent agricultural revolution—particularly with arable cropping—there are periods of intense activity in the autumn and then relatively long slack periods. The marriage of these two factors gives a major impulse for DIY farm buildings.

It is to the credit of the agricultural workforce that they are usually enthusiastic about any new development with which they are involved. Imagine an industrial worker being asked to shovel concrete! Nevertheless, there are one or two cautionary points to be made. Firstly, if DIY projects are engaged upon to use spare labour, then perhaps too much labour is employed within the farm business. Secondly, although there is some very creditable building work produced by farm staff, in general it would be unfair to expect them to produce the results of a skilled building worker, or for the work to progress as quickly.

The obvious approach to any job for which staff are not competent is to call in an expert—perhaps a bricklayer or a plumber. For some reason the subcontract bricklayer is something of a prima donna in the building industry. When engaged in agricultural work they, like others, make the mistake of thinking it is only a 'farm job' and will cut any corners they can.

Most assistance required will be available from local tradespeople who are well known. Good advice when employing unknown specialists is to show them an example of how the finished job should look. Agree a rate for the job and fire them if they cannot produce the results. For any very specialised work it is worth the trouble to visit a recently completed contract and see how that looks, or at least telephone previous customers.

Another approach for the large farm or estate is to directly employ its own skilled building workers. This is a traditional approach perhaps, but supervision becomes crucial since it is a very expensive operation and lacks the competitive element.

A midway approach may occur on an expanding pig farm where a resident builder may be employed, much as a farm fitter is employed on arable farms. The difficulty is that a building gang really consists of a minimum of three people.

Does DIY Save Money?

Having considered the points above, it must be decided whether the project should be DIY, left to a contractor or a combination of both. It is usually assumed that DIY is cheaper, and if farm labour is not charged to the building work DIY certainly ought to be. In practice, this is not necessarily true and in some cases the reverse may occur if farm management is also charged.

Assuming that a competent contractor is approached for a quotation, he would calculate the materials and labour involved and add 15–20 per cent to cover overheads and profit. As a DIY operation, this 15–20 per cent on the cost of the building would be expected to be saved (even if the material and labour element remained constant). In practice this is not always the case. It would be reasonable to expect a well-equipped contractor to be 15–20 per cent more efficient than farm staff and on most DIY projects the farmer still incurs considerable overheads.

Generally farmers will accept lower quality work on a DIY basis than they would from a contractor. If a contractor was not laying 150 mm thickness of concrete where it had been specified there would soon be a fuss, and quite rightly so. However, if farm staff lay a bay of concrete and it is roughly 150 mm thick, but happens to reduce to 100 mm at the edges, and the concrete is not cured properly because it is milking time, the situation is accepted, even if the concrete fails after only five years.

On a DIY basis there is always an element of make-do. This is not wrong, but it does lead to some poor buildings when taken to extremes, and poor buildings are not cheaper in the long term.

In view of the lack of planning controls and regulations, farmers ought to produce buildings which are at least tidy in their construction and appearance. In order to achieve this it may not necessarily be more expensive to employ a contractor.

Farm Buildings Contractors

Construction contracts will not be dealt with too deeply here, but it is worth remembering that a very simple specification or description of what is required, together with dimensions, can form the basis of a contractor's quotation. Generally, of course, it is wise to obtain more than one quotation.

For a multitude of reasons a good farm buildings contractor is very much a specialist in his field. The very large construction companies do not usually get involved in farm building contracts, as most are extremely small by their standards and they find great difficulty in producing the fine detail required in farm buildings due to the long lines of communication. At the other extreme, the jobbing builder with a truck, a trowel and a wheelbarrow who can work wonders with any domestic building will not necessarily have the ability or equipment to produce the required results in a modern livestock building. One such character was heard to lament after he had been made to correct some very poor work at considerable expense that he would now stick to building dwellings, since none of his work showed after a house had been plastered, painted or carpeted.

As a final point, the etiquette of building contracting has changed, and not for the better. In times of recession it has become customary for the larger organisations to quote very keenly for a new contract by reducing their allowance for overheads and profits, sometimes to nil. Since, with any large contract, there are always alterations and additions as work progresses, these extras, which are unquoted, are charged at a very high rate. Having obtained the contract on a low tender, profitability is recovered by hiking the extras, so beware and obtain a quotation for any additional work.

Plant and Equipment

Discussion about the choice of available plant and equipment for constructional work is far beyond the scope of this book. Nevertheless, the application and operation of even the largest

Plate 3.1   The invaluable tractor-digger-loader. Even an older machine will have lots of DIY work left.

Plate 3.2   A tracked machine will cope with most situations—but is expensive to operate.

equipment will hold little mystery for today's mechanised farmer and his staff. There are other similarities too, in that generally it is fair to assume that the bigger the item of plant the lower its cost per unit output. Also timeliness in carrying out excavation work can be as crucial as it is with arable cropping.

There are some machines which should particularly be mentioned since their use could be regarded as essential to produce the desired results. Other machines can be easily borrowed from the farming operation, such as fork-lift trucks or tractors and trailers to cart away excavated material.

Excavators
The most useful and versatile machine for this scale of work must be the tractor-digger-loader (Plate 3.1). It can excavate a site, level hardcore, dig foundation holes, dig trenches for drains and backfill. It is particularly useful with a wide rear bucket for excavating accurately down to formation level and for clearing very small areas.

Where considerable excavation is necessary, a crawler loader is a faster machine (Plate 3.2). Its output is not restricted by the roughest materials or site, and will find traction in conditions unsuitable for wheeled machines. It can perform well in restricted areas and has the ability to crush and compact hardcore in a way unmatched by any wheeled machine or roller. The skilled use of the opening front bucket can produce an accurate surface to the sub-base, especially with fine granular materials. It is usually necessary to carry out all crawler work in one operation since the expense of return visits to the site with specialist transport may become prohibitive.

Compactors
One of the constant difficulties is to recompact the subsoil after excavation for services, or to compact backfill to footings and sumps, etc. Also, it is necessary to compact hardcore and blinding to provide a smooth surface to the underside of concrete floors. The need for careful compaction of materials cannot be over-emphasised since any

Vibrating rollers

These machines are usually pedestrian-controlled and have either one or two drums which have a heavy eccentric shaft within the drum (Plate 3.3). The shaft is rotated at high speed which causes the drum to vibrate as it is driven forwards. This produces a compacting effect many times greater than the static weight of the machine.

The twin-drum machines have a high capacity and can work on rougher hardcore but cannot be turned or manoeuvred in small areas. They are superb for road construction. Single-drum vibrating rollers are ideal for this scale of work, producing good results and able to work in confined areas. The 'edge' roll machines can compact directly alongside walls or roadforms.

Plate 3.3   A single drum vibrating roller is very manoeuvrable and ideal for working between roadforms.

uneven settlement can only result in floor failure. Fortunately there is a variety of equipment which can be used.

Rollers

The agricultural flat or Cambridge roll is useless for building works. A heavy road roller is little better.

Vibrating plates

These are used in a similar way to vibrating rollers but have a flat heavy base which is caused to vibrate and create a compacting effect (Plate 3.4). They are able to compact deeper layers of material than rollers although they are not so manoeuvrable. Plate compactors 'bounce' along by the reactive force to the vibrator unit, but curiously the more sophisticated machines also have a forward and reverse mechanism. Plate compactors are particularly useful for crushing brick hardcore or materials too rough

Plate 3.4   A vibrating plate compactor—an alternative to a roller.

for a drum machine. There are also similar narrow machines designed specifically to re-compact excavated material from trenches. It must be remembered that with all backfilling operations material should be placed in layers of 200 mm to 300 mm and thoroughly compacted.

Vibrating beams and pokers
A vibrating beam is essential in the production of best-quality concrete floors and slabs since it quickly produces the results no amount of hand tamping can match. The same is true of vibrating pokers for use within formwork (Plate 3.5 and Figures 3.1 and 3.2).

Electrical power tools
Power tools now form an enormous range of equipment for an enormous range of tasks. Only

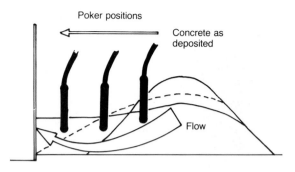

Figure 3.1   Filling corners.

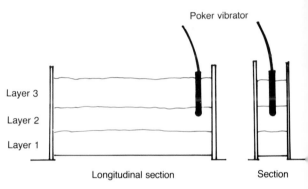

Figure 3.2   Compacting—depths of layers in a lift.

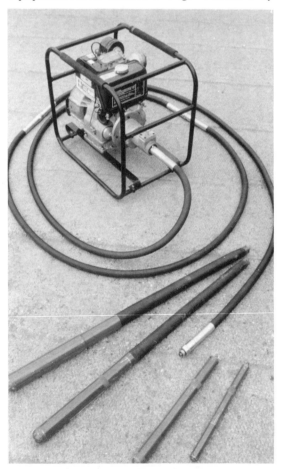

Plate 3.5   A vibrating poker is used to compact and regulate concrete within formwork.

two will be mentioned, but these are particularly versatile. The first is a 9 inch angle grinder; this is a powerful, robust machine intended mostly for grinding and cutting metal but, with a suitable disc, is invaluable for cutting concrete, blocks, stone and asbestos cement. It is generally rec-ommended that asbestos cement is sawed to reduce the dust output (Plate 3.6). The second most useful tool is a jig-saw. Small perhaps, but invaluable for cutting plywood for formwork and all forms of sheet or lining materials. For all site work it is recommended that 110 volt equipment is used. This simply means that all the equip-ment is run from a small transformer which, in turn, runs from the mains supply. Equipment of 110 volts cannot kill, no matter what faults occur nor how wet the equipment is. Once the trans-former is acquired there is no increase in the

Plate 3.6   An angle grinder with 'stone' disc cutting a dense concrete block.

Plate 3.8   Tractor-mounted concrete mixer (*courtesy of AC Bamblett Ltd*).

purchase price of any equipment, one simply specifies 110 volt (Plate 3.7).

Concrete mixers
The range of mixers to choose from is enormous—from the tractor-mounted models suitable for the smallest jobs such as patching, repairs and mortar mixing (Plate 3.8)—to the self-propelled, self-loading versions with load cells under the mixing drum to help batch the quantities (Plate 3.9). The mixer should be selected to suit the job.

Plate 3.7   A few examples of a very wide range of electrical power tools available. Note also the 110V transformer.

Plate 3.9   Self-propelled, self-loading concrete mixer (*courtesy of Metaquip Ltd*).

Loading the materials into the drum by hand is a very time consuming and laborious process and can only be justified when small quantities of concrete are required or when mortar is being mixed (Plate 3.10). The tractor-mounted models really come into their own if the materials need to be transported some distance. Electric motor driven or petrol/diesel driven, 100 l or 150 l, half-bag mixers are uneconomic for concrete laying on a large scale.

The old imperial dimensions, e.g. 5/3½ or 10/7 are now replaced by metric dimensioned mixers. The 5/3½ mixer accepted 5 cu. ft of unmixed ingredients and delivered 3 cu. ft of mixed concrete. This is now designated a 100 l mixer.

If it is decided to weigh-batch the materials on-site, then the one-bag mixers with hydraulic loading (Plate 3.11) or the self-propelled self-loading models with drum capacities—in the latter case—of 1 cubic metre and more, are worth while. With concrete, take care to work out the actual costs of mixing (including hire costs) and transporting the concrete, compared with ready-mixed concrete, before buying the equipment, even second-hand, or hiring it.

Breakers and hammers
Pneumatic breakers need little introduction or skill in their handling—their universal acceptance stems from the fact that they are very, very effective. Recent years have seen the introduction of similar hydraulic machines driven from a power-pack—a digger, or even a hydraulic vibrating roller. Hydraulic machines are much quieter and more efficient in terms of power required, although their working range from the power unit is a little less.

There are similar impressive looking electrically-powered machines available. In our experience these machines are fairly ineffective for any 'serious work'; however in their other guises as heavy masonry drills they are unmatched.

Plate 3.10 Loading materials by hand can be time-consuming unless only small quantities are required.

Plate 3.11   One-bag mixer with hydraulic loading.

Equipment—Buy Or Hire?

The equipment needed for DIY building work is considerable and, as has been suggested, much equipment will already be held on most farms. Even hand spades, shovels and hammers are expensive to purchase for a gang of men. Almost all the equipment necessary can be very readily hired, but that is not always a cheap operation either. If a piece of specialist equipment is required such as a floor scabbler for a short period, then there is no doubt that it should be hired. If a concrete mixer is required for three months then there are several options. Unless a large machine is needed it will probably be too expensive to hire. If it is possible to manage with a small machine, it would be economical to buy an electric tip-up mixer. As a third option a reasonable second-hand machine could be bought and most of the purchase price could be expected to be recouped at the end of the project. In the case of a medium-sized mixer, this would easily be the cheapest option, always assuming that it would not be kept, in the hope that it would be 'useful' in the future.

With a vibrating beam, perhaps the problem is not so easy. It has been said that it should be regarded as essential equipment, yet it may only be needed for 20 minutes a day and may not be used every day. It is expensive to buy and is not readily available second-hand.

This then is the dilemma of the DIY builder and is an example of where his costs can exceed those of a well-equipped small builder. Hire charges will mount daily for a machine which cannot necessarily be used daily. Living in rural areas it is not possible to just pop round the corner and return the machine at the end of the day's work and re-hire if required again for more concrete. The net result is that often work is carried out in an unhelpful sequence in order to be able to return hired equipment at the earliest moment and avoid excessive charges.

Machinery costs may in themselves influence the decisions regarding the use of a contractor, especially for larger projects. For a DIY operation there can be no hard and fast rules concerning buying or hiring machinery. If buying, buy the best possible because machinery which is unreliable soon wastes precious building time.

Chapter 4

MEASUREMENT

THOSE OF us who have been educated since metrication should have little difficulty with metric building calculation. Those of us who are a little older cling affectionately to the imperial system, and three feet still make a yard of course!

However, it is still an advantage if one is conversant with both systems, and can convert easily from imperial to metric or vice-versa.

There are some disadvantages to the metric system but there are also major advantages. This book will be almost exclusively metric for reasons which will become apparent. The one disadvantage is that the numbers we deal with have many more digits, and the units themselves become much larger (or smaller), and thereby more difficult to comprehend.

For example, a piece of 4 in by 2 in timber becomes 100 mm by 50 mm. It has cross-sectional area of 8 sq. in or 5000 mm²—mental arithmetic becomes more difficult.

Secondly, if π is taken as being $3\frac{1}{7}$ as a fraction we have an exact measure; 3.14159 in decimal language is still only an approximation, although for all practical purposes 3.142 is quite accurate enough.

The metric system is of course built upon units (or a base) of ten, as follows:

10 millimetres	=	1 centimetre
10 centimetres	=	1 decimetre
10 decimetres	=	1 metre
10 metres	=	1 decametre
10 decametres	=	1 hectometre
10 hectometres	=	1 kilometre

A fair proportion of the units above are irrelevant. For all farm building work only two units are considered: the metre and the millimetre. These are denoted as m and mm. This is because with the metric system the decimal point is crucial. A wrongly placed point gives us an error by a factor of 10 or even perhaps 100.

The metre is used because it is a convenient unit not too different from the yard, and the millimetre is used as the 1000th part of the metre. One millimetre is the smallest unit which could be envisaged to be used for building works. Hence measurements are written 2.46 m or sometimes 2460 mm. The only occasion upon which a decimal point is used is to distinguish between metres and millimetres. Using centimetres as an example, in 2.5 cm the decimal point is crucial, whereas if 25 mm is written there is no decimal point to consider.

Within this chapter care has been taken to indicate which units have been used. On-site it may be very different. Drawings soon become damp and easily torn, altered or written on with a blunt pencil, or a pen that does not write properly. They blow across the slurry lagoon in a stiff wind, but they are still of vital importance. Any convention which can ultimately reduce confusion and mistakes is to be welcomed. When using the preferred system, if a number is read with no decimal point and no units indicated, it is unlikely, for example, that 25 m will be mistaken for 25 mm when one is one thousand times larger than the other.

To summarise, if there is a decimal point it can only mean metres to the left and millimetres to the right. Thinking and working in centimetres should be avoided at all costs.

A few metric tips
It is a great mistake to try and convert imperial units to exact metric equivalents, and such accuracy is never necessary anyway. The following suggested conversions are quite adequate for all our needs:

25 mm	=	1 in
100 mm	=	4 in
150 mm	=	6 in
300 mm	=	12 in or 1 ft
900 mm	=	3 ft or 1 yd

900 mm is not quite 3 ft and as longer measurements are used the error begins to become significant; whereas at 4 in it is negligible.

To convert longer measurements to metric, the accurate standard of 305 mm to 1 ft should be used. Hence a 60 ft long building (60 ft × 305 mm) is an 18300 mm building. Shift the decimal point and call it 18.3 m.

One must use one's judgement as to when an accurate or approximate conversion is required. If the above example had been worked with 300 mm to the foot the answer would have been 18 m, which shows an error of 300 mm or 1 ft. This is a serious discrepancy on a 60 ft long building, but it may not be so important on a 60 ft long earth bank. To convert from metric to imperial simply divide by 0.305; hence 4.575 m = 15 ft.

The Advantages of Working in Metric

Many of the advantages will become obvious as setting out and calculating quantities are discussed, but a major benefit comes within volume measure. For example, the quantity of concrete for an apron 10 m wide by 30 m long by 150 mm thick is calculated as follows:

$$10 \times 30 \times .15 = 45 \text{ m}^3$$

Note how the thickness is expressed in metres simply by moving the decimal point, which gives an answer direct into cubic metres of concrete.

You can forget that there are 9 square feet in a square yard and 27 cubic feet in a cubic yard. How would you do the calculation if the concrete was 5 in thick instead of half a foot?

There are other small advantages for metric measurement. You no longer have the problem of misreading 36 in instead of 3 ft 6 in or reading 96 in instead of 69 in by looking at the tape from the wrong side. However care is still needed when reading a metric tape because of the tendency to miss a zero digit after the decimal point; 3.025 m can become 3.25 m especially when someone transmits the dimension verbally.

Another useful facility with metric measurement is the ability to divide a given dimension into any number of equal parts. To divide 64 ft 7½ in by 5 is not easy; it is not so easy with a pocket calculator either. Dividing 19.50 m by 5 with a calculator is easy!

Metric Mass, Force and Volume

Having suggested that metric linear measurement holds a number of benefits for us, the same is not necessarily true for the remainder of the metric system, although it is fair to say that the new 'system international' (SI system) is a more logical mathematical system than has been devised before and takes into account the fundamental changes in mathematical thinking in recent years.

Mass

The first thing to attempt to understand is that mass is different to weight. An object may have a mass of 1 kg, a brick perhaps, and it may also have a *weight* of 1 kg on planet earth. However on the moon the brick would not weigh 1 kg, because the gravitational pull is lower. Nevertheless, if it is the same brick then it must have the same mass as it started with—1 kg.

Force

Mass, as described above, will cause little difficulty because we shall still refer to the weight of building materials even though the terminology is wrong.

When considering the loads within a building (or more correctly the forces), in the SI system there is a separate derived unit of force called the 'newton'. A newton is named after the man who first understood some of the physical laws of motion and one newton is defined as being the force necessary to accelerate a mass of 1 kg by 1 m per second. This is very different from the old method of considering both mass and forces in pounds. The important point to grasp is that it requires the *same* force to move, or more correctly accelerate, our 1 kg brick on earth as it does on the moon. This is fundamental stuff to any space traveller but leaves us lesser mortals with a small unit of force the size of which it is difficult to comprehend.

As a comparison a newton is equivalent to about ¼ lb, and a pressure of 1 N/mm² is equivalent to roughly an apple on a pin head. (Apples seem strangely appropriate to this subject.)

The units are either expressed as N/mm^2 or kN/m^2. Thus a concrete may have a crushing strength of $28 N/mm^2$ which is equivalent to 4000 lb/sq. in; a soil may have a bearing pressure of $100 kN/m^2$, roughly the old yardstick of 1 ton/sq. ft.

Volume
The metric unit of liquid volume is the litre, of which there are approximately 4½ to the gallon. The litre is another derived unit although not too complicated in that 1 kg of water occupies a volume of 1 litre. Apart from paint and fuel, the litre is of little interest in agricultural building work since the volume of sumps or lagoons is better expressed in cubic metres.

The metric system is more logical in the way units are derived so that $1 m^3$ is 1000 litres or 1000 kg of water (a metric tonne).

Pocket calculators
Often very large or very small numbers have to be used which do not make for easy arithmetic. A pocket calculator can not only sort out the numbers it can also put the decimal point in the right place. This obvious advantage caused the demise of the slide rule, an otherwise excellent device.

It is interesting to reflect that metrication paved the way for the advent of the electronic calculator. The electronic calculator in turn may have paved the way for VAT which causes more work than ever feet and inches did!

Tape measures
There is a wide variety of tape measures available in a range of qualities and prices. The usual lengths are 3 m, 5 m, 10 m, 30 m, and 50 m.

Plate 4.1   Use of two tape measures to directly establish the third corner of a building.

These are manufactured in steel or fibron material, the old linen tape having been superseded.

Usually a steel tape is to be preferred as it is more accurate and will often have both imperial and metric graduations. A steel tape is more expensive in longer lengths and is very easily damaged. The fibron tape, 50 m long with an open winder frame, is strongly recommended for all farm building work. It is robust, accurate, and the whole tape can be swilled in a tub of water if it becomes soiled with mud or cow muck. However, fibron tapes are expensive and for some setting out two such tapes may be needed (Plate 4.1).

It increases efficiency and decreases mismeasurement to equip everyone on site with identical 3 m steel tapes for detailed work. These tapes are very cheap and are graduated in both metric and imperial.

Setting Out

Careful setting out is fundamental to any successful building project to ensure that each element is correctly positioned and will work properly with the neighbouring component. This is true even for the very simplest building because components which are not correctly aligned can become highly stressed, particularly if forced into position.

A building must always be set square, not just for the sake of being square but because it becomes very difficult to sheet the roof of an out of square building.

Setting out always demands great attention to detail and a considerable degree of judgement. Sometimes it is enough to work to the nearest 100 mm. At other extremes it is necessary to struggle for ± 2 mm. Normal building contracts allow a maximum error of 5 mm in 50 m.

It is sobering to realise that most of the serious mistakes made will occur during the process of setting out. Most of these mistakes occur in the first few hours of work. The laws of statistics dictate that dimensional errors will be made from time to time. How many and how often will depend upon the individual, his equipment and methods, but remember that mistakes *will* occur. It is therefore important to assume that measurements made are basically incorrect and to employ a system of constant checking and re-checking as the building progresses, and to build up accuracy as various elements are fitted.

Accepting then that mistakes will be made in setting out, it is vital that they are recognised at an early stage. Staff should be encouraged to admit if they have made a mistake or to report when something does not appear correct. A decision can then be made upon any corrective action if necessary.

The objective of this chapter is to suggest how a system of setting out can be developed to suit individual needs and developed as the buildings become more complicated.

Setting Out Parallel Lines
Problem To construct a wall parallel to an existing building and 5 m away from it (Figure 4.1).
Solution If one end of the tape is held against the existing building in the two positions A and

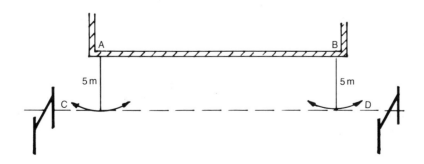

Figure 4.1 Use of a tape measure.

B then the points which need to be established will be 5 m along the tape at right angles to line AB.

Because it is not easy to tell when the tape is at right angles, the technique is to swing it in a curve and move the building line CD until it is at a maximum from AB. This gives us accurate parallel lines AB and CD.

Setting Out a Concrete Base
Problem   To set out a rectangular 5 m × 6 m concrete base for a bulk feed bin adjacent to an existing building.
Solution   To be able to construct a square or rectangle it is necessary to be able to construct a right angle at each corner and to check the results by measuring each diagonal to ensure they are the same length (Figure 4.2). There are several geometric methods of constructing a right angle, but the Pythagoras theorum is the only practical answer available on-site. Pythagoras stated that for a right-angled triangle the length of the longest side squared is equal to the sum of the squares on the other two sides (Figure 4.3).

In our example $5^2 = 4^2 + 3^2$
$$25 = 16 + 9$$
$$25 = 25$$

Thus a 3, 4, 5 triangle is a universally known figure because it so happens that each side contains 3, 4 or 5 whole units and has a right angle opposite its longest side. A right angle can be constructed using any units, be they inches, metres or even bricks. Because the units are in simple ratio a triangle 15 m × 20 m × 25 m could be constructed if it were more convenient. In this example each factor of our 3, 4, 5 triangle has

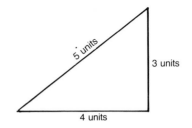

Figure 4.3   A 3, 4, 5 triangle.

been multiplied by five. The larger the triangle is, the more accurate it is likely to be.

Method 1
To return to the problem, the classical solution would be to construct a 3, 4, 5 triangle to produce one of the right angle corners of the base (Figure 4.4). First mark 4 m along the wall A to B. Hold the tape at A and measure the 3 m offset to C,

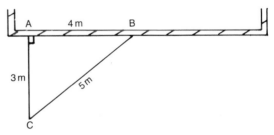

Figure 4.4   Establishing a 3, 4, 5 triangle on site.

double the tape back to B which an assistant holds on the 8 m mark (3 m + 5 m), by tensioning the tape at C two measurements are taken at once and line AC is now at right angles to AB.

The lines AB and AC are now extended to the dimensions required of 5 m and 6 m (Figure 4.5).

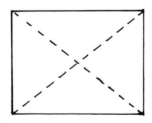

Figure 4.2   The accuracy of any square or rectangle is checked by ensuring the two diagonals are of equal length.

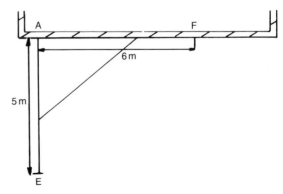

Figure 4.5   Using the 3, 4, 5 triangle for setting out a concrete base.

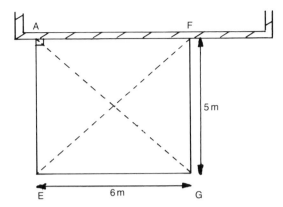

Figure 4.6 Checking the rectangle.

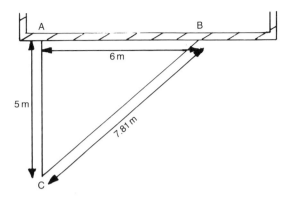

Figure 4.7 The 'pocket calculator method'.

This gives us the positions of E and F, the other two corners. From each 5 m and 6 m is measured again to close the rectangle at G (Figure 4.6).

Having established the rectangle AEGF, the result is checked by comparing the diagonals AG and EF. They should have the same value but in practice it will depend upon how accurately the above procedure has been carried out.

If the diagonals are not correct it can only mean that one or more sides have been mismeasured or a right angle has not been constructed.

A reasonable tolerance on any diagonal would be $\pm$ 10 mm, but on longer dimensions over rough ground with a stiff breeze $\pm$ 25 mm may have to be accepted. The dimensions can be tightened up as conditions improve.

The above is a traditional but very tedious method of setting out, and not to be recommended unless necessary because accuracy is difficult to maintain when lines beyond AB and AC are extended to positions F and E in Figure 4.5.

Method 2
The improved method results from the metric system and a pocket calculator.

Firstly mark positions A and B 6 m apart (Figure 4.7). Then using Pythagoras again, calculate the total diagonal length to position point C, the third corner.

$$\text{e.g. } 6^2 + 5^2 = \text{length of diagonal } x^2$$
$$36 + 25 = x^2$$
$$61 = x^2$$

Using a calculator with square root facility the square root of 61 is found to be 7.81. Using a tape measure, or preferably two measures, point C can be directly established by measuring

from points A and B (see Plate 4.1).

From points B and C the fourth corner can easily be established as before. Then the diagonals can be checked, as in Figure 4.6 again.

The saving in time and trouble is significant and all the necessary calculations can be made before arrival on site.

This method, by triangulation, is basic to the building trade. There are no other instruments or equipment able to produce the desired result.

Note though how it is always desirable to measure to the outside of the peg during setting out. This is not only a good convention, because if the line is attached to the wrong side of the peg there is instantly an error of 25 mm, but once the peg is established the concrete formwork can be positioned directly against the outside of the peg (Plate 4.2).

Problem To set out for a framed building 27 m long by 13.5 m wide.

Calculate total diagonal
$$13.5^2 + 27^2 = \text{diagonal}^2$$
$$182.25 + 729 = 911.25$$
$$\sqrt{911.25} = 30.187$$

Profiles

When dealing with buildings with footings or stanchion foundations, corner pegs cannot be maintained in position because of the need to excavate and pour concrete into the corner holes, yet accuracy must be maintained and building lines positioned quickly when required.

The method is to set up a series of corner profile boards as in Figure 4.8. Once established

Plate 4.2   When setting out for small areas of concrete it is useful to measure to the outside of the peg. The lines and roadforms can then be positioned without disturbing the peg.

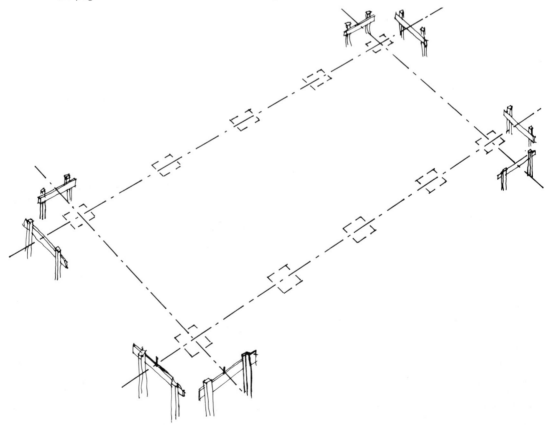

Figure 4.8   An example of profile boards set out.

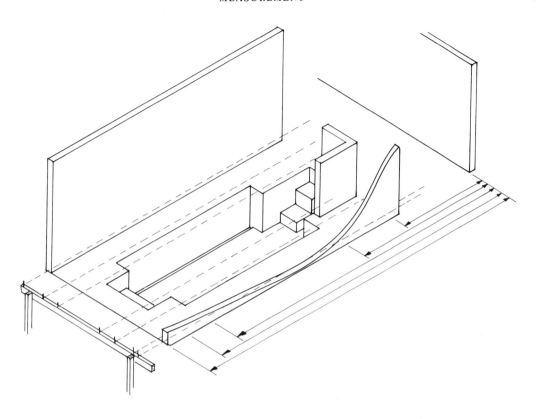

Figure 4.9 A milking parlour pit is an exacting structure with many important dimensions and complicated by various gradients. A profile board set at both ends is helpful as would be a series of running dimensions noted on the drawing.

the lines are positioned on the board with a nail or saw cut. The building lines can then be taken down and refixed as often as necessary in the sure knowledge that they are accurate once set.

Profile boards can be set as far as 3.5 m to 5 m from the corners of the building if necessary to allow ample room for site traffic. Profiles should also be set at the same level.

The most efficient way to set out a building using profile boards is to measure the length and width, and place accurate corner pegs using the calculated diagonal technique. The building lines are then stretched from the profile boards and adjusted laterally until they kiss the corner pegs. The corner pegs can then be removed and work can commence. In a high wind or other difficult circumstances the lines can be rechecked and the accuracy tightened up when conditions improve.

A profile board technique can also be adopted when there are many important dimensions to control such as with a herringbone milking parlour. Simply by marking the required dimensions along the profile boards at both ends of the parlour the walls and pit can be accurately positioned (Figure 4.9).

Actual methods may vary greatly and a degree of improvisation is called for. Constant checking is necessary and it is advisable to transfer measurements to part of the structure as soon as possible; for example, once walls appear above ground level there is a physical edge, or base line to work from. It is very easy for a milking parlour fitter to find fault when the pit and side walls are completed, and the equipment does not fit. He has physical elements to measure from. He would be less vociferous if he had to accurately produce the desired result from an initial start in the bottom of an excavated hole.

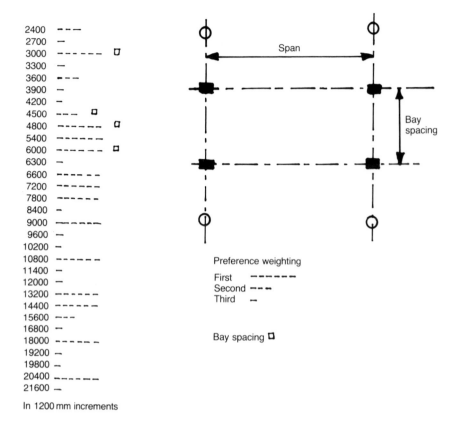

Figure 4.10 (a) Horizontal spacing of structural zones for span and bay spacing.

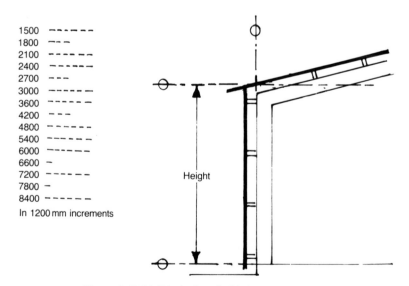

Figure 4.10 (b) Principal vertical height preference.
Source: *Farm Buildings Digest*, Vol. 5, No. 4, 1970/71.

Running Dimensions

If a number of items have to be set out at regular or even irregular intervals, (such as stub stanchions in a bunker silo) rather than measure from first to second stanchion and then second to third etc., it is far more accurate to measure first to second, first to third and first to fourth etc. This prevents any build up of error if slight mis-measurement to stanchion two occurred perhaps. Even though stanchion two will remain incorrect, stanchion three and those after will not be thrown out. Again the various dimensions can be summed before arrival on site.

Our milking parlour drawing (Figure 4.9) would be easier to follow if a series of running dimensions were noted starting from a fixed point such as the front wall of the parlour building.

Dimensional Co-ordination

Dimensional co-ordination establishes a measurement framework from which buildings and fittings can be sized. Although grandiose in name, dimensional co-ordination has been with us for many years in the form of the standard 15 ft bay spacing for framed buildings. This spacing suited both timber, steel and concrete buildings with the advantage that secondary items such as thrust wall and cladding panels could be made to a standard form by a second manufacturer and be expected to fit a standard bay.

During the change to metric under international agreement size multiples of 300 mm were chosen as a basis for standardised buildings.

Thus as in Figure 4.10(a) there is a range of dimensions for span or bay spacing, but the more appealing dimensions are given a preference weighting in the hope that they will gradually become standard.

Curiously farm buildings are often still specified in imperial measure and the 15 ft bay is still popular. Nevertheless it is reasonable to expect that bay widths will tend to increase with ever bigger machinery on farms and a 6 m (20 ft 4 in) bay will hopefully become the norm.

Bay spacing is, of course, measured from centre to centre of the stanchions and the total length of the building is taken to be the sum of the bay spacings (Figure 4.10). Therefore, most framed buildings will in fact be slightly longer overall—by the thickness of one stanchion.

Span, however, has normally been measured from outside face to outside face of the stanchions, whereas BS 5502 now recommends that span is measured to the centre line of the stanchions for modular buildings. This may be a point of confusion between farmer and building supplier—so beware.

Not perhaps so obvious is the position of eaves height which is taken from the finished floor level to the plane of upper side of the roof purlins, i.e. to the underside of the cladding material.

For traditionally constructed buildings span and length will continue to be measured to the outer faces of the walls, which is sensible.

Chapter 5

LEVELLING

THE TECHNIQUE of calculating levels and establishing falls and gradients is another fundamental skill for the DIY farm builder to master. The provision of falls may be more critical in agricultural rather than industrial or domestic building because inevitably gradients are being constructed to encourage run off of water or effluents, whereas a factory floor must be level. Conversely, steps or steep ramps are undesirable if livestock are to move freely about. Water which lies on concrete aprons and freezes in winter to become a sheet of ice is a particular hazard.

Again the techniques can be altered to suit the job in hand. For example a concrete farm road may simply be allowed to follow the ground contour and a minimum crossfall of 25 mm maintained to ensure surface drainage. However, with a new dairy complex a complete plan of all important floor and drainage levels will be required.

It is perhaps worth stating that a level line or level surface is equivalent to that taken up by an area of still water such as a lake. Therefore a level line follows the curvature of the earth.

A flat, or horizontal line, or surface, is tangential to the earth's surface and the force of gravity will act perpendicular to it.

The distinction between these two is important to comprehend although perhaps of little real consequence to a farm builder. All types of level produce a horizontal line of sight and for long distances it is normal to apply a correction to allow for the curvature of the earth and also for the refraction of light.

The sum of both corrections is about 170 mm for the first mile. At 100 m, the maximum recommended line of sight, the error is negligible.

Levels

Levels work either by means of a bubble tube or by a pendulum-mounted mirror to produce a horizontal line of sight. The layman must not confuse levels with theodolites. Whilst the latter do measure relative heights they do so by trigonometric means.

Spirit level

A spirit level can be used with a straight edge to level small areas. Over greater distances it is impractical and inaccurate. It is sufficiently accurate to check the falls on formwork prior to laying concrete since it needs little skill in use and the direction of fall can be instantly seen. It is invaluable for checking for perpendicular.

The Cowley level

This is an ideal and essential piece of equipment for small-scale work. The action of placing the level on its tripod unlocks a pendulum-mounted mirror. A second operator moves a special target on a staff by direction from the instrument operator until a level reading is obtained. The use of the Cowley level is highly recommended. Its advantages are:

- It is completely automatic, enabling rapid setting up.
- Accuracy over 50 m plus.
- It is very easy to read with a staff which is graduated in both imperial and metric.
- Virtually 'solid state' and difficult to damage when removed from tripod.
- Inexpensive to purchase and requires little skill to operate.

Plate 5.1 A Cowley level in use.

Dumpy levels

These are basically telescopes with crosshairs in the lenses. The telescope is accurately levelled by a bubble tube mounted alongside the telescope and a reading taken by aligning the crosshairs onto a staff. The advantages include greater accuracy at distance, plus the ability to measure large differences in level because the staffman does not have to move a target.

Quickset level

This is a very similar instrument to a Dumpy level. However its mounting and adjustment mechanism is better and it can often be set to a gradient.

Automatic levels

These are again similar in appearance to a Dumpy level but have a pendulum-mounted mirror so that they are approximately set by hand and then automatically adjust for each reading.

Staffs

The level is aimed at a graduated staff from which the readings are taken. A staff would historically be graduated in feet with subdivisions of one tenth of a foot. Since a tenth of a foot is a nonsense, obtain only a metric staff and operate in metric.

Unfortunately most Dumpy levels produce an image which is upside down and care is needed to read the staff, especially with the figures 6 and 9.

Other levels

There are other types of level available, one of which uses a rotating laser beam. This instrument has the advantage that it produces a horizontal plane or collimation over the site rather than a horizontal beam. Once the level is set an operator can work on his own, referring to the 'level' as he wishes without the help of a second operator. Moreover he can obtain a level wherever he may roam on the site which is a considerable advantage.

Use of Levels

Datum

It is important to establish a datum from which to calculate the relative heights of each part of the building. Datum point should be positioned away from the immediate building site and may be an area of concrete or drain gulley or other point of fixed height which can be readily returned to as often as necessary.

On a large project datum would normally be taken to an Ordnance Survey bench mark. Within agricultural works it is suggested that a datum height of 10 m is assumed, for most projects. This is an arbitary height which simply removes the need to work in negative figures. If the datum were zero and it was necessary to excavate for drains 2 m deep, drain height would be minus 2 m. By using an assumed datum height of 10 m it is easy to visualise the drains laid at a height of 8 m.

Height of Collimation

Collimation height can simply be thought of as the height of the line of sight of the level. Collimation height must always be established relative to a back sight taken from the datum point, and of course must be re-established whenever the level is moved. It is certainly easier if the instrument can be positioned centrally to view the whole site including the datum point in one sweep. It is a useful trick to leave the tripod, once set, and just remove the instrument at the end of the day's work.

Mistakes in levelling can occur all too easily. The most fundamental is that the instrument is inadvertently knocked or moved. For this reason it is strongly recommended that work should proceed in a circular fashion around the site, but before the level is moved a final reading is taken to the back sight above the datum. Provided the instrument remained secure the same reading should be obtained as from the start.

Reduced Level

Figure 5.1 indicates some staff readings obtained at 5 m intervals over an area of ground adjacent to a concrete apron at points A, B, C, D and E. The edge of the concrete apron is chosen as the datum, the level set and a back sight reading on the staff of 1.6 m is obtained. By turning to point A, a reading of 1.5 m is obtained which indicates the ground rising by 100 mm. Therefore, the smaller the staff reading the higher the ground. The larger the staff reading the greater the distance from collimation and the lower the ground. If a roadform is to be erected 100 mm above the concrete apron then all that is necessary is to compare the two relative heights in this way.

If however the site needs to be surveyed and levels planned accordingly these new readings must be related back to the datum and a reduced level calculated. This is best achieved in tabular form, which will enable errors to be rapidly

STATION	READING	COLLIMA-TION	REDUCED LEVEL	REMARKS
Datum	1.6	11.6	10	Assumed Datum
A	1.5	11.6	10.1	
B	1.38	11.6	10.22	
C	1.46	11.6	10.14	
D	1.52	11.6	10.08	
E	1.76	11.6	9.84	

Figure 5.2   Tabulating the reduced levels.

identified (Figure 5.2). By adding the back sight of 1.6 m to the assumed datum height of 10 m the height of collimation of 11.6 m is reached. By subtracting all the staff readings from the collimation a reduced level can be achieved for each point (Figure 5.3). It is only by calculating a reduced level and marking it on the plan that it is possible to visualise the ground contour.

As an example a bunker silo is to be constructed on this area. For convenience the silo is to be 20 m long with a 3 m wide apron at the front to meet with the existing apron. The silo floor is to fall 300 mm to the front and the apron is to fall 50 mm back towards the silo so that the effluent runs into a channel discharging into a 1.5 m deep effluent tank. (It would normally be essential to arrange a crossfall to direct the effluent into the tank but in this example crossfall is omitted.)

Working from the datum it is easy to fix the finished floor levels (FFL) at the two crucial points, the edge of the 3 m apron and at the end of the site. The formation level of the effluent tank is also established from the edge of the 3 m

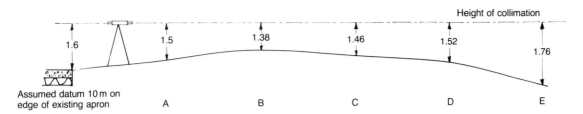

Figure 5.1   Level readings taken at 5 m intervals.

Figure 5.3   Calculated reduced levels.

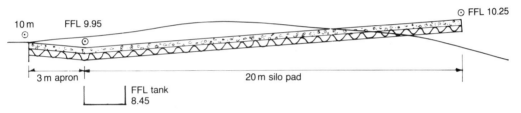

Figure 5.4   Calculated finished floor levels (FFL) relative to existing ground levels.

apron. To give the level at the edge of the apron subtract the fall required from the existing concrete (our datum at 10 m); 10 m minus 50 mm gives 9.95 m (Figure 5.4). Similarly add on the required 300 mm rise over the silo floor; 9.95 m plus 300 mm gives 10.25 m

Assuming now that 150 mm of concrete is to be laid over 150 mm of hardcore (Figure 5.4) excavation must be carried out to reduce the levels accordingly and to remove topsoil and vegetation. It is to this formation level that excavation is needed. Too shallow may result in failure and too deep is wasteful of materials.

It can be seen that near station E the formation level exceeds ground level. This may sometimes force reconsideration of the proposed levels or size of building feasible on the site, but on this occasion there would only be approximately 100 mm of extra hardcore required, plus whatever amount is needed once the topsoil is removed. For most projects it is desirable to

mark the finished floor levels on a plan of the site. Surprisingly few points need be marked, generally at the high and low points of the floors, intermediate positions being boned in (Plate 5.2 and Figure 5.6). From this information the amount of materials to be excavated can be calculated, as described in Chapter 6.

Gradient

Within farm building work it is better to express gradients as a rise or fall over a given distance. Thus the silo floor has a gradient of 300 mm over 20 m. Nevertheless, gradient is usually expressed as a ratio when given as a general recommendation. It is always preferable to use the maximum gradient possible to minimise the risk of water ponding. The ideal for a silo is 1 in 60–70, but where wall panels are used in a roofed silo a lesser fall may be necessary to facilitate easy fitting of the panels. A minimum fall to facilitate drainage is about 1 in 180 which corresponds to 1 inch in a 15 ft bay. A maximum gradient for general work, excepting ramps, is about 1 in 30.

It is becoming common practice to express gradients as a percentage. This is another non-sense when applied to agricultural buildings except that some sophisticated levels work to a gradient which must be expressed as a percent-age. For this silo floor (Figure 5.4) divide the fall required (300 mm) by the length (20 m) and multiply the result by 100.

$$\frac{0.3}{20} = 0.015 \times 100 = 1.5\% \text{ fall}$$

A minimum gradient of 1 in 200 equals 0.5 per cent and 1 in 30 fall equals 3.33 per cent.

For drains a minimum of 1 in 800 is possible (0.125 per cent) with great care.

Grid Levels

For most agricultural buildings a very simple site survey is all that is required. Relatively few measurements will provide all the information necessary, although the position and height of any drains, cables and poles or other immovable objects must be carefully noted.

Occasionally it may be necessary to survey a site for a new layout where the levels change dramatically and the site is overgrown with rub-bish. The only alternative then is to engage upon a grid survey. The site is marked out in a 5 m or 10 m grid and levels are taken at the intersections. Figure 5.5 gives the results of an actual survey. A reduced level is calculated for each inter-section and marked on graph paper. Contour lines can then be drawn at 0.5 metre intervals or whatever is suitable.

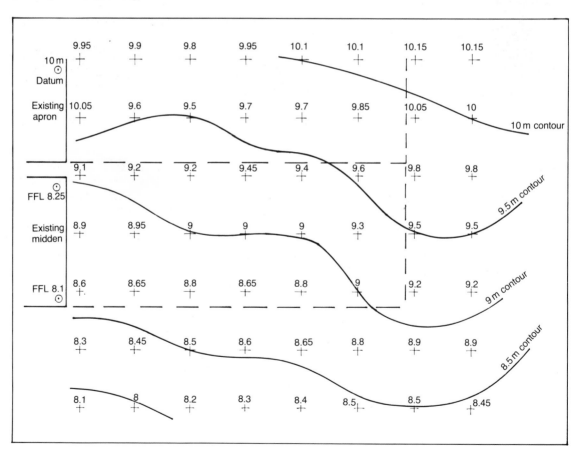

Figure 5.5   Plotted reduced levels of 5 m grid survey.

Plate 5.2   Boning in roadforms. Note steel pin under concrete block which is set to finished floor level. The bricks merely support the block.

Setting Roadforms

As it is seldom necessary on farms to lay concrete level it follows that quick and easy methods of setting roadforms to falls are required.

For small areas a spirit level and straight edge are all that are needed. It is also good practice to check all other formwork with a spirit level prior to concreting.

For formwork up to about 10 m in length, roadforms may be placed using a building line fixed taut between two pegs set at the required height. For longer runs, with a mimimal fall, it is necessary to bone each roadform into position.

Classically a boning rod and sight rail is set up as in Figure 5.6 just as might be used for laying drains.

For roadforms a boning rod and sight rail are

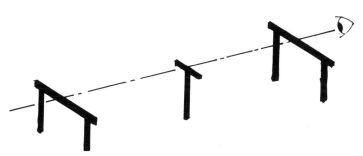

Figure 5.6   Boning rod and sight rails.

sometimes impractical due to the setting up time and the restrictions they impose on the machinery operator. At least one of the sighting frames may have to be set well away from the immediate site. Instead it is suggested that steel pegs are set to the correct height at each end of the concrete bay. Two identical concrete blocks are then set on the pegs and supported with packing bricks and the roadforms boned in between (Plate 5.2). Roadforms can be adjusted above the subgrade by use of suitable packing pieces although a little more hardcore can be placed under the form if preferred. The form is then tapped down to the correct level. In any event well supported roadforms are essential, especially on minimal gradients, or they may shift under the vibrating beam.

Chapter 6

EXCAVATION AND EARTHWORKS

MOST BUILDING works will require some excavation if only to remove topsoil and vegetation. Normally however it will be necessary to excavate to level the site and, of course, footings and sumps, etc. will need excavation to specific depths. Sand/gravel soils will need little excavation because they need little sub-base, as does shallow rock. Any black vegetable soil or soft material should always be removed, and considerable pockets may occur where ditches and farmyard ponds have been filled in, often many years ago. The aim is always to build on an undisturbed subsoil or material of known characteristic. On black fen soils, for example, special attention will always have to be paid to foundations and sub-base, and certain types of buildings may be undesirable in such a situation.

Generally speaking, excessive excavation and earthworks should always be avoided for farm building, partly on grounds of cost but more so because changes in level should be used to assist the flow of materials by gravity. Also livestock buildings which are cut deeply into a hillside will invariably suffer from poor ventilation. For example, one new dairy unit was planned so that slurry was pumped to tanks above the buildings, whereas if the arrangement had been reversed, the change in level would have been sufficient to allow it to flow by gravity.

Cut and Fill

Cut and fill is an obvious method of levelling ground, whereby material is removed from high areas and placed in lower areas, as used in railway and motorway construction. Unfortunately, except perhaps with certain granular subsoil, this is not a technique to be recommended for the DIY farm builder, since it is not easy to compact excavated material back to a density similar to its undisturbed state; 95 per cent being possible only with specialist rollers and compactors.

Strangely enough a degree of natural settlement under 'rigid' farm buildings will be more serious than slight embankment settlement of a 'flexible' motorway carriageway. Any necessary large-scale cut and fill operations must therefore be carried out under guidance from a qualified engineer. This particularly applies to embankments for lakes, reservoirs and large slurry lagoons, or indeed any bunded area (see p. 212).

Most farm buildings are relatively small structures and, because of the difficulty of cut and fill, if there is a deficiency in level it should be made up with hardcore which can readily be compacted into a stable condition. For bulk fill, clean, crushed brick hardcore or crushed concrete are ideal and usually cheap.

Volume of Earthworks

With any less than perfect site, it is advisable to calculate the amount of material to be removed, but more importantly, to calculate the volume of hardcore required. Figure 6.1 is really a poor choice of site with excessive gradient, but useful to illustrate the volume of excavation needed and the volume of hardcore necessary to construct a concrete apron 40 m long by 10 m wide.

The existing ground rises from a level of 8.75 m at the lower end to 10.35 m at the upper end and, for various reasons, the concrete apron is to have a finished floor level (FFL) of 9.45 m. Assuming the cut begins along half the length of the apron, then the volume of cut will be half ×

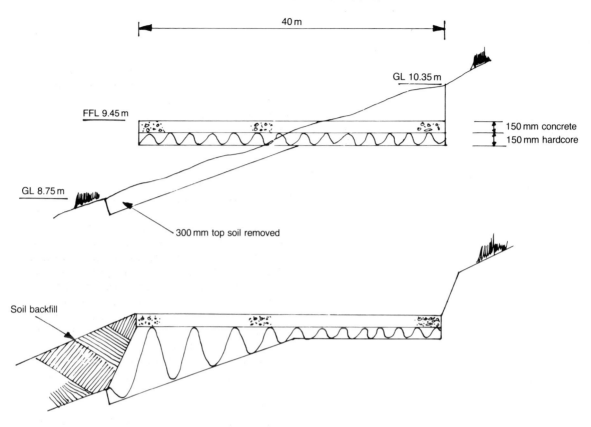

Figure 6.1   An example of calculation of excavation and hardcore fill.

height × width × length. The height will be: 10.35 m − 9.45 m = 900 mm. Add on a thickness of concrete of 150 mm and a minimum 150 mm thickness of hardcore and this gives a vertical height of 1.2 m:

0.5 × 1.2 × 20 × 10 = 120 m³ (Area of triangular section to be removed × width of site)

At the lower end of the site the top soil (300 mm) will have to be removed to provide a stable base for the fill. This part can be calculated by simple cubic measure: 20 × 10 × 0.3 = 60 m³. Therefore the total excavation required is 180 m³.

To calculate the amount of hardcore required the same method should be used but altered slightly in this example. Since a minimum of 150 mm hardcore is required over the whole site, then 0.15 × 40 × 10 = 60 m³. This now leaves the volume for the lower part of the site as 9.45 − 300 mm (concrete + hardcore) =

9.15 m. Ground level of 8.75 − 300 mm (top soil removal) = a formation level of 8.45 m:

9.15 − 8.45 = 700 mm
0.5 × 700 × 20 × 10 = 70 m³
Total fill required = 130 m³ approx

For most sites it will only be necessary to take levels at representative points at the higher and lower end of the site and assume a uniform gradient between. Whilst the ground will not be uniform, the difference will be immeasurable to the amount of excavation required.

Volumes of awkward sites may be calculated by subdividing them into smaller shapes. Figure 6.2 lists useful formulae.

For the ambitious there is a formula known as Simpson's Rule which is particularly useful for volumes of ponds and lakes or other irregular areas. A surveying textbook should be consulted for information on this.

- Area of rectangle =
  length × width
  (l × w)

- Area of triangle =
  $\frac{1}{2}$ length of base ×
  perpendicular height
  ($\frac{1}{2}$ × l × h)

- Area of circle =
  π × radius squared
  (πr²)

  $\pi = \frac{22}{7}$ or 3.142

- Circumference of circle =
  π × diameter
  (πd)

- Area of sphere = 4πr²

- Volume of sphere = $\frac{4}{3}$πr³

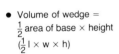

- Volume of wedge =
  $\frac{1}{2}$ area of base × height
  ($\frac{1}{2}$ l × w × h)

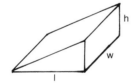

- Volume of prism =
  $\frac{1}{3}$ area of base ×
  perpendicular height
  ($\frac{1}{3}$ l × w × h)

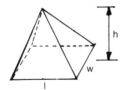

- Volume of cone =
  $\frac{1}{3}$ area of base ×
  perpendicular height
  ($\frac{1}{3}$πr²h)

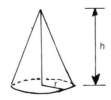

Figure 6.2 Areas and volumes of common figures.

Hardcore and Fill

It is difficult to fully describe materials for hardcore for a sub-base to building works because there are so many local variations and names of material. In most localities it probably pays to follow the crowd and use the same materials as everyone else. Nevertheless, there are basically two groups of materials—either quarried in some form, or derivatives of other materials.

Quarried materials

These consist of crushed granites and limestones or as-raised gravels or hoggin. Granites and limestones are graded by the top size down so that a 100 mm crushed stone would all pass through a 100 mm screen. This would constitute a first-rate material at a premium price. For farm building a waste or screened out material of 40 mm down is most useful since it is cheaper, often self-blinding and easy to work. Screened materials often contain clays and other 'impurities' but this is not normally detrimental.

Quarry waste, hoggin or 'as raised ballast' are similar sized materials giving excellent results.

Other materials

Other suitable materials include slag, crushed concrete and brick, colliery shale, ashes and railway ballast. Ashes and colliery shales must be checked for excessive sulphate levels before use.

Some rules of thumb:

- Apart from fill, it is rarely necessary to use more than 150 mm of hardcore provided a good subgrade exists.
- Most DIY problems occur when the site is not properly stripped and fill materials become contaminated with mud from the underside.
- Farmers in particular are lax about proper compaction of hardcore. A properly compacted cheap material may perform better than a poorly compacted expensive material.
- In difficult wet ground, the bigger the stone the better, and the cleaner the stone the better, i.e. no clay or fines. A graded 100 mm to 50 mm stone will give an excellent sub-base similar to a hand-pitched base in this situation.
- Most quarried materials will weigh about 2 tonnes/m³.

Plate 6.1   Excessive earthmoving is expensive and its necessity may indicate poor choice or utilisation of site.

Membranes

The advent of ground membranes is of particular help in poor site conditions. Membranes support the hardcore and prevent it punching into the subgrade whilst, at the same time, preventing mud rising from the subgrade and lubricating the hardcore to the point where it fails to bind and support the applied load. Apart from the tremendous benefit in wet areas, the use of a membrane can make significant savings in the cost of stone used to construct hardcore roads and aprons.

For very small areas of poor ground the outer sacking of 1 ton fertiliser bags can be used to good effect.

Chapter 7

DRAINAGE

DRAINAGE SYSTEMS in and around buildings are either 'separate' or 'combined'. This means either that storm water and sewage effluents are piped in separate systems or they are run together combined in one drain.

It is strongly recommended that for farm buildings work, storm water be kept as clean as possible so that it may be directly discharged into a soakaway, ditch or watercourse. Effluents will normally have to be collected and contained until it is possible to spread them on the land. Any dilution of effluents by storm water can dramatically increase the storage capacity required and the cost of disposal.

One inch of rain per square yard of concrete apron will produce 4½ gallons of storm water, which is a massive dilution if allowed into a slurry system. The metric equivalent is 1 millimetre of rainfall per square metre gives 1 litre of storm water, or 10 mm on 100 m² giving 1 m³.

It is important to note that whilst slurry and silage effluents can be stored and handled by normal agricultural means, domestic sewage cannot. Thereby any toilet must discharge to a septic tank or sewer and will need approval under local authority regulations.

Septic Tank

For most agricultural situations the installation of a septic tank will be the only available means to treat sewage. In a septic tank the material is digested over a period of time by bacteria in anaerobic conditions until it is safe to discharge. It is now common to install a proprietary GRP tank which has greatly simplified many constructional difficulties, although careful siting and installation are necessary due to the fragile nature of the tank.

The other main considerations for a sewerage system are:

- Adequate falls—neither too steep nor too shallow. A minimum gradient for a 100 mm drain is 1 in 50.
- Pipe joints must be sealed and pipes laid deep enough to be protected from seasonal ground movement and traffic above.
- Foundations to buildings must be bridged so that no load is taken by the pipe. Also drains under buildings may need haunching in concrete but a granular bedding may be better.
- Manholes and rodding eyes must be placed frequently to enable blockages to be cleared. Sharp bends should be accommodated within chambers wherever possible and the sides to the channel within the chamber haunched to maintain flow of sewage.

Storm Water

It is normal to calculate the appropriate sizes of gutters and drains to cope with storm conditions. Whilst the annual rainfall varies greatly over the country, strangely enough the volume of water falling during a storm of given duration does not alter significantly from place to place.

Roof drainage is normally based on a rainfall rate of 75 mm per hour. This rate may occur for five minutes once in four years on average and, if it is exceeded, the gutter will simply overflow. Overflowing occasionally will be of little significance for a farm building, except for a grainstore where it may be prudent to design for a rate of 150 mm per hour, which may occur for three minutes in fifty years or for four minutes in a hundred years.

The correct design for rainwater systems is

beyond the scope of this book due to the variable factors involved—types of gutters and sizes, fall sizes and position of rainwater pipes and frequency and position of bends. However, the Building Research Establishment publishes a series of excellent digests which describe the design of roof and storm drainage systems.

Many similar factors affect the discharge rate of an underground storm drainage system. However, since 100 mm drains will cope with most situations, 150 mm pipes will be suitable for mains and 225 mm pipes will normally be adequate for whole farmstead discharges with shallow falls.

Storm water drainage systems
Storm water systems comprise a range of options from a simple land drain to a complicated network of a civil engineering nature. It is important to maintain a gradient throughout the system and the excavation will need checking with boning rods (Chapter 5, Figure 5.6). It is usually easier to check the trench gradient with boning rods and then set each pipe with a spirit level to ensure a continuous fall. Also (sometimes in conflict with the above) drains should be kept to a reasonable depth if possible where they terminate near the building, because any subsequent extension of the building may be accommodated by simply extending the existing drains.

Whilst there is less chance of a storm water system blocking, inspection chambers should be provided at strategic locations. They are particularly useful if several minor pipes have to be jointed together (Figure 7.1). By contrast to a sewerage inspection chamber, it is better not to channel and haunch the bottom of the chamber but to leave it as a silt trap.

Gulleys can be constructed in a similar way which is cheaper and enables a larger cast-iron grid to be used.

Inspection chambers can be constructed of semi-engineering bricks, concrete blocks or precast concrete rings. Generally the deeper they are and the more services that are connected, the larger they have to be. When chambers have to be situated under heavily trafficked areas, e.g. lorry access, special consideration may have to be given to the design of the concrete cover and to encasing the walls of precast rings in concrete.

Pipes

Underground drainage pipes are available made either of clay, concrete or plastic (UPVC) and each have their advantages. Whilst some collared or spigot and socket pipes are still used, the difficulty in producing a sealed joint has resulted in the advent of other systems. A similar looking

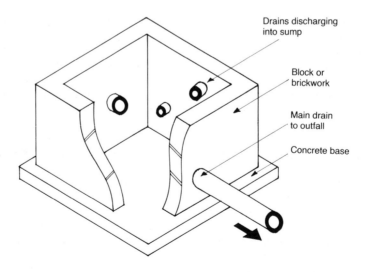

Figure 7.1   Stormwater inspection chamber with concrete, steel or cast iron cover.

Plate 7.1 Drainage pipes.
From left to right: 150 mm collared pipe; 150 mm concrete pipe with 'ogee' joint; 100 mm clay pipe with sleeve coupler 1.6 m long; 100 mm UPVC pipe 6 m long with coupler.

clay product with plain spigot ends is becoming common; this uses a separate plastic collar with rubber seals to produce an effective joint.

Concrete pipes are excellent in that they are available 'porous' which assists general ground water drainage over the site and have simple 'ogee' joints (Plate 7.1). Concrete pipes begin to become significantly cheaper from 150 mm diameter upwards. Larger, dense concrete pipes with sealed jointing systems are available, but these are intended for mains sewer construction.

UPVC pipes are available in long lengths up to 6 m and are easily transported and worked on site. As these pipes are thin walled they rely on the bedding material and surrounding backfill material to a fair degree to maintain their integrity. It is normally necessary to provide a 50 mm bed of granular material (10 mm gravel) upon which to lay the pipes and if there is any significant ground loading above, the pipe should be completely surrounded by bedding.

The bedding of pipes and subsequent backfilling is a difficult problem to overcome. It is important that pipes are laid on an undisturbed subsoil or a gravel or weak concrete bed where poor support conditions exist. Any low places in the excavation should also be filled with gravel or weak concrete.

Where pipe runs become shallow or terminate inside buildings, it may become desirable to bed and haunch the pipes in concrete to protect them from surface loadings. However, if there is any resultant settlement of the building, it may crack the haunching and take the pipe as well. A more flexible pipe may therefore be desirable.

Backfilling should always be carried out by hand until 100 mm above the pipe using a regular sized material. Backfilling with any hard, large or angular material should be avoided as it could produce a point load on the pipe and collapse it. In difficult situations imported material will have to be used to cover the pipe. Initial compaction of fill material must be by hand due again to the danger of crushing the pipe, before a trench rammer or vibrating plate or roller can be used on the upper layers. Alternatively the trench can be filled with foamed concrete.

In truth, few of the comments above will apply to a farm situation, but the inevitable settlement of roads after excavation for services must be remembered. Therefore it is as well to be aware of the above when laying pipes, bearing in mind subsoil, type of pipe, depth of excavation and floor construction or subsequent trafficking of the area above the pipe.

Land drains
The laying of land tile drains to convey storm water from buildings is not really to be recommended because of the likelihood of roots entering the pipe joints, and the fact that tiles can become so displaced that rodding becomes impossible.

Perforated plastic pipe in long coils is very cheap and may suffice in some situations, although for any shallow gradients it must be machine laid because of the difficulty of accurately finishing the base to the trench by hand.

On rare occasions land drains or stone drains will be necessary to intercept ground water approaching the site of a building.

Soakaways

In permeable subsoils it is possible to construct a soakaway to disperse storm water into the surrounding land and thereby save the cost of an expensive drainage system. Often 'drains to soakaway' is seen on drawings as an easy option, whereas the designer has no notion of whether the subsoil is suitable for a soakaway. In clay soils or soils with a high water table, a soakaway is unlikely to be successful except for the smallest discharge. Where there is uncertainty, it is desirable to bore a test hole and time how long a given quantity of water takes to disperse. Again, the Building Research Establishment has some excellent information on tests for and the construction of soakaways.

In our experience soakaways are rarely successful since the largest volumes of water normally need to be discharged when the land is in the worst condition to receive it (winter). The whole concept is contrary to the farmer's normal desire to improve land drainage.

Sumps

Sumps or underground tanks are an invaluable

Figure 7.2   Some surface drainage systems.

(a) 100 mm Porcupipe

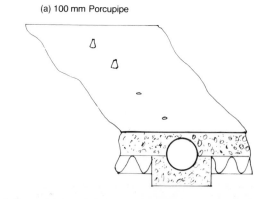

A Porcupipe is installed with polythene 'quills' protruding through the finished concrete. The quills are cut off to floor level at a later stage which leaves a small conical duct into the top of the pipe.

(b) Slot pipe

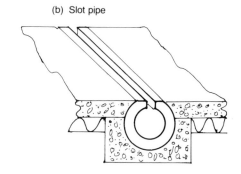

A slot pipe is bedded into position on concrete and then used as a permanent roadform for the remainder of the floor or apron.

(c) Kerb drain

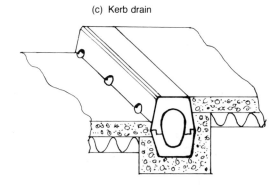

A kerb drain is fitted in two halves to form a duct or drain as shown. Water enters through a side hole which makes them a useful alternative for roads and aprons.

(d) Channel drain

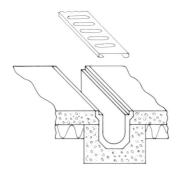

An example of a 1 m section of channel drain which is part of a sophisticated system of polymer concrete drainage products. The channels are lightweight and suitable for silage and other effluents if the end joints are sealed to prevent leakage. The channels are available with a constant internal depth or with a 0.6% slope to the invert when laid in a sequential arrangement. Various galvanised or cast iron grids fit the channel rebate.

(e) Precast channel

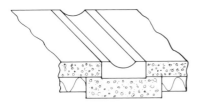

A precast concrete dished channel is very useful in situations where minimal falls occur. Dished channels are laid with a spirit level to slight gradient which ensures the subsequent surrounding paving is adequately drained.

means of collecting slurry and effluents and preventing pollution. Unfortunately they are not easy to construct and surprisingly, the larger they are the more expensive per unit volume they become, because the engineering becomes more complex.

Sumps will normally be constructed on a 150 mm concrete base and be built of bricks, concrete blocks reinforced and rendered, reinforced mass concrete or precast concrete panels or rings. Unless the proposed sump is modest in size (maximum 4.5 × 4.5 × 2.5 m deep) the services of an engineer will be necessary. The main consideration will be of ground water pressure leading to flotation or collapse of the walls whilst the sump is empty. A sump situated beneath a concrete apron will also need an engineer to design the cover to withstand vehicle loadings.

Surface Drainage Pipes

Slot pipes, Porcupipes and kerb drains are of special interest for draining roads and aprons, and sometimes for livestock buildings (Figure 7.2, page 60).

Discharge to Sewer

Any discharge to Water Service Company sewer, other than for domestic sewage, is under the category of 'trade effluent'. Whilst under a 1937 Public Health Act there is right of use for all, the water companies have the right to impose certain conditions, and a formal consent from them is necessary to discharge trade effluent.

The conditions the companies are allowed to impose are mostly to prevent wastes or effluents damaging the sewer installation, affecting the treatment system at the sewage works, or carrying harmful effects through into the environment. The same applies to surface water discharges to a water course. As an example silage effluent discharged to a sewer (unlikely though it is) might damage the concrete pipes and would probably overwhelm the local (small) sewage treatment works with its high BOD loading. The water companies themselves may then be in trouble with the NRA if the treatment works failed to cope and the resulting discharge polluted the watercourse. The water service companies are therefore within their rights to refuse to accept such trade effluent because the above conditions cannot be met. Existing consents for dirty water may cause similar problems and are under pressure to be phased out. Charges are certain to rise nevertheless.

In an apparent overlap with NRA responsibilities water supply companies are similarly able to prohibit discharges of trade effluent without treatment where supplies of potable water, licensed abstractions, wildlife and conservation are at risk.

Chapter 8

FRAMED BUILDINGS

ALMOST ALL farm buildings are now factory made. Traditional construction of local materials is uneconomic for all but the smallest buildings. Factory-made buildings fall into two distinct groups, both of which leave ample opportunity for DIY.

The first group is the intensive livestock building, usually timber-framed and clad with timber, steel or fibre cement. Such buildings are relatively small, lightweight and normally require only a simple concrete base as a foundation and floor. Bases to prefabricated buildings can be readily constructed as a DIY operation, even when complicated by slatted floors and slurry channels. The only difficulty is to maintain dimensional accuracy whilst constructing the base. The buildings are often termed 'package deal', since the package will usually include internal pens and divisions, troughs and feeding equipment, fans and ventilation control equipment. As stated, these buildings are predominant for intensive livestock systems and their choice is usually determined by animal husbandry considerations. For a pig farrowing house, the insulation, ventilation and internal fittings are predetermined to a high standard and difficult to match on a DIY basis. Yet DIY baseworks for such a building could make significant savings. It is also worth noting the longevity of most package-deal buildings.

The second group consists of framed buildings and, since the advent of the portal frame, it has become predominant because of the economy of labour and materials in its construction. Portal buildings are competitively available in timber up to 15 m span, concrete up to 24 m span and steel up to 45 m or more. The relative price difference between materials varies due to economic factors from time to time, but a survey by the Farm and Rural Buildings Centre in 1970 found that there was a greater difference between competing companies than there was between construction materials.

It is common practice for a farmer to purchase a building frame and then to fit it out himself. The purchase of a frame building will normally also include roof, gutters, doors and side cladding down to a specified level. In addition, a building frame manufacturer will usually be responsible for excavating and constructing his own foundations and this avoids many difficulties for the purchaser.

The two major advantages of the portal frame are the high internal clearances for tipping lorries and trailers, and their ready adaptation for barns, bunker silos, grain stores and buildings for cattle and pigs just by alteration to walls, floors and doorways. Little alteration to a building's frame is necessary which makes for a standard item produced at economic cost. The popularity of framed buildings on farms is enhanced because they are considered a capital asset which might be converted to other uses not possible with package-deal buildings.

When deciding upon the size of a portal building it is important to consider the economies of scale, i.e. that the bigger the building the lower its unit cost. Since any portal building will have two gable walls, perhaps with doors, walls and cladding, it follows that the cost of the gable wall will be the same whether the building is three bays long or ten bays long. Hence the longer building becomes cheaper per unit area. The same argument applies to the width of a building and an extra 600 mm on the eaves height may incur only a very small additional charge compared to the total cost.

The above must not be taken to extremes, however, since other factors such as ventilation considerations affect permissible width, as does airflow speeds in lateral ducts in grain stores. It is for the reader to balance all these factors.

BS 5502

Although, as discussed in Chapter 2, BS 5502 is a wide-ranging document embracing many aspects of farm building construction and use, it has particular relevance to the purchase of a building frame. As described in Chapter 2, farm buildings enjoy relaxation from many of the planning and building regulations and controls since the view is taken—quite rightly—that the structural failure of a farm building is unlikely to endanger human life. Consequently, farm buildings have always been constructed to a lower integrity and more cheaply than their industrial equivalents.

In recent years it has become difficult to establish, for example, whether a vegetable packing plant should be an agricultural or an industrial building. BS 5502 solves this problem by offering four Classes of building (see Chapter 2, Figure 2.6). A Class 1 building is very similar in its structural requirements to an industrial building. Most framed farm buildings will fall into Class 2; simple pole barns or temporary structures into Class 3 or 4.

Within the British Standard a Class 3 building has a 'design life' of ten years but this does not mean that it will fall down after only ten years. Design life takes into account statistical weather information for all regions of the country and suggests that a Class 3 building may only face extreme conditions of wind and snow loadings once in ten years on average. If these loadings are exceeded some damage might occur. For a Class 2 building, such a combination of loads should only occur once in twenty years on average. Since this part of the code is based on actual weather information, it theoretically allows for a building of lower integrity (hence cheaper) to be constructed in lowland England compared with its equivalent in highland Scotland, though both are of the same Class.

Choosing a Framed Building

If it is decided to purchase a building frame, and the size is established, it is then necessary to decide on the material. Steel is very versatile, concrete is more resistant to fire and needs no maintenance, and timber is naturally sympathetic,

easy to work and much favoured in coastal areas where steel corrosion is more of a problem. It is then advisable to obtain at least three quotations for the building in question. Having received the quotations, unless choice is based on price alone, it may be very difficult to decide between them.

Variations occur in size of steel work, amount of bracing, type of purlins, type of roof and side-cladding, position and number of rainwater pipes and, above all, protective finish of steelwork. It can be very difficult to assimilate all these features and it is suggested that they are listed in descending order of importance in each case (Chapter 2)—much as might be done when trying to decide which new tractor to purchase. Some features to be considered are:

- Near to the top of the list should come the manufacturer's local reputation for a good product completed on time.
- The sizes of steelwork should be considered. They may vary from manufacturer to manufacturer even though each building fulfils the same requirements within the British Standard. In recent years building stanchions have become larger in dimension but slimmer in terms of kilogrammes of steel per metre of length. Whilst this undoubtedly meets the structural requirements, consider the effect of corrosion over the years on a thin column—the larger area of exposed surface is more susceptible to being weakened by corrosion.
- Timber purlins may be preferable in livestock buildings because of possible corrosion of galvanised steel purlins. 'The trade' may not always agree since, unless good quality timber is available, shrinkage, twisting and warping of timber purlins could be a problem.
- With the exception of grainstores, too many rooflight sheets can never be fitted in a building. Always insist on an open ridge for a livestock building; crown-cranked ventilation sheets are unlikely to give adequate ventilation.
- The quality of paint finish is tremendously variable from manufacturer to manufacturer. A cheap job will consist of one coat of red primer applied directly to the steel as it is fabricated. A good manufacturer will shot or grit blast the steel to remove the mill scale and rust, and then paint with primer and top coat, and touch up as necessary on-site. However, it is becoming more common for steel building

frames to be galvanised after fabrication to eliminate this problem—galvanising may cost a little more but the additional protection may be well worth while.

• Assess the requests or demands for payments and deposits, etc. A request for a small deposit at the time of ordering is usually justified, especially when a manufacturer is to make the necessary planning applications, and even more so if any detailed design work is needed. However, significant amounts of money should not be paid until the building is delivered on-site, and on time; then 75 per cent of the money should be paid promptly. The remaining 20 per cent or so is usually paid when the building is erected to the customer's satisfaction.

Plate 8.1   A pin jointed stanchion foundation prior to grouting.

Steel Buildings with Anchor Bolt Foundations

Pin jointed foundation designs have been in common use with industrial buildings for many years and agricultural buildings are now mostly constructed in the same way. The advantages stem from speedier construction on site because of easier foundation work and rapid erection of the frame with stanchions quickly bolted into position. (Plate 8.1)

The special foundation bolts with plate washers are assembled onto a plywood template (Plate 8.2) and positioned as accurately as possible in the wet concrete foundation (Plate 8.3). Subsequently the template and polystyrene are removed which gives the bolts clearance within the tapered holes allowing for small lateral adjustment of the columns as required. Some manufacturers may survey the level of the foundations 'as cast' and correct any relative differences by fabricating stanchions to appropriate length as a factory operation.

During erection of the building any small discrepancy in height can be corrected by placing steel shims under the stanchion. Final alignment and plumbing of the building is usually carried out once the frame is fully erected which helps produce a more accurate result than the conventional method of casting the stanchions into the concrete base. Once completed the final operation is to grout the bottom of the stanchion with a sand cement mix which fixes the components in position and protects the bolts from corrosion. The grout must be encouraged to fill the tapered holes and cover the base plate and

Plate 8.2   Foundation bolts are assembled through a polystyrene sleeve (or similar) and attached to a plywood template.

Plate 8.3   The template with pins attached is placed into the surface of the concrete foundation as accurately as possible.

nuts. Being the last job on site and being diffi-cult and tedious grouting is often skimped par-ticularly if it's Friday afternoon. Alternatively it may unfairly become the general builder's responsibility and he should be in no doubt about the importance of the operation. It is the writer's opinion that unless grouting is meticu-lously carried out this successful technique for industrial buildings is cause for concern in agri-cultural buildings where effluents may enter the foundation bolt pockets and rapidly cause cor-rosion in a critical location where inspection is impossible.

Re-erected Buildings

Occasionally, second-hand buildings may become available on industrial sites which are suitable for re-erection as farm buildings, especially as a DIY venture. Whilst such a building might seem very attractive and be attractively priced, the pros and cons should be weighed up carefully:

- A re-erected building which costs more than 60–70 per cent of the price of a new building is hardly worth the trouble.
- The cost and work involved in putting up a used building are exactly the same as for a new one.
- The cost of dismantling an existing building, transport, allowances for breakages and re-newal of cladding fixings, etc., have to be added.
- A coat of paint will be desirable before re-erection.

All these factors may leave little margin to pur-chase a second-hand building and it is difficult to understand the inflated prices often asked.

Nevertheless, where an agreement has been reached, the frame must be carefully marked before it is dismantled and carefully taken down. Generally the purchaser would be advised to dismantle it himself since more care can be taken and breakages reduced. At all costs avoid any agreement to clear the site completely or engage in demolition work. Buildings most suitable for re-erection will be of steel and these can usually be unbolted, and then handled and transported in manageable units.

Concrete buildings are difficult to dismantle because each item—purlins included—needs to be lifted by crane. For some buildings two cranes will be necessary. Stanchions will need crane support whilst the concrete foundation is broken out—not a speedy job. Concrete components will need careful handling at all stages with specialist slings if chips and fractures are to be avoided.

Timber buildings are relatively easy to dis-mantle, although with a portal frame it will prove very difficult to remove the plywood gussets since the galvanised nails cannot be withdrawn. In some circumstances, it may be possible to nail a new gusset over the existing one.

Kit of parts

As an alternative to second-hand buildings, but as a means of reducing costs, many manufac-turers will supply on to the site all the com-ponents for a building for DIY erection. Although this is not a difficult job, it must be tackled in a safe manner, and even DIY enthusiasts would be unwise to attempt anything with over 15 m span.

Erecting Framed Buildings

Foundations

The size of foundation depends upon the size of the building, the loading it will apply to its foundation and the allowable bearing pressure of the subsoil. Manufacturers will make rec-ommendations for self-erected buildings, but for re-erected buildings the services of a structural engineer might be necessary. With a trussed building (Figure 8.1) the downward load on the columns is supported by the upward forces in the footing.

A portal frame (Figure 8.2) is more compli-cated in that it also imparts a lateral load to the foundation, and there is an overturning moment to be resisted at the top of the column. It is important that no excavation is carried out at point X (for drains perhaps) without proper advice because of the lateral forces involved.

To construct the foundations, the site is set out and profile boards erected to carry the build-ing lines. The centre position of each hole is then pegged and the foundation excavated to a suitable size and depth. As it is sometimes difficult to maintain the correct position on a hole during excavation and to check its correct size, a cross should be made to the correct size and registered

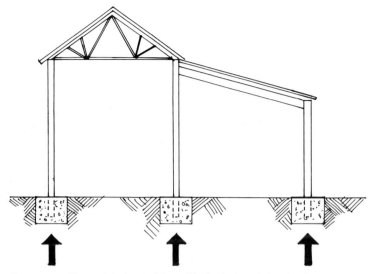

Figure 8.1   Trussed design building with simple foundation loadings.

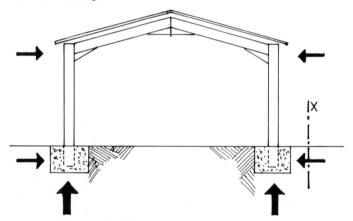

Figure 8.2   Portal frame building with more complicated foundation loadings.

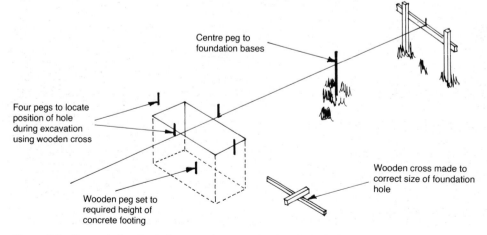

Figure 8.3   Suggested method of accurately excavating foundation holes.

with four pegs as shown in Figure 8.3. Wooden pegs are then driven into the base of the hole to the correct height to gauge the height of the footing concrete.

The structure

It is strongly recommended that the first row of columns is erected and concreted into posi-

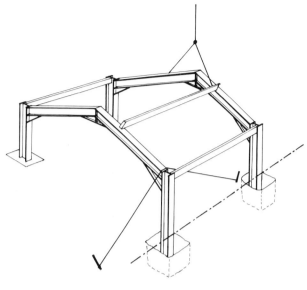

Figure 8.5   The first frame is set into position, guyed and then subsequent frames spaced by eaves beams and purlins.

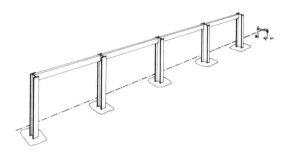

Figure 8.4   First row of stanchions concreted in position.

Plate 8.4   A timber portal frame building being erected.

Plate 8.5   For a concrete frame building it is necessary to construct a socketed foundation using a tapered box.

tion with the eaves beams attached (Figure 8.4). Subsequently each portal is lifted into place with the second stanchion and fixed with some of the purlins and second eaves beam.

This is not the fastest method of erection but it is the safest. The danger of collapse is much reduced with one row of stanchions having been concreted in. The first portal is trued into position and guyed, the remainder are then lifted into position (Figure 8.5). Any diagonal roof bracing must be fitted to the first bay before erection of the remaining frames.

A crane will be necessary for all the lifting operations, and since rough-terrain cranes are extremely scarce, it will usually be necessary to provide a hardcore standing from which the crane can operate. Improvised means of lifting with a forklift truck or other machinery can be extremely dangerous.

Timber Portal Designs

Within the timber industry there are a number of manufacturers who specialise in producing hardwood timber portal frames to TRADA designs. These frames are similar in performance to steel or concrete frames and will cope very well in an agricultural environment of condensation, slurry, silage effluent and fertiliser.

They are especially useful in coastal areas where salt spray is a problem. Whilst they are relatively simple for a manufacturer to construct, it is not really a DIY job, because it is difficult to produce the necessary strength at the dense nailed ply joints. Designs can accommodate a full range of spans, heights and bay lengths. Because of timber's flexible nature, these buildings can often be constructed to special requirements at no premium (Plate 8.4).

Chapter 9

THE USE OF TIMBER

EVEN A MODERATE treatise on current timber technology is beyond the scope of this book. Nevertheless, some agricultural requirements for structural timber are advanced as it is important to appreciate the factors involved. Specific advice is available from the Timber Research and Development Association, but some of the more general considerations are listed here.

Availability of Timber

Far from declining in use over recent years with the onslaught of 'new materials', the use of timber is actually increasing. This may well be due to improvements in preservative treatments, gluing, laminating and the selection of species with higher strength properties. Also timber invariably looks good.

Timbers are divided into two distinct groups: hardwoods and softwoods. Hardwood is produced by broad-leaved trees and softwoods by coniferous trees. Confusingly then, some softwoods can be harder than hardwoods and vice versa.

Timber is normally dried or seasoned before use as the natural drying process will result in shrinkage. The resultant moisture content of wood will eventually equate to the moisture in the surrounding atmosphere. In the 'green' state timber will have a moisture content of at least 30 per cent but this will often be significantly higher. Timber used for fencing, or more particularly set in the ground, will have an equilibrium moisture content of around 20 per cent; the threshold for rot is 22–25 per cent. Most joinery timbers will be seasoned to about 18 per cent, whereas timber for the furniture trade will be artificially dried down to 8–12 per

cent, which hopefully equates to the environment in which it will eventually reside.

Most of the world's virgin forest has been consumed and in a changing pattern more timber is cropped in regenerated forests. Some of the large timber sections are now unavailable. For example, 225 mm is the maximum depth of European softwood with a length of 4.8 m or 5.4 m as an absolute maximum. Larger sections are only available in hardwood, although a few large softwood sections are still available from North and South America.

Tropical hardwoods are available from very large trees, either as logs up to 10 or 12 m long or sawn to size, but in long lengths.

Sizes
The European timber industry is metricated but the American is not. This does not cause too much difficulty since most sizes approximate to each other. Timber which is planed or prepared will always be 3 to 5 mm under the nominal sawn size.

Durability
Durability of timber relates to the rate of fungal decay and varies between species. Very simply put, hardwoods are less permeable to moisture and are usually considered more durable than softwoods, even though there are still great differences between species.

Preservative Treatment

Pressurised preservative treatment has been very successful in increasing the resistance of timbers, particularly softwoods, to decay and insect attack; it should always be specified for farm buildings. The most common material used

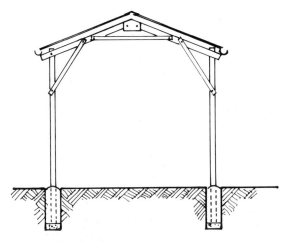

Figure 9.1   A simple pole barn.

treatment of softwoods can improve their durability so that they are better than many hardwoods. For example, a hardwood such as
Greenheart is classified as very durable and
extremely impermeable, and is used for heavy
constructions, marine installations, bridges, etc.
However, a water-borne treatment has little
extra effect since the preservative cannot enter
the timber. In contrast, the European Redwood
which is often used for joinery, etc. is classed as
non-durable and only moderately impermeable.
But here a dramatic increase in durability
following treatment can be seen since the timber
is permeable enough to allow ingress of the
water-borne preservative.

Stress Grading

The stress grading of timbers is of increasing
consequence for agricultural buildings—particularly thrust walling, portal frames and purlins.
Gradings for cladding and secondary framings
are unnecessary. Timber is either hand-graded
or machine-graded to produce material with
similar strength characteristics. Hand-grading
consists of a visual check on knots, splits, shakes
and slope of grain for each piece of timber.
Machine-grading measures the stiffness of each
timber which correlates to its ultimate strength.
Each timber is then marked as having been
graded either visually or by machine and the
grade achieved. The grades are: GS—General
Standard; SS—Special Standard. Hardwoods
are all one grade: HS. North America has its
own grades which are acceptable in the UK.

The average DIY builder should have little
concern over stress grading but be aware if a
specification calls for graded timber. Since stress
grading is specific to each species, similar grades,
or more accurately, strengths of timber are now
being bound together in strength classes, e.g.
SC3 includes Redwood GS and Whitewood SS.

Hardwoods are also either specified as grades/
species, or as strength classes. SC 8 includes
Balall, Ekki, Kapur and Kempas. Thus it can be
seen that timber can be supplied by species if
specific features such as durability override
other considerations; or an engineer can specify
in strength classes for structural work, and the
purchaser has the freedom to obtain the
cheapest timber available to meet the specified
strength class. Since all timbers are rated on the

is a water-borne copper chrome arsenic which
gives the highest degree of protection. The
timber is placed in a vessel and the preservative
forced into the timber under pressure. Thus the
timber is treated throughout its thickness and
subsequent sawing or machining does not
remove the protection. Nevertheless, it is
desirable to cut material to size initially to aid
penetration of the preservative. The treatment is
very cheap considering the benefits obtained,
although there are a couple of drawbacks. The
timber should be seasoned to allow ingress of
the water-borne salts (saturated timber will not
admit more water) and it will again be very wet
at the end of the process.

After processing, some free salts may appear
on the surface of the timber which can simply be
washed off. However with metal cladding, particularly aluminium on treated timbers, corrosion
may occur. Therefore it is desirable to isolate the
two materials with a layer of bitumen or pitch.

Another treatment of preservatives in organic
solvents is available and this is applied in a
broadly similar manner, but has the advantage
that it does not re-wet or swell the timber.
However this treatment is not fixed in the timber
cell and can leach out. It is therefore better
where there is no rainwater, or alternatively the
component is painted or stained to prevent
leaching.

It is important to realise that the preservative

Plate 9.1   A typical well-engineered and well-built timber building.

same scale, SC5 contains an overlap of three hardwoods plus the higher grade softwoods.

Fire

Contrary to popular belief timber is an excellent structural material when exposed to fire. Although all timbers burn, they do so at a fixed or controlled rate on each exposed face. The rate of burning or charring is little influenced by the severity of the fire and hardwoods perform best as the charring rate is lower than softwoods. The charring process protects the interior wood and thus there is no bending or warping of structural members, and collapse does not take place until a very advanced stage of the fire. Timber should therefore not be underrated for farm buildings use and may have particular application in livestock buildings where stock could be at great risk due to fire.

Plywoods

Plywood is in many ways an underrated material for agricultural use as it can be used for numerous tasks such as a simple cladding for partitions, walls, gates, etc., or as a structural component as in a box ply beam (Plate 9.3). The most significant aspect of plywood is the durability of the glue bond between the laminates. For all agricultural uses an exterior grade is necessary which may also be pressure treated if necessary. Nevertheless, the term 'exterior grade' can be misleading since it is loosely applied. The Canadian and Finnish Ply Industries adhere to a similar standard whereby each board will be marked WBP. This refers to a standard test for plywoods meaning 'weather and boil proof' and it is the only material likely to stand full weather exposure. Other plywoods marked 'exterior' may be as good and cheaper, but then perhaps not so unless they are used in a more protected environment.

Due to the nature of plywood, in harsh conditions water is absorbed into the edges of the board through the end grain more easily and more quickly than through the face. This can cause swelling and delamination of the edges which is also associated with discoloration and eventual decay. To prevent and minimise this effect it is necessary—although often neglected— to seal the edges of boards. Proprietary sealants are available for this purpose.

Plate 9.2   Plywood is a very versatile material with many uses as this novel design of farm gate shows.

Plate 9.3 An example of a ply box beam in use (*courtesy of TRADA*).

Other Boards

Hardboard
Oil-tempered hardboards are excellent materials which are able to withstand fairly harsh conditions within agricultural buildings. Their use, along with other composite boards, finds favour with package-deal building manufacturers who employ the correct procedures as to studdings and fixings.

Chipboards/blockboards
Only a few of these materials will have sufficient integrity for agricultural use due mainly to swelling from moisture and the failure of the glue bond. Nevertheless, there are exceptions and it would be wise to check with the manufacturer concerning their proposed use.

Decorative finishes for timber
Over recent years a dramatic change in the protection of timber has taken place with the advent of exterior woodstain. For agricultural use stains can be assumed to supersede creosote because they do not fade, and supersede paints and varnishes because they do not flake or lift off. Stains are easy to apply and prevent ingress of water whilst still allowing the timber to breathe naturally. They fail over the years simply by a general loss of surface which is easy to re-apply and maintain.

There are two types of stain, both available in a range of colours. One is for general application and the other, a heavy body stain, is a semi-varnish for doors, window frames, etc., and helps stop timber swelling due to moisture.

In a similar vein, there are now micro-porous paints available which break down slowly rather than peel off.

These products can only enhance the use of timber for claddings and doors, since the old adage about it being 'difficult to make timber look bad' is still true!

Fasteners for Timber

Nails
There are many varieties and shapes of nails available. Round wire nails are the most common for general work, but galvanised nails are far superior for any structural work or indeed any fabrication that is expected to last. Galvanised nails also exhibit considerable resistance to withdrawal. Among many specialist nails is a new group with a square-twisted or square-grooved shank. Also there are annular rink-shanked and helically-threaded nails. These nails are particularly intended for structural work.

Screws
Woodscrews are available in as many materials and finishes as are nails, although perhaps screws play a lesser role with farm builders. The coach screw should not be underestimated though, especially when used with timber connectors (Figure 9.2).

Coach bolts
This is a traditional fixing for light general work which begins to suffer severe limitations in use as demands become more sophisticated. The square shank under the head of the bolt is

Figure 9.2

Coach screw.

Coach bolt.

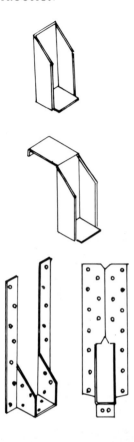

Figure 9.4   Some examples of joist hangers.

designed to bite into the timber and prevent rotation. This it will normally do initially, but often fails on subsequent disassembly. For any structural work the head of a coach bolt is unlikely to be large enough and a washer will be required under the nut and under the head of the bolt. Annoyingly, the washers will need to be of different inside diameters. Because of the limited thread length available on most coach bolts, life becomes difficult when trying to 'pull up' on several timbers together or where timber connectors are used.

Figure 9.3   Timber connectors.

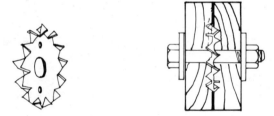

A double sided connector used for permanent joints.

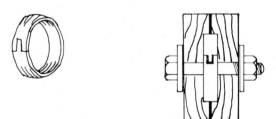

A split ring connector for heavy duty use.

Another difficulty occurs with joints made from poles which are invariably irregular in dimension, making a wide selection of bolt lengths necessary. The answer is to buy threaded rods in 1 m lengths with nuts and heavy washers and make your own bolts as required.

Timber connectors
The use of timber connectors permits the transfer of load from one timber directly to another in the strongest of configurations. The bolt simply stitches the joint together and is not normally considered in calculations. This is a slight oversimplification since there are many types and arrangements of timber connectors and single-sided connectors would pass sheer forces through the bolt (Figure 9.3).

The design of joints using connectors is complex and further advice should be sought if necessary. Nevertheless for a DIY construction following a standard design it is imperative that connectors are used exactly as specified.

Chapter 10

CORRUGATED SHEET CLADDINGS

IN A CONSTANTLY changing situation, sheet cladding materials have made a major impact on farm buildings by being efficient in use and economic to buy and fix. They also allow the supporting structure to be light weight and therefore much cheaper than traditional slate or tile construction.

When new sheet materials took over from traditional roof construction, beginning in the 1930s, agriculture may have taken a wrong turn, and still perhaps has not always discovered the right track. What was not realised at the time was the extent to which natural ventilation took place through the gaps between slates and tiles. The early replacement of these roofs with sheet materials was in many cases disastrous and methods of creating adequate ventilation (see Chapter 16) only began to be developed in the 1960s. Nevertheless, buildings are still being erected today with inadequate ventilation. For livestock buildings keeping rain out should be secondary to the ventilation requirement.

As indicated, corrugated cladding materials are extremely effective in creating a weather-proof envelope and a wide range of accessories is available. All corrugation profiles can be matched with rooflight sheets. Rooflights are extemely effective and it is difficult to fit too many into buildings, except perhaps for grainstores

Plate 10.1   Carrying roofsheets is a difficult job but a forklift only helps if it can reach above the eaves.

where darkness discourages birds from entering. Rooflights are only rarely cleaned, which is unfortunate.

All cladding materials are available with various colour finishes and, for a large building on a sensitive site, it may be worth consulting an expert. The only rules of thumb are that the roof should be darker in colour than the walls, and that bargeboards to the roof should be in the same colour as the roof and not the gable cladding. This has the effect of giving the roof thickness. Generous eaves and gable overhangs or oversails create interesting shadow areas which can make a very ordinary building look much better.

Bitumen Mineral Fibre Sheets

On a first cost basis these sheets are very attractive and are available in several colours. However, there are several disadvantages in that sheets are only available in 2 m lengths and they require purlins to be spaced at about 600 mm centres. Also they are at a considerable disadvantage to other materials in the event of fire.

Bitumen mineral fibre sheets are suitable for re-roofing in place of slates and tiles, but only where the existing timber roof structure is sound. They may also be laid over the top of a corrugated steel roof which is beginning to corrode, provided adequate fixing can be ensured.

Fibre Cement

Fibre cement sheets look and perform similarly to the asbestos cement sheets they are about to replace. The common sizes have either 3 in or 6 in corrugations and are available up to 10 ft long and exactly match asbestos cement sheets.

Fibre cement sheets have a life expectancy in excess of 40 years and are usually guaranteed for at least 25 years. Furthermore no routine maintenance will be necessary in that time save for inspection of the fixings for corrosion.

The standard 3 in sheets have an effective cover width of 2 ft 1½ in allowing for 1½ corrugations side lap, whereas the 6 in corrugated sheets have an effective cover of 3 ft 4 in and only need one corrugation side lap. Both sheets need a minimum 150 mm end lap and this may need increasing for shallower roof pitches; all

side and end laps may need sealing in some circumstances. A maximum purlin spacing for standard 3 in sheets is 3 ft (900 mm) and for 6 in sheets is 4 ft 6 in (1.37 m). A full range of fittings and accessories is readily available.

Fixing fibre cement sheets

Because of their fragile nature, fibre cement sheets must always have the bolt holes drilled 2 mm oversize (never punched) and need their corners mitred in order to lay flat against each other. A professional roofer will mitre the sheets on the stack and drill some of the fixing holes before carrying them on to the roof. However, the amateur may prefer to lay the sheet in position and mitre the two sheets together with an angle grinder (Plate 10.2).

When fixing fibre cement sheets (Figure 10.1) or indeed any sheet cladding, it is imperative that the first sheets in each course are set square

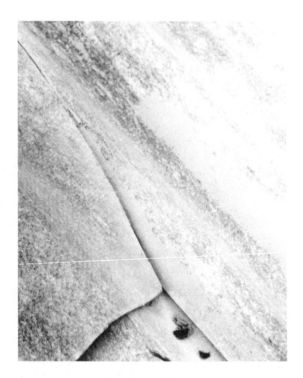

Plate 10.2   Two fibre cement sheets mitred to fit together. The next sheet covers this joint. The length of the mitre is equal to the end lap of the sheets and the width is equal to the side lap.

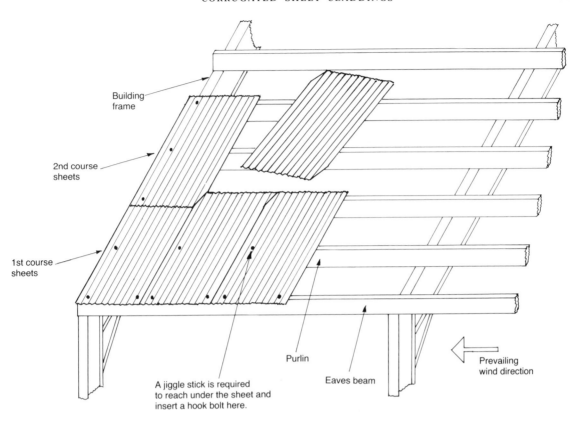

Figure 10.1 The alignment of the first few roof sheets is very important.

Plate 10.3 With any roofing sheets it is important to check for 'square' against the building frame as work progresses. For pitched roofs both halves must be maintained to the same dimension if a close fitting ridge is too be used.

Plate 10.4 A 'jiggle' stick is used to reach under the sheet and poke the hookbolt through the drilled hole. Bolts for use with concrete purlins have a lesser crank to the end and may be inserted from above.

to the building frame and as work progresses, a check is made as each building frame is passed (Plate 10.3). If this point is not observed, the eaves overhang into the gutter will begin to increase or decrease significantly as work progresses, resulting in a very untidy job. Also the side laps in the corrugations will wander, so constant checking is necessary.

It is also good practice to lay the sheets towards the prevailing wind if possible, as this reduces wind and rain problems with the side laps.

A fibre cement roof is fairly garish when new and is often the subject of some controversy. However, it soon mellows with the growth of moss and lichen on the roof surface and looks most attractive. It is sometimes suggested that an application of slurry can speed up this process or indeed that the sheets be fitted upside down since the reverse texture is supposedly more suitable for lichen.

There are alternative colour treatments for natural fibre cement roofs and these include the use of through-coloured sheets with colouring included during manufacture, or a paint which is applied either at the factory or to the whole roof upon completion. Coloured sheets are only usually available to special order which also takes longer, so the most flexible approach is to paint the whole roof on completion. However there is little difference in total cost between the two approaches.

The use or otherwise of coloured fibre cement sheets has been the subject of much debate, but

there can be no doubt that a coloured roof looks good when new, but may be less so if colour fades or goes 'patchy'. (A coloured sheet also tends to inhibit growth of moss and lichen.) On the other hand, a natural, grey coloured roof only improves with age. To compromise though, a light colour treatment to side cladding may give excellent results since vertical asbestos cement does not weather in the same manner, and may show unsightly stains. The roof can be left to weather naturally.

Steel Sheets

Agriculture suffers a unique situation where metal cladding is used since the sheet can be seriously affected by corrosion from the underside rather than its life being limited by corrosion of the weather side, sometimes accelerated by atmospheric pollution. This corrosion of the underside results from the normal farming operations where silage effluent, milk, slurry and some foodstuffs, associated as like as not with condensation, produce a very aggressive environment for the sheet. These corrosive elements comprise mostly of carbon dioxide, methane, hydrogen sulphide and ammonia which may be combined with liberal amounts of diesel fumes. It would be unfair to overstate the situation in general terms but problems have arisen particularly in cow kennel buildings where ventilation may be poor and the sheets were not isolated from the salt-treated timber purlins. If all the above conditions accrue serious corrosion within 3 to 8 years may occur. Other factors associated with premature failure may be contained within the checklist below. There is now a considerable range of protective treatments for steel sheets and longevity is probably related closely to purchase price in what is a very competitive market. However for agriculture, sheets with a minimum 350 g/m^2 of zinc together with plastic or painted coatings top and bottom sides should be specified.

Corrugated Steel

Corrugated steel sheets perhaps need little introduction since they are so readily available and find universal use. They are available in different thicknesses from 22 gauge to 28 gauge and in stock lengths of 6–12 ft; 2 ft 6 in wide 10

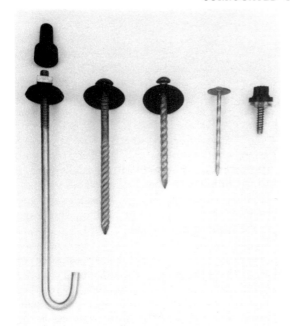

Plate 10.5 Some examples of fixings for cladding materials.
Left to right: Hook bolt sealer washer and top hat; 140 mm drive screw and sealer washer for 6 in fibre cement sheets; 80 mm drive screw and sealer washer for standard fibre cement sheets; spring head nail for corrugated steel; self-tapping sealer screw for valley fixing box profile steel sheets to galvanised metal purlins.

by 3 in corrugations or 3 ft wide with 12 by 3 in corrugations. All corrugated steel sheets are available up to 8 m long by order, which makes for very efficient usage.

Plain galvanised sheets look unsightly when new and paint will not adhere to their surface until they have weathered somewhat. As an alternative, factory applied primer painted sheets are available which look satisfactory in the early stages and will take a paint finish as necessary, although it is essential to check which paints can be used.

Box Profile Sheets

A range of box profile sheets is available which look better and, depending on profile, allow a much greater purlin spacing than other materials. Box or trapezoidal profiled sheets are available with a range of primer, polyester or PVC coating materials. The primered sheets are as for the 3 in corrugated but a recent inno-

vation has been the polyester/organosol coated sheet which has a similar coating top and bottom over the galvanised layer. This product should give good results at reasonable cost.

Plastic coated sheets are a very high quality product, albeit at a premium price. They are galvanised on both sides and have a PVC plastic coating to the upper side and a grey painted finish to the under side. The plastic coated sheets are only available in box profile but in a wide range of colours and gauges of 26 g or 28 g.

Additional factors associated with steel roofs

- All steel sheets must be stored in dry conditions on-site or they will discolour or even weld themselves into a solid block in time.
- Corrugated sheets should be fixed through the crown of the corrugation by hook bolts or spring head nails (Plate 10.5).
- Box profile sheets should be fixed in the valley of the corrugation by self-tapping sealer screws (Plate 10.5).
- Mastic sealing tape may be necessary for side and end laps where roof pitches are below 10°.
- Ensure that there is sufficient ventilation in a livestock building to minimise any condensation and eventual attack to the underside of the sheet.
- Avoid fixing steel sheets, particularly box profiles, to steel angle purlins since corrosion of the purlin will also corrode the sheet. Galvanised metal purlins are far superior in this respect.
- Salt-treated timber purlins must be isolated from the sheeting by a layer of bitumen or DPC material.
- Always pop rivet side laps to sheets, particularly with wider purlin spaces.

Aluminium

Aluminium cladding is similar in many respects to steel cladding and is available in 3 in corrugated and box profiles in a range of colours. Its main disadvantage is its initial cost, although this can be partly offset by the use of lighter structural members to support the lighter weight. Corrosion above salt-treated purlins can again be a problem, and sheets must be isolated by bitumen or DPC as for steel sheets.

Chapter 11

FOUNDATIONS AND WALLING

FOUNDATIONS

Introduction

THE FOUNDATIONS of a building, on which the walls are built, are usually below ground level and are required to carry walls, roof and other loads from a structure and transmit them safely to the ground. Almost all farm buildings are exempt from the control of the Local Authority Building Inspectorate and of the Building Regulations themselves; the suggestions in these documents, however, which are based on the Building Regulations, make good building sense and will always achieve their objectives. They are not cheap though; but as a building or floor for a building is only as good as its foundations it is not worth skimping at this point. Start as you mean to continue and try to get it right!

There are a few very simple rules to determine how thick and how wide the foundations of a wall should be, and how deep they should go into the ground.

- In Figure 11.1 X must not be greater than T.
- The footing must be wide enough to spread the load over a large enough area so that settlement or movement will not cause damage to the building or threaten its stability.
- It must be deep enough to safeguard the building against damage by swelling, shrinkage or freezing of the subsoil.
- The concrete must not only be correctly proportioned but must also be capable of resisting attack by sulphate and other chemicals which may be present in the soil.
- The walls below ground may also need protection. The Local Authority Surveyor will probably be able to advise on the soil conditions in the area and on the precautions required.
- Often the floor slab is laid before the walls are built. In such cases a foundation consisting of a thickened edge to the slab is sufficient.
- If the ground level on the site has been raised by fill material, it may be necessary to carry the foundations down into the undisturbed ground below.

Soil Types

On clays of all types, the bottom of the foundation should normally be at least 1 m below ground level. On soils which are susceptible to frost and tend to expand and contract with freezing and thawing, such as silt, chalk and silty sands, this depth should be 450 mm. In sandy soils and gravels the recommended depth is 350 mm. The concrete should all be well above the ground water table if possible, especially in sandy soil.

Table 11.1 based on the 1985 Building Regulations gives the minimum widths of foundation recommended for various types of soil, and for three values of wall loading. For normal walls these loadings can be related to the height of the wall (see first footnote); thus, for a 4 m high wall not supporting any part of the roof structure, founded in soft clay, the minimum

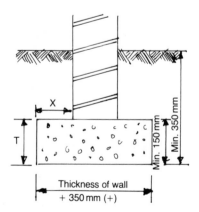

Figure 11.1   Design of strip footing.

Table 11.1 Minimum foundation widths

Type of soil	Condition of soil	Field 'test' applicable	Minimum width* (mm) for load† indicated		
			15 kN/m	20 kN/m	30 kN/m
rock	not inferior to sandstone, limestone or firm chalk	requires mechanical excavation	equal to width of wall		
gravel, sand	compact	requires pick for excavation	300 (b)	300 (c)	300 (d)
clay, sandy clay	stiff	cannot be moulded in fingers; requires pick or mechanical excavation	300 (b)	300 (c)	300 (d)
clay, sandy clay	firm	can be moulded (just) in fingers; can be excavated with spade	300 (b)	300 (c)	350 (d)
sand, silty or clayey sand	loose	can be excavated with spade	300 (b)	450 (c)	600 (d)
silt, clay sandy clay silty sand	soft	easily moulded and excavated	350 (a)	450 (c)	650 (d)
silt, clay sandy clay,‡ silty sand	very soft	exudes between fingers when squeezed	450 (a)	600 (b)	850 (c)

* The minimum widths apply only if the walls do not exceed the following heights:
  (a) 1.8 m
  (b) 2.5 m
  (c) 3.0 m
  (d) 4.0 m

† The load on a foundation is produced by the weight of the wall and of the foundation itself. This table does not strictly apply to buildings in which the wall supports any part of the roof structure, although the 30 kN/m loading can be assumed to apply to small single-storey buildings with a light, small-span roof.

‡ Avoid these sites if possible.

foundation width is 650 mm.

The concrete should not be less than 150 mm thick. In most circumstances the minimum thickness will be determined by the width of the wall, the type of soil, and the requirement that X should not be greater than T (Figure 11.1). Thus, for a 150 mm thick wall in soft clay (foundation width 650 mm):

$$X = \frac{650 - 150}{2} = 250 \text{ mm.}$$

Therefore the minimum thickness of T must also be 250 mm.

Strip Foundations

In a normal strip footing (Figure 11.1) the wall rests on a relatively thin concrete pad. This type is more economical in materials but is probably more expensive to build as it is more labour intensive. The width of the strip footing is normally determined by the necessity for a man to get into the trench to build the wall. (See also Table 11.1.)

In a trench fill foundation (Figure 11.2) the concrete comes up almost to ground level. This type is more suited to the use of a mechanical digger, and is probably cheaper than the

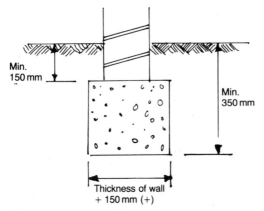

Figure 11.2 Trench fill foundation.

traditional strip footing if labour is costed. It has a number of other advantages:

- The trench will not have to be dug any wider than the minimum width given in Table 11.1.
- The trench can be filled with concrete as soon as it is dug, thus avoiding cave-ins and flooding.
- Time is saved on brick or block laying since the concrete in the foundations extends almost up to ground level.

Thickened Slab Foundations

On soils of low bearing pressure, such as the soft clays with interbedded peat layers of the East Anglian Fens, a common type of foundation consists of a thickening of the floor slab (Figure 11.3). Its use may also be economical on other soils.

The thickened edge should be at least 300 mm thick, and up to 400 mm thick on frost-susceptible soils. The slab should extend at least 100 mm beyond the outer face of the wall and the thickened section should extend at least 100 mm beyond the inner face of the wall.

The Trenches

The trenches should be excavated to the correct depth and the bottom made level and firm. Pockets of soft material may have to be dug out and tightly filled with concrete, stone or ballast. If possible, trenches should be kept free of standing water which will soften the soil. This may involve digging a sump in the bottom of the trench and using a pump. If the bottom is softened by rain, the soft layer of soil should be removed before placing the concrete. Concrete should never be placed in pools of standing water as the water will wash the cement out of the underside of the concrete and seriously reduce its strength. If excavation has to go below the level of ground water, it must be pumped out before, and even during, concreting.

Where deep trenches have to be dug in very soft or unstable ground, it may be necessary to support the sides of the excavation. Two methods of doing this are shown in Figure 11.4. The method shown in (b) can be used where only nominal support to the trench sides is necessary.

If it is necessary for a man to go into a deep trench for final trimming and levelling, then supports prevent cave-ins while he is working.

To ensure that the foundation concrete will be level and the right thickness, a line of pegs should be driven along the centre of the trench so that their tops indicate the level to which concrete is to be placed. The top of the foundation concrete must be a whole number of courses of bricks or blocks below damp-proof course level.

On sloping sites it may be easier and more economical to form the foundation in steps (Figure 11.5). Each step in the foundation must be equal in height to a whole number of bricks or blocks. It is also wise to see that the distance

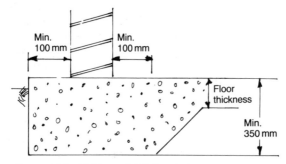

Figure 11.3 Thickened slab foundation.

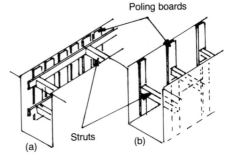

Figure 11.4 Trench support in unstable ground.

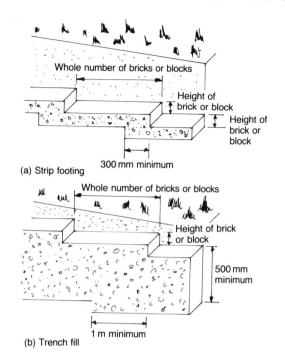

Whole number of bricks or blocks

Height of brick or block

Height of brick or block

300 mm minimum

(a) Strip footing

Whole number of bricks or blocks

Height of brick or block

500 mm minimum

1 m minimum

(b) Trench fill

Figure 11.5 Stepped foundations.

between steps is equal to a whole number of bricks or blocks to ensure that cutting will not be necessary. Traditional strip footings should be stiffened by lapping steps for a distance at least equal to the footing thickness.

The Concrete

If ready-mixed concrete is to be used, a GEN3 or ST4 mix with ordinary Portland cement and 20 mm maximum-sized aggregate is suitable. The workability should be high (125 mm slump) for trench fill foundations or medium (75 mm slump) for strip foundations. It is slightly richer than the traditional '1:3:6' mix and should give good durability.

If mixing is to be done on-site, batches should be done by weight if possible. With every 50 kg of ordinary Portland cement, 115 kg of damp concreting sand and 195 kg of coarse aggregate (gravel or stone maximum size 20 mm) should be used. Just enough water should be added to enable the concrete to be compacted thoroughly. If batching is done by volume, 3 parts of

cement, 5 parts of sand and 9 parts of coarse aggregate should be used.

In sulphate bearing ground use the mixes shown in Chapter 2, Table 2.3.

After placing the concrete, it should be tamped thoroughly to remove any trapped air, then levelled carefully and the surface finished with a wood float.

WALLING

There is a lot of mystique about brick laying and block laying. High-quality facing brickwork, in particular, certainly requires much skill and even more practice. But it is not necessary to know the meaning of all the words used in a building textbook or even the complicated bonding patterns illustrated to make a 'tidy, efficient job'. Care and commonsense will go a long way.

Some of the traditional bonding patterns are illustrated in Figure 11.6. Most of these can only be used if the wall is at least 205 mm thick in brickwork. Stretcher, or half-bond, is the normal method of bonding for 102 mm thick walls and for single-skin concrete block walls. Three simple rules apply:

• No vertical joints on one course should be exactly over the one in the next course above or below it
• To achieve a tidy appearance, the vertical joint in every other course should be aligned one above the other
• Have a lap not less than ¼ the length of a brick or block.

The role of mortar in a wall needs to be understood as well. Its primary job is to allow a wall to be built with small building units which is absolutely 'true'—that means true to line and level and perhaps, of most importance, that the wall is truly vertical. It is obvious how much extra vertical load the wall in Figure 11.7(a) could withstand compared with those in Figure 11.7(b) or 11.7(c). In a sense the mortar keeps the blocks and bricks apart so that the wall can be built upright.

Of course, the mortar also helps to some degree to stick the units together and to distribute the load the wall receives from one unit to the next, and also to keep the building dry and warm.

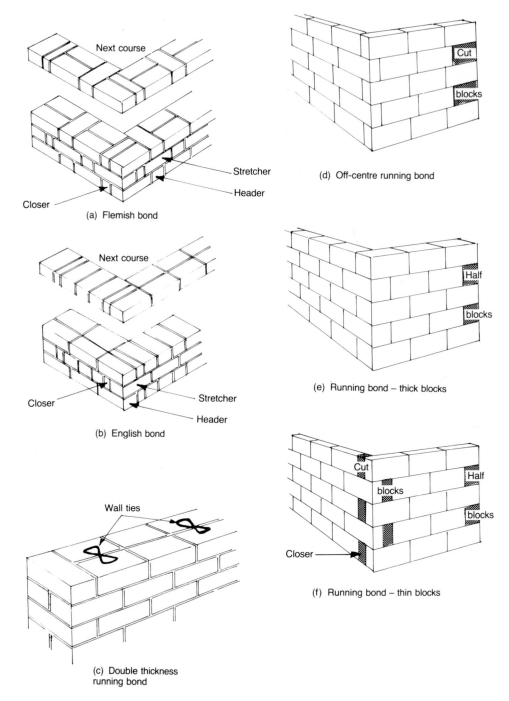

(a) Flemish bond

(b) English bond

(c) Double thickness
running bond

(d) Off-centre running bond

(e) Running bond – thick blocks

(f) Running bond – thin blocks

Figure 11.6 Bonding patterns.

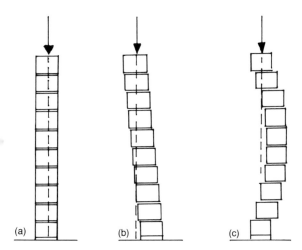

Figure 11.7 Building a wall 'true'.

Some Building Terms Defined

Bricks Normally made to the dimensions 215 mm × 102.5 mm × 65 mm. Some are made 73 mm thick. Special shapes are also available.

Blocks Anything bigger than a brick! Usually 440 mm or 390 mm long, 215 mm or 190 mm deep and 215 mm, 200 mm, 190 mm, 140 mm, 100 mm, 90 mm or 75 mm thick. A range of special shapes is available.

Dense concrete blocks Blocks made with normal dense aggregate—i.e. gravel, crushed rocks of various kinds.

Lightweight concrete blocks Blocks made using specially manufactured or selected aggregate which have a honeycomb like structure—these include Aglite, Foamed slag, Glic, Leca, Lytag, Pumice.

Autoclaved aerated concrete blocks Blocks made from a light, foamed material which are steam-cured after manufacture. Different densities are available.

Solid blocks Blocks that contain no formed holes except cutting slots.

Hollow blocks Blocks with one or more formed holes which pass right through the block.

Cellular blocks Blocks with one or more formed cavities which do not pass wholly through the block.

Facing bricks or blocks High quality units made with sharp edges and in colours and textures to give an attractive appearance. More expensive than common bricks or ordinary dense blocks.

Engineering bricks Bricks made to a high strength and low water absorbency.

Common bricks These are suitable for general building work. They make no claims for appearance.

Course A row of bricks (or blocks) between two horizontal joints.

Stretcher A brick laid with its length parallel to the face of the wall.

Header A brick laid with its end parallel to the face of the wall.

Lap The horizontal distance between two vertical joints.

Bond The arrangement of bricks in a wall which by lapping them prevents vertical joints between bricks falling one above another.

Bed joint The horizontal mortar joint.

Perpend The vertical mortar joint.

Bats and closers Pieces of brick used to fill in spaces in the wall which are too small to take a whole brick; they may be required to maintain a lap.

Quoin The external corner of a wall.

Jamb The vertical sides of a door or window opening—it is covered by the frame.

Reveal The vertical side of a door or window opening not covered by the frame.

Racking The stepped arrangement at the incompleted end of a wall—see Figure 11.8.

Toothing Allowing alternate courses of bricks to project, tooth-like, from a wall to provide a bond for brickwork which is to be added at a later date.

Piers A rectangular thickening (or pillar) built as part of the wall to provide stiffening.

Pointing Applying a 'facing' to a mortar joint using a mortar of either a different quality or even a different colour to that used in the rest of the joint.

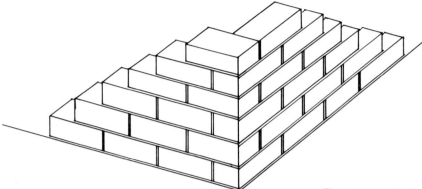

Figure 11.8   Racking the corner of a wall.

Finishing (joints)   A treatment given to mortar joints after the bricks or blocks have been laid.

Spot board   A 600 mm–900 mm square board onto which mortar is placed for subsequent transfer to a trowel.

Mild steel reinforcing bars   Plain round steel bars with a lower strength than high yield steel bars.

High yield reinforcing bars   Round-ribbed or square-twisted bars with a higher strength than mild steel.

Starter bars   Short lengths of reinforcement which protrude from the concrete foundation.

Reinforcement cage   A rigid (or nearly rigid) assembly of reinforcing bars and/or reinforcing mesh put together in a predetermined way to the designer's specification. It can be lifted into

position for a wall or a floor.

Kicker   A 75 mm high strip of concrete which projects upwards from floor level at the point on the floor where a wall is to be made of in-situ concrete (Figures 11.9 and 11.10).

Selection of Materials

Well-built walls of clay or concrete bricks can be depended upon for strength and durability as well as resistance to rain penetration. They have a high degree of fire resistance and good sound insulation. They are made in a wide range of colours, and carefully built walls will result in a good-looking building. But for the do-it-yourself builder, brick walls are more difficult to build, and will almost certainly cost more, than walls built with concrete blocks.

If bricks have traditionally been used for farm

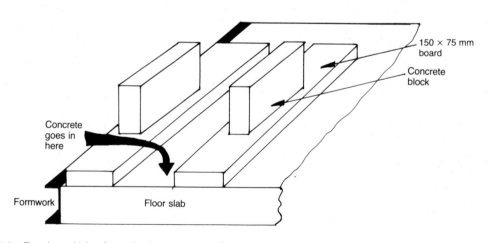

Figure 11.9   Forming a kicker for an in-situ concrete wall.

Steel portal with reinforced brick/flint panelling in Norfolk.

Cavity walling to RC frame—a beef unit in west Yorkshire.

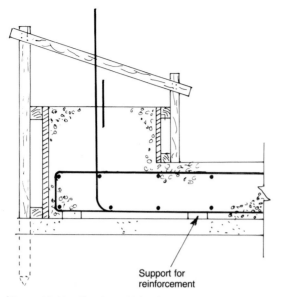

Figure 11.10   Forming a kicker in a reinforced floor.

buildings in the area, this will apply in parts of East Anglia, the Midlands, and the North West where concrete bricks are popular, to maintain uniformity of appearance there is a good case for sticking to that traditional material, despite the cost. Elsewhere concrete blocks are quicker, easier and cheaper to use.

Table 11.2 suggests where different types and thicknesses of blocks and bricks should be used in farm buildings.

Insulation

For walls in pig buildings and potato stores, for example, the normal block or brick walls will allow heat, or cold, to pass through them. Insulation in some form will be required to reduce this heat loss or cold penetration. Lightweight concrete blocks made with specially manufactured aggregate or selected materials, or made with a foamed-type of concrete, can be used for this purpose, possibly in conjunction with ordinary dense blocks or bricks. Foamed concrete, more correctly defined as autoclaved aerated concrete, is now available with a density of only about one-fifth that of ordinary concrete—475 kg/m³ against 2400 kg/m³—and these can be used to provide a high degree of insulation. Alternatively, or in addition to this, an insulation layer may be incorporated in the cavity in the wall, see Figure 11.11 (a), (b), (c) and (d) and Figure 11.12 (a) and (b).

The amount of heat or cold passing through the wall is reduced by having cavities (or air spaces) in the wall and it is further reduced if these cavities are filled with a very low density material (glass fibre, polystyrene, polyurethane, etc.).

The thermal transmittance of a wall, that is the rate at which heat is transmitted through it,

Table 11.2   Where to use the different types of dense concrete blocks

Application	Loading	High strength (7 N/mm²) 215 mm thick 215 mm thick Hollow	Cellular or Hollow	140 mm thick Solid	Cellular	Hollow	90–100 mm thick Solid	Cellular	Hollow
Retaining walls		★ (depending on height)	★						
External walls	some horizontal (e.g. muck)		★ (depending on height of storage)			★			
External walls	no horizontal some vertical			★	★	★		★	
Internal walls	no horizontal some vertical			★	★	★		★	

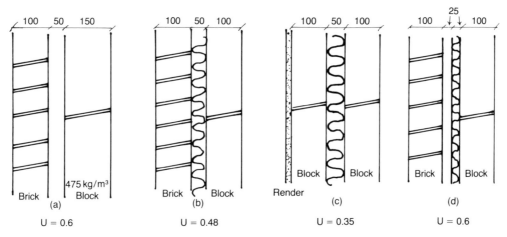

Figure 11.11   Insulating cavity walls (using 475 kg/m³ blocks).

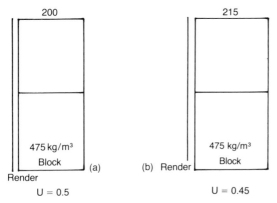

Figure 11.12   Single leaf insulating walls.

is known as its 'U value'. The lower the U value the lower the heat loss. The units used to measure this figure are watts (a measure of heat) per square metre of the wall, per degree Celsius (or Centigrade) (W/m² °C); the difference in temperature between the inside and the outside of the wall. If the U value is reduced from 1.0 to 0.5 W/m² °C then the rate of heat lost is halved. Values of 0.6 or less are considered acceptable on all farm and domestic buildings where insulation is needed. A 140 mm thick, solid, dense concrete block has a U value of 3.0, whereas a 215 mm thick, hollow, dense concrete block has a U value of 2.4.

Other Materials and Equipment

In addition to the bricks or blocks and the cement, lime, sand, etc., a mixer will also be needed for the mortar (see later section). The usual range of bricklayer's tools will include:

- 250 mm trowel
- Pointing trowel
- 2 kg hammer
- 100 mm bolster (a wide chisel for cutting masonry)
- A length (300 mm) of 12 mm plastic pipe
- Buckets
- Shovels
- Sundry hand brushes (wire, stiff bristle, soft bristle)
- Sweeping brush (stiff bristle)
- Wire cutters, wire ties, pincers, hacksaw (for cutting reinforcing bars)
- Hammer and nails
- Builder's level (1 m long or more)
- Nylon string line
- Tape and/or rule

For cavity work wall ties are usually placed at 900 mm centres horizontally and 450 mm centres vertically with additional ties at openings (this works out at about 300 ties for each 100 m² of wall). High yield and mild steel reinforcing bars should be cut to length and bent to shape. This is discussed in detail in a later section.

Damp-proof Coursing Material

A damp-proof course (dpc) is not necessary in the wall of a farm building. Its presence will reduce the stability of the walls subject to horizontal loading. However, in a pig building, constructed using traditional methods, it will be necessary to prevent moisture moving upwards in the wall. In these buildings the wall is carrying mainly vertical loads from the roof.

A dpc normally comes in rolls of bituminous or polythene-based material which can be unrolled onto a 12 mm thick bed of mortar at the required level in the wall. The joints should be lapped at least 100 mm. The next course of bricks or blocks is then laid on its normal bed.

Alternatively, in unreinforced walls two courses of class A engineering bricks can be used as a dpc, using a rich mortar in the joints.

In reinforced walls for grain or potato stores the dpc is best laid as a continuous membrane with the floor dpm, using a minimum of 250 μm (1000 gauge) polythene. This passes right under the foundations. Sticky tape should be placed along the joints of the polythene if possible, though this is not always easy to do. If the polythene is wet or dirty, taping it is almost impossible—it is always tricky. If you cannot tape the joints make sure you have a good lap (450 mm).

Handling and Storage

If the work is to look good at the finish, good care must be taken of materials whilst building. The bricks and blocks should be stacked carefully and kept dry (Figure 11.13).

Mortars

The role of mortar in a wall has already been mentioned. Because of the tendency for mortar and concrete blocks to shrink, the mortar used for block laying should be weaker than the blocks so that if cracks occur, by shrinkage or other movement, they will be in the mortar joints and will not pass through the blocks themselves. The cracks can then be filled and will not be unsightly. In reinforced walls a stronger mortar should be used as the reinforcement in the bed joints will prevent cracks from opening.

The properties of a good mortar are very difficult to define. Terms such as 'consistency', 'cohesiveness', 'workability' and 'plasticity' are

Figure 11.13 Take care when stacking materials and handling them.

Table 11.3 Table of mortar mixes

Mortar designation	Cement:lime:sand			Masonry cement:sand			cement:sand with plasticiser		
	by volume	Yield (m³ per 50 kg cement)	Mean water demand (litres per 50 kg cement)	by volume	Yield (m³ per 50 kg cement)	Mean water demand (litres per 50 kg cement)	by volume	Yield (m³ per 50 kg cement)	Mean water demand (litres per 50 kg cement)
1	1:¼:3	0.14	40	—	—	—	—	—	—
2	1:½:4–4½	0.19	50	1:2½–3½	0.15	35	1:3–4	0.16	40
3	1:1:5–6	0.25	70	1:4–5	0.21	45	1:5–6	0.24	50
4	1:2:8–9	0.37	100	1:5½–6½	0.27	55	1:7–8	0.30	60

all used to describe the properties. The type of sand, the mix and the proportions of cement, sand, lime and other additives used will affect all these properties. The ideal mortar is one which readily slips from the trowel and is easily spread, but hangs onto the brick or block. A less workable (less sloppy) mortar should be used for blocks than for bricks as the heavier blocks tend to settle in sloppy mortars. Under no circumstances should the mortar flow like a liquid. Once it starts to stiffen, on the other hand (as long as it is less than two hours old) re-mix it with a little water.

Many skilled bricklayers still use lime in their mortar. It makes the mix sticky but workable and tends to improve both the water retentivity of the mix and its water resistance (water shedding) properties. Water retentivity is desirable because it reduces the instant loss of water and thus the loss of flow characteristics, which is sometimes experienced when mortar is placed on highly absorbent surfaces. Two alternatives to lime are available—a chemical, which is added at the mixer to ordinary Portland cement mixes, called a plasticiser; and one which is added by the cement manufacturers to produce 'masonry cement'. Both work well. The instructions provided by the manufacturers of the chemical plasticiser should be followed carefully. Mortar plasticisers or masonry cement should not be used in concrete mixes—only in mortars (mixes with no coarse aggregate or stone in them).

Washing-up liquid is sometimes used by bricklayers on building sites as an additive for mortar. This is not a good idea and is a very dangerous practice for the DIY builder. The proprietary chemical plasticiser resembles washing-up liquid, but it is not exactly the same formulation and the DIY builder will not have the first idea how much washing-up liquid to add to the mix. Excessive foaming is bad for the strength and durability of the mortar and the wall.

Mixes (by volume) are given in Table 11.3.

Table 11.4 Quantities of units and mortar needed per 100 m² of wall

Unit work size (mm)	Number of units	Wall thickness (mm)					
		90	100	102.5	140	190	215
		Volume of mortar (m³)					
440 × 215	988	0.59	0.66	—	0.92	1.25	1.42
390 × 190	1250	0.67	0.74	—	1.04	1.41	—
215 × 65	5926	—	—	1.76	—	—	4.52
290 × 90	3333	1.17	—	—	—	3.34	—
190 × 90	5000	1.31	—	—	—	3.62	—
190 × 65	6667	1.59	—	—	—	4.18	—

Use Mix 1 for load bearing and reinforced work; Mix 2 for work below ground and below damp-proof course level; Mix 3 for unreinforced external walls and single-leaf walls of insulating blocks; and Mix 4 for internal leaves of cavity walls and lightweight partition walls.

The number of concrete blocks of different sizes that are required for 100 m² of wall and the quantity of mortar needed for these units are given in Table 11.4.

Batching and mixing
It is common practice to batch mortars by volume but batching by shovel-fulls cannot be relied upon to give consistent results. A shovel full of damp sand is likely to have more sand on it than a shovel full of dry sand, and will certainly be larger than a shovel full of cement. It is better to use buckets full of materials using a separate bucket for cement so that it is kept dry. Using buckets can be tedious, but the following technique can be used.

If a 1:1:6 mix is being batched, count the number of shovel-fulls of cement taken to fill up a bucket, the number of shovel-fulls of lime it takes to fill a bucket, and the number of shovel-fulls it takes to fill up six buckets of sand. The numbers of shovel-fulls recorded for cement, lime and sand in this operation can be used for batching purposes.

The proportions given for lime in Table 11.3 may be increased by up to 50 per cent to obtain the workability required. The range of proportions of sand given is to allow for variations in the type of sand. Generally the higher value is used for a well-graded sand—see definitions in Chapter 13—and the lower value for coarse or uniformly fine sand.

The stated volumes in Table 11.3 are officially for dry sand and compacted cement—that is cement in a bag. Fortunately, for damp sand and loose cement (cement tipped or shovelled into a bucket) the figures still apply. The quantities quoted may need to be increased if wastage is excessive.

Consistency is the key to good proportioning, batching, workability and even mixing time. Mixes with plasticisers in them should have a uniform mixing time as the mix will 'foam up' more with longer mixing. Once all the ingredients are in the mixer, 3–5 minutes of mixing is about right.

Most of the sand and most of the water should be put in the mixer first. If a plasticiser is being used all of it should be put in with the first batch of water. The lime and cement is then added, followed by the rest of the sand and finally plain water is added to give the required workability.

Setting Out

The quality of the finished job is largely dependent on the care that is taken during the laying process—uniformity of joint thickness, alignment of vertical joints and prevention of mortar smearing and staining. But it is also necessary, particularly with concrete blocks, to work out the arrangement of the units, the position of the reinforcement, the position and the size of openings to fit in with the coarsing and length of standard blocks, and also the position of joints and piers.

The best way to do this is to have a dry run—literally. Using whole blocks or bricks and half blocks or bricks lay the first two courses, inserting a 10 mm timber lath between the units to allow for joints. For reinforced work make up a timber template to mark the centres of the hollows in the blocks accurately and to enable starter bars to be positioned in the foundations or floor. A few minutes at this stage in the process could save hours later on (Figures 11.14, 11.15 and 11.16).

Cutting bats and closers in a brick wall is normally done as work proceeds—using the back of the trowel, after some practice. Cutting concrete blocks into anything but halves is to be

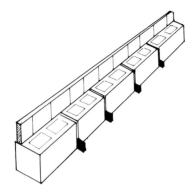

Figure 11.14   Timber template on dry laid blocks to mark position of reinforcement.

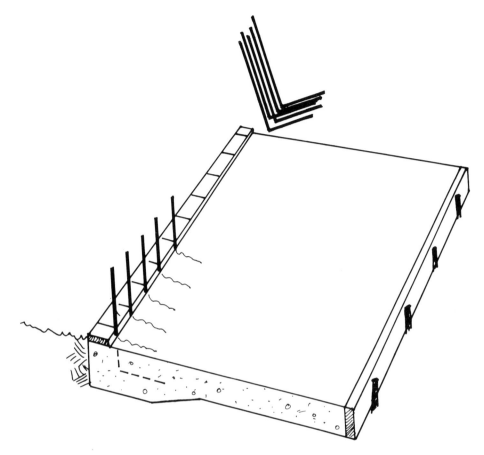

Figure 11.15   Template used to position reinforcement in base.

avoided if possible. Some manufacturers provide half blocks for bonding, others supply blocks with cutting slots preformed in them. These should be used if possible.

If a lot of cutting has to be done it might be worth hiring an electrically driven masonry saw for a day or so; most of the work can then be done in advance. It is possible, of course, to use a bolster and hammer but it is a much slower process. If hand tools have to be used, first score the position of the cut on all faces of the block with the bolster. Sharper hits will break the block along this line (Plate 11.1).

Laying

After the dry run, the first course in the wall can now be laid, taking particular care that it is straight, level, and plumb. The corners are the most important point. These should be built up first; the damp-proof course and reinforcement should not be forgotten.

A string line should be stretched from corner to corner, or column to column if the wall is being built up between columns. The top outside edge of each brick or block should be level with this string line. The line is thus the height of the unit plus a mortar joint above the course below. Continue working from both corners towards the centre until only one unit, the closure unit, is left to complete the course.

Mortar is then spread on the bed joint and up the perpends on each side of the opening. A thin layer of mortar is applied on each end of the closure unit and then it is inserted into position in the wall (Plates 11.2, 11.3). All surplus mortar should be struck off as work proceeds with an upward motion of the trowel to leave the wall

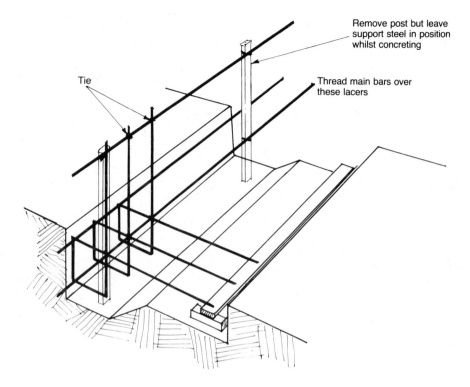

Figure 11.16   Fixing reinforcement in the foundation for concrete block on in-situ concrete walls. Support the 'cage' on blocks and timber during assembly. Remove timber before concreting.

Plate 11.1   Splitting a concrete block.

clean. This mortar can be put back on the spot board, but mortar which has fallen onto the floor should not be so replaced.

It is generally quicker and easier to handle the mortar in small quantities—one shovel full on the spot board at a time and only as much on the trowel at any one time as is needed.

Bricks or blocks should not be hammered into position. If this is necessary the mortar being used is too dry; if they sink in the mortar after positioning, it is too wet. Blocks can normally be tapped into position with a 2 kg hammer—but be gentle (Plate 11.4). Bricks can be tapped into position with the edge of a trowel. Mortar should not be spread on the bed joint too far in advance—not more than 2 or 3 units. The mortar should be spread on the end of the brick or block to be laid immediately prior to putting it into position in the wall, checking line, level, alignment and plumb-ness frequently as work proceeds (Plate 11.5). All joints should be filled solidly (Figure 11.17). Deep furrows in bed

Plate 11.2 'Buttering' the last joint.

Plate 11.3 Inserting the closure block.

Plate 11.4 Tap the blocks into position with a 2 kg hammer. Check for level.

Plate 11.5 Take care that the corners are plumb.

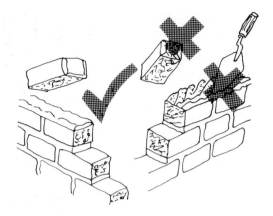

Figure 11.17   Do not 'tip and tail' units or make deep furrows in bed joints. Fill all joints solidly in brickwork.

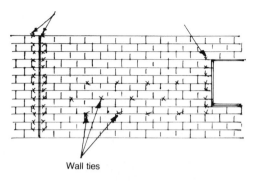

Figure 11.18   Position of wall ties.

joints and 'tip and tailed' perpend joints will let more water through.

Cavity Walls

Cavity walls are built in the same way as single-leafed walls—corners first and then infilling. Both leaves of the wall should be brought up together, not forgetting the wall ties (Figure 11.18). The cavities should be kept clean and no mortar should be allowed to drop onto the ties, as it would transmit moisture from the outer to the inner leaf. Ties should be laid 'drip' down as illustrated (Figure 11.19) and should slope downwards towards the outer leaf so that moisture does not move towards the inner leaf. To prevent mortar dropping onto them a 40 mm wide piece of timber should be suspended from

Plate 11.6   In 215 mm thick unreinforced walls mortar can be spread on the outside surfaces of the joints only— called 'shell bedding'.

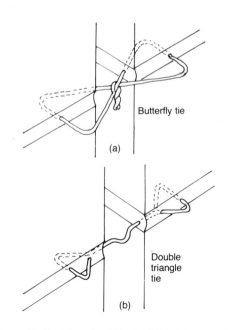

Figure 11.19   Ties should be laid 'drip' downwards and slope towards the outer leaf.

Plate 11.7   To prevent mortar dropping into the cavity suspend a timber batten from strings and lift it occasionally.

strings down into the cavity and lifted as work proceeds (Plate 11.7). Alternatively, a tool can be made as illustrated in Figure 11.20 to clear the mortar from within the cavity.

If insulation is to be built into the cavity ensure that it is properly fixed and is not dislodged during building. In cavity walls weep holes are required at the bottom of the walls or where a cavity is bridged by the dpc to allow water which runs down the inside face of the

inner leaf to drain away. These weep holes are best provided by putting a small piece of wood in the vertical joint at the required level every 1.0–1.5 m (Figure 11.21).

Movement Joints

If an unreinforced concrete block wall exceeds 6 m in length it should have contraction joints

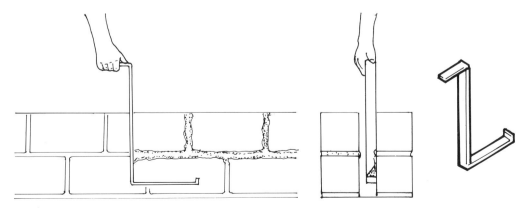

Figure 11.20   Tool for cleaning wall cavities.

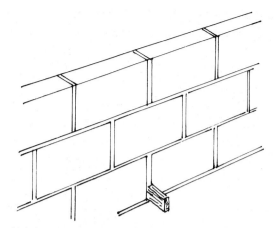

Figure 11.21   Forming a weephole.

Plate 11.8   Filling a joint with sealant.

built in to allow movement resulting from changes in temperature and moisture content. If the joints are omitted the wall will crack. In reinforced walls these joints should be at 12 m centres. In brickwork expansion joints should be provided at 12 m centres. If a concrete wall is very long (36 m) expansion joints may also have to be provided. The joints are illustrated in Figures 11.22 and 11.23.

The bonding pattern is 'broken' and a continuous vertical joint is formed. A galvanised strip, 3 mm thick, 25 mm wide and about 250 mm long is often laid in the bed joint across the movement joint, with one end of the strip greased to allow it to slide. The strip will act as a dowel allowing movement parallel to the blocks but preventing the wall being thrown out of line. These strips must not be too long and must be placed parallel to the wall or they will prevent movement by 'stitching' the joint.

The mortar in the continuous vertical joint is raked back 20 mm with the point of the trowel and the groove is filled with a sealant (Plate 11.8).

In the expansion joint the mortar is left out and replaced with a compressible filler (usually a proprietary bitumen-impregnated fibreboard). Again sufficient space should be left on the outer face, and sometimes the inner face, to apply a sealant.

Piers and Intersecting Walls

A number of ways of providing additional

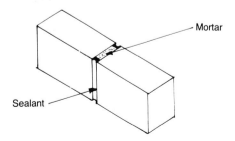

Figure 11.22   Contraction joint.

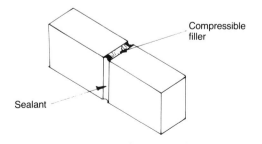

Figure 11.23   Expansion joint.

support to single-leaf walls are shown in Figure 11.24. In hollow block walls a pier can be stacked on the inner or outer face of the wall and tied to the main run of the wall with bent metal bars (Plate 11.9).

Dowelled joints should be used in concrete blockwork where long walls intersect. This allows the partition or intersecting wall to contract without the risk of cracking in the main wall. If the intersecting wall is 2 m long or less it can be tied to the main wall (Figure 11.25).

In brickwork the normal method is to bond the intersecting wall to the main wall using the normal toothing technique, bonding brick with brick.

Finishing

The mortar joints have to be 'finished' in one of a number of different ways. Time will be saved if this is done during building rather than 'pointing'

Plate 11.9 Tying a pier to a main run of wall.

the joints afterwards. If the wall is not going to be rendered or painted the mortar should be compacted into the face of the joint so that it will shed water. This can be done when the mortar is thumb-print firm, using either a pointing trowel to form a 'struck' joint (Plate 11.10), or a round

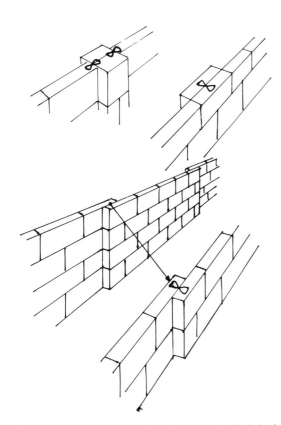

Figure 11.24 Providing additional support in single leaf walls.

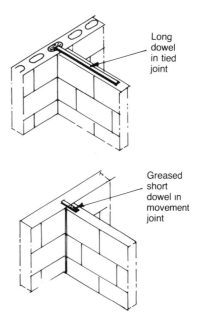

Long dowel in tied joint

Greased short dowel in movement joint

Figure 11.25 Dowelled joints in blockwork.

Plate 11.10   'Struck' joint.

Plate 11.11   'Bucket handle' joint.

metal bar or a short length of plastic hosepipe to form a 'bucket handle' joint (Plate 11.11).

If the wall is to be rendered, the joints should be raked out to a depth of about 12 mm to provide a key for the render (see Chapter 12). On open-textured lightweight aggregate blocks this will not be necessary as the open texture in the face of the block itself will give the required key. On aerated concrete blocks the 'cuts' in the block face give a good key and the mortar is simply struck from the joints flush with the face of the block.

If the wall is to be painted or 'rub and fill' applied to the surface (see Chapter 12), the joint should be 'flush' finished—not simply struck off. Additional mortar may have to be put into some joints to achieve a tidy result. It is poor workmanship to finish with mortar smeared all over the face of the joints.

REINFORCED WALLS

The Principles

In most instances it will be much cheaper to include reinforcement in a wall than to achieve

the required stability by an increase in thickness of the wall. However, the latter is a possible economic option if the resistance of an existing wall to overturning is to be increased. In this case an additional leaf should be constructed about 4–6 in away from the face of the existing wall and concrete poured down between the two leaves.

It is not within the scope of this book to give detailed guidance on the design of retaining walls, but it is important to know the basis of the design which you are building. The reinforcement must be in the right place in the wall if it is to be successful.

Masonry walls and in-situ concrete are strong in 'compression'. This really means that they can withstand heavy loads which squeeze or attempt to squeeze the material from which they are built—this is a *compressive force*. However, they are relatively weak in tension—they can relatively easily be stretched or pulled apart—this is a *tensile force*. A designer has to consider other forces as well but for the purpose of clarity these will be omitted here.

In a simple beam which has a positive thickness (Figure 11.26) and is supported at each

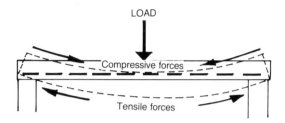

Figure 11.26   Forces in a simple beam.

end, when a load is applied in the middle, the top surface tries to become shorter, it is squeezed, and thus experiences a compressive force. The bottom of the beam tries to get longer, it is stretched, and thus experiences a tensile force.

Concrete and masonry perform well in compression but poorly in tension, whereas steel performs well in tension. Reinforcing steel is therefore included near to the surface of a beam and in a wall which is experiencing tensile forces. In a simple beam that would be near the bottom surface. A wall which is built between two columns is really a very wide beam. The steel should be included near the surface which is being stretched—the outside face of the wall, away from the load. The tensile and compressive forces in an L-shaped wall unit—called a cantilever design—are such that the inside face

is being stretched and the back face is being squeezed—the reinforcement in this instance should be toward the inside face, nearest the load (Figure 11.27).

In each case most reinforcement is put at 90° (right angles) to the direction that the cracks are likely to travel (Figure 11.28). The steel is there to prevent the wall from cracking, or more precisely, to prevent large cracks from occurring; acting like a very strong piece of elastic it will stretch. As it stretches, the concrete or masonry will crack a little bit, but the steel prevents the cracks from becoming too big.

From this simplified analysis of how reinforcement works it is possible to understand why reinforcement is never placed centrally in a structural unit. It is always towards one face or the other. In a well designed cattle slat for example, the steel is in the bottom of the unit. But there is also some steel in the top. The slat is subjected to forces which tend to push it sideways towards the next slat lying alongside. These forces occur if the cow walks forward and actually pushes the slat in the direction opposite to its own movement. So there is a bar near the top of the slat and along each side.

Wall Design

Free-standing walls, 0.9 m high, with no supporting columns, which are to be used to retain farmyard manure, soil or sugar beet should have L-shaped starter bars cast into the foundation at intervals of about 450 mm. These protrude up into the wall (Figure 11.29). In brickwork the starter bars can be in the cavity between two 102.5 mm thick leaves of the wall and the cavity filled with concrete. In concrete blockwork the starter bars are positioned to project into the hollows (see Setting out—an earlier section in this chapter).

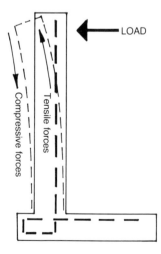

Figure 11.27   A cantilever wall.

Figure 11.28   Steel is placed at 90° to the likely direction of cracks.

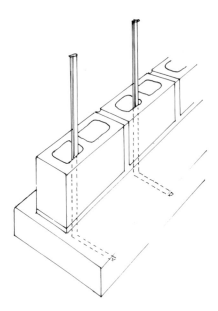

Figure 11.29   Starter bars in lightly loaded blockwork.

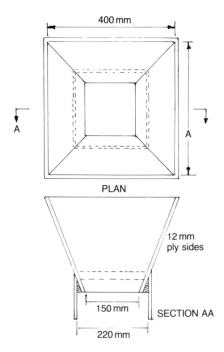

Figure 11.30   Hopper for pouring concrete into one hollow core of a block. Dimension 'A' increases for multiple hollows.

The bars should be of high yield deformed steel, 12 mm in diameter and 1.2 m long including a 0.3 m toe. This toe is pushed 75 mm below the surface of the foundation concrete (Figure 11.15). The bricks or blocks are then built up around them and the cavities or hollows filled with a sloppy (150 mm slump) 1:3:2 mix of cement:sharp sand:10 mm maximum-sized aggregate.

Quite a lot of concrete may be needed to fill these cavities. A chute or series of hoppers should be made up so that a tractor bucket can be used for quick and efficient filling (Figure 11.30). For brickwork, if the cavity is 100 mm wide 4 cubic metres of concrete (possibly from a ready-mixed concrete supplier) will be needed for each 0.9 m high section of the wall of three sides of an 18 × 9 m building. In 440 × 215 × 215 mm blockwork about 2 cubic metres of concrete will be needed for the same building. The cavity or hollows above this level should also be filled with concrete to increase the overall weight of the wall and thus improve its stability. The mortar shown in Table 11.3 should be used for the joints. For this type of work common bricks and normal (3.5 N/mm²) dense concrete blocks can be used.

Heavy Duty Retaining Walls

Retaining walls for slurry stores, grain and potatoes, are usually reinforced both vertically and horizontally. Designs must be very carefully followed, and unless the design states otherwise, it would be advisable to use either engineering bricks or high-strength concrete blocks with a compressive strength of 7 N/mm². A rich mortar mix should always be used (1:¼:3). Plasticisers should not be used for this quality of work.

The type, position and frequency of reinforcing bars would be scheduled in the design. The bars should be bent to the required shape by the steel supplier if possible, as he can do it quickly and accurately with special bar bending equipment. Unless these tools are available it is a tedious and time-consuming operation.

Two courses of bricks or blocks should always be set out before starting this type of work. The reinforcement must be put in the right position (Plate 11.12) in relation to pockets in brickwork and hollows in blocks. The timber template

Plate 11.12 Make sure the steel is in the right position in the foundation and lay on intermittent course of bricks or blocks to coincide with the vertical joints in the first course of blockwork.

Figure 11.31 Proprietary reinforced binders are easy to use.

should be used to keep work accurate (Figure 11.15).

The reinforcement cage should be made up first and all the bars tied firmly either with wire 'twists' or with the specially made reinforcement 'binders' from a specialist manufacturer (Figure 11.31). The latter are easier to use but give less stability to the cage. The foundations need to be excavated deep enough to put a blinding layer of concrete in the bottom, and pieces of concrete or bent reinforcement should be put on the blinding layer of concrete to hold the cage up from the floor of the trench. The foundation concrete is then placed in position using the correct quality concrete which should be specified on the drawings. If it is not, use at least an RC 40 or even an RC 45 mix from BS 5328 mix and compact it with a poker vibrator. The joints may need to be formed so that they can be sealed (Chapter 13). The surface should be finished flat with a wood float where the bricks and blocks are to be laid, and as the rest of the floor elsewhere. The concrete must be left to cure.

Constructing Reinforced Blockwork

Most of the methods used to build reinforced concrete blockwork involve threading the blocks over reinforcing bars for every course all the way up to the wall. This is hard work and slow, but has been necessary to ensure properly filled cores or hollows in the blocks which are filled a few courses at a time.

An alternative method was developed in the early 1980s which makes this technique out of date.

Before starting to build in blockwork but having set out the walls as described and filled the foundations with concrete, the next step is to lay an intermittent course of concrete bricks or engineering bricks at 450 mm centres, or another relevant dimension, so that the centre line of the bricks in this course coincides with the vertical joint of the blockwork (Plate 11.12). These bricks will eventually become part of the wall.

When the mortar joint beneath this brick course has stiffened, the first course of blocks can be threaded over the 'starter bars' bedding them on a full bed of mortar on the bricks. Then the horizontal reinforcement is put in. The threading of blocks over bars is continued and courses of blockwork are laid in the usual way until the starter bars are covered. The nibs of projecting mortar inside the hollows should be knocked off as building proceeds.

At this stage it would be normal to fill the hollows, push more reinforcement down beside the starter bars into the concrete infill, and either tie the bars together with wire to make them rigid so that the next few courses of blocks can be laid over the bars or alternatively leave the concrete to harden so that the bars are held in the vertical position.

In the 'new' method the wall is built with a full bed of mortar for each block but without any additional vertical reinforcement. The horizontal steel is put in the joints, movement joints are formed and the nibs or mortar projecting into the hollows are broken off as before.

Scaffolding will be needed for a job of this scale. It might be possible to manage on short lengths with a tower scaffold or even by operating from a tractor trailer, but it will be a time-consuming job moving these around the wall, so proper scaffolding will pay in the long run.

When the wall has been built up to its full height, it should be left to harden up. The next job is to clear away from the bottom of the wall all the dried mortar that has been pushed down the hollows. The hollows will now form a series of clean, full height tubes all the way along the wall. At this stage several 100 mm × 250 mm × 1 m or so long pieces of timber will be needed, each being as long as the hopper to be used for putting the concrete into the hollows, is wide. A hopper which fits onto the wall will also be needed, and a tractor loader with a hydraulically controlled tipping bucket.

The final operation before the hollows are filled with concrete is to thread reinforcing bars into each hollow from the top to the bottom of the wall (Plate 11.13). These can be tied to the starter bars at the bottom of the wall although this is rather an awkward job. It is important that this bar stays in the correct position in the hollow—normally towards the face of the wall which is to be loaded.

The 1:3:2 mix or cement:sharp sand:10 mm maximum-sized aggregate should be ordered from a ready-mixed concrete supplier or mixed on the farm. It needs to be very sloppy— 150 mm slump—so it will need to be contained in some way if it comes ready-mixed so that it does not spread out all over the yard. The concrete is then loaded into the hopper with the tractor bucket. The concrete should flow down the hollows and when it begins to run out at the bottom, the timber is put over the gaps to stop

Plate 11.13   Thread reinforcing bars from the top to the bottom of the wall lapping the starting bars.

the concrete from continuing to flow out. One piece of wood is put on each side of the wall and anchored in position with blocks. To ensure that the cores or 'tubes' are full and that the full height rod is in the correct position another rod should be used to prod the concrete as it is poured into the hopper. The hopper must not be overfilled at this stage or excess concrete will have to be shovelled out before the hopper can be slid over for the next series of hollows.

After twelve hours the timbers can be removed for re-use and the bottom of the wall tidied up with a trowel. The wall is then ready to receive its 'rub and fill' coat or render or other form of finish, but should be left for a week before starting this work.

Lintels

In most farm buildings lintels will not be required for wide openings as these will extend the full height of the brick or blockwork. Storey high panels at doors and windows can be used elsewhere to avoid lintels and provide suitable positions for movement joints. There will be

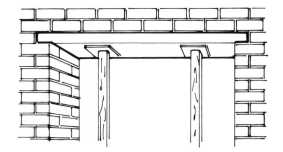

Figure 11.32 Support reinforced concrete lintels.

some doors and windows however that do need lintels. In solid walls, with no cavities, reinforced or pre-stressed concrete lintels are usually most convenient. Reinforced concrete lintels need supporting for about a week to prevent the fresh mortar at the supports from being squeezed out by the weight of the unit (Figure 11.32). Pre-stressed lintels are stronger for a given weight than plain reinforced ones and will only need to be propped if they are over 1.5 m long.

Reinforced aerated concrete lintels are lighter to handle than the normal concrete variety and seldom need propping (Figure 11.33). Their insulation value is comparable to aerated concrete blockwork.

For cavity work use either a composite lintel with a concrete beam inner-leaf and a galvanised steel tray to carry the outer leaf of the wall, or an all-metal lintel with trays for inner and outer leaves. These are much lighter in weight than the concrete lintels and are more convenient for larger openings.

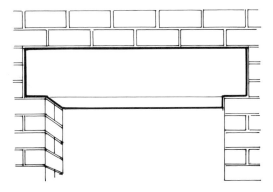

Figure 11.33 Aerated concrete lintels seldom need support.

The aerated concrete lintel and the all-metal lintel will require internal and, for aerated concrete, external finishes on the walls.

SURFACE BONDED BLOCKWORK

Using good-quality blocks, facing quality with clean sharp edges and preferably of uniform size, it is possible to build a strong wall for partitions or as walls to a milking parlour where a rendering is required using the surface bonding technique. In this technique the first course of blocks is laid on the horizontal mortar bed on the foundation—a levelling course—with no mortar in the vertical joints.

Subsequently the blocks are built 'dry', with no mortar in either the vertical or the horizontal joints. They are stacked, half-bond, one on top of the other. If a block rocks during this process a shim of formica or a dab of mortar may have to be put in the joint to stop this rocking, but apart from this, they are simply stacked dry.

Before the end of the day—the blocks must not be left as a stack too long, it may be blown over by the wind—a 3 mm thick coat of a glass-fibre reinforced render or 5 mm of plastic fibre reinforced render must be applied to each face (Plates 11.14 and 11.15). The materials in this surface bonding coat are special—a mix of

Plate 11.14 The mix for surface bonding.

Plate 11.15 The 3 mm thick coating spanning the joints.

Plate 11.16 'Play out' a thin uniform layer of fibre reinforced mortar.

very fine sand, waterproofers, special alkali-resistant fibres, etc., are used—but the method of applying them is just the same as a second coat of rendering. A firm, even pressure is used on the trowel, playing out a thin, more or less uniform, layer of material behind it (Plate 11.16). The layer should be tightened up and the surface finished with a trowel (Plate 11.17) and then cured with polythene.

This type of wall is suitable to carry vertical loads and can be insulated by using solid aerated concrete blocks. It is not normally used if the wall is less than 140 mm thick and if the wall will have to take horizontal loads.

In-situ Concrete Walling

For the experienced do-it-yourself builder or the inexperienced but adventurous type, in-situ concrete walling is a good method of construction for many farm jobs. It would be unwise to tackle this type of work though without first obtaining detailed design plans and drawings of the proposed construction.

If a slurry tank, a silage effluent tank, or a retaining wall for silage in particular is being built, this form of construction has much to recommend it however. Leakproof walls, if that is what is needed, are likely to be easier to construct this way than with other materials.

Plate 11.17 Finish the wall with a steel trowel.

Assuming suitable plans have been obtained, they must be studied in detail so that the requirements are known; for instance the size of reinforcing bars and/or mesh required. The catalogue of the specialist formwork suppliers should be studied to find out exactly what formwork is also needed. The representatives of the formwork suppliers will be happy to help with this. Scaffolding, a tractor bucket with hydraulic tipping, a chute to get the concrete into place and a poker vibrator (Plate 11.18) to compact the concrete will all be needed.

Once the requirements on paper have been familiarised a reinforcing cage can be put together and the foundations or foundation/floor cast as specified around the reinforcement, as described on page 103. A 'kicker' may have to be made on the floor all around it, where the floor will join the wall.

The easiest way to do this is to finish the surface of the foundation/floor in the usual way and then leave it for about 1½ hours until the concrete is 'firming up'. Then lay 150 mm × 75 mm timbers in an accurate line on both the outside edges of the line of the wall (see Figure 11.9). These should be fixed together with timber 'straps', weighted down with blocks and then filled in between with concrete, the concrete being carefully and thoroughly compacted.

After a further two or three hours when this concrete is stiff, using a watering can with a rose fitted to it and a soft hand brush, wash away the cement and fine sand—the laitance—from the top surface of the kicker to leave clean stones exposed. If the concrete is left too long this washing-off process will be difficult and the laitance may have to be removed later with a wire brush. This is not to be recommended as a standard practice because it takes too long. It will work in an emergency though.

The object of this operation is to achieve a leakproof bond between the concrete in the kicker and the concrete in the wall which will subsequently be cast over the kicker. When the removal of the laitance is complete the timbers are removed and the following day the formwork for the wall can be erected.

Alternatively 'kickerless' construction may be used in which the floor slab is cast, the wall/floor joint is prepared by pressure washing the grout off, setting up the formwork to line and locating it in position using timber blocks with shot

Plate 11.18   A poker vibrator.

fired fixing into the floor or shot fired fixing of specially prepared precast concrete blocks within the shutters (Figures 11.34a and b).

Setting Up the Formwork

Unless a lot of in-situ walls are to be built, it is best to hire the formwork. There are now a number of national companies specialising in formwork for this type of wall. If they are told how thick your wall is going to be, they will supply a complete system and provide instructions for assembling it. A dry run with formwork and accessories is worthwhile as well. The accessories should be looked after, as an extra charge will be made if they are not returned at the end of the hire period.

Before erecting the formwork the inside face must be coated with oil—a special concrete mould oil or release agent, as it is sometimes called, is best, but diesel oil will do as a stand in. It is important not to overdo it. The thinnest smear of oil is all that is needed but it must go all over the face of the forms. The oil will allow removal of the forms, usually the next day,

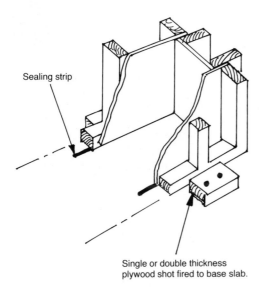

Sealing strip

Single or double thickness
plywood shot fired to base slab.

Figure 11.34a   Shot fired plywood battens for
floor/wall joints.

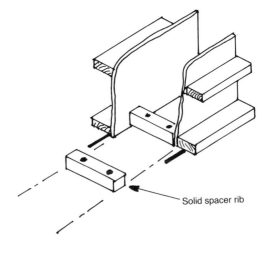

Solid spacer rib

Figure 11.34b   Prefixed purpose made concrete
ribs for wall applications.

without pulling the face of the concrete away. Builders' merchants should be able to supply this oil.

'Bar spacers' should be clipped onto the reinforcement before erection. These are plastic propeller-like objects which ensure that the reinforcement does not move too close to the face of the forms when the concrete is put into position (Plate 11.19). The bar spacers are normally bought direct from the manufacturers—addresses are available from the British Cement Association.

The formwork should be fixed securely, as any gaps between forms will allow liquid from the concrete mix to run out and produce 'honey-combed' areas (open textured patches with only stones in them). If this is likely to be a problem then it can be solved by sticking ordinary domestic draught excluder strips of foamed polyethylene between the offending panels. Ensure that the formwork is in line by using G clamps and scaffold tubes provided by the formwork suppliers (Plate 11.20) and props to ensure that the formwork stays vertical during the filling process.

When the formwork is rigid the concrete can be placed. An RC 40/45 mix should be used for most work if other types of concrete are not specified in the drawing. A 75 mm slump mix is ideal for this type of work. As soon as the concrete is in the forms, it should be vibrated with the poker vibrator, using it to make the concrete flow (Chapter 3, Figures 3.1 and 3.2). If the mix is a good one it cannot be overvibrated. Stones will not 'settle out'. The poker should be kept vertical if possible and lifted out slowly, so that the concrete closes in around it as it is removed. Avoid the steel too, because if the steel is rattled about with the poker, particularly if the concrete is stiffening up, it is possible to cause voids to be formed around the steel. The bars will then be standing up in hollow tubes with no contact with the concrete.

Joints will need to be formed in long runs of concrete just as with blockwork. Columns which intersect the work act as joints, but if there are no columns, then the wall can be broken into sections with dowels to transfer the load from one side of the joint to the next. For completely leak free joints waterstops may need to be incorporated into these joints. These are described in more detail in Chapter 18. Provision should also be made for sealing.

After casting the bottom section of the wall (the first 'lift') wash away the laitance using a soft brush and a watering can as on the kicker (Plate 11.21). The forms can be removed the

Plate 11.19   Bar spacers on reinforcement.

Plate 11.20   Proprietary formwork systems.

next day. All the formwork may not need to be dismantled. If a forklift is used the formwork can be left in large sections and moved to its next location as a pre-formed section. It is advisable to cure the concrete for the same amount of time as for floors.

The formwork must be thoroughly cleaned. Remove all the loose concrete, brush it down well and regrease it ready for re-use.

If there are honeycombed areas the gaps should be made up with a 1:1½ mix of cement:fine sand (Plate 11.22). A small area should be done at a time, pushing the mortar well into the pores in the concrete, trowelling it and then a sponge rubber-faced float can be used to blend in with the appearance of the rest of the wall. The same should be done with any holes in the wall which form when formwork ties are broken off. In some cases the holes will go right through the wall and it will be necessary to use a semi-dry mix of 1:1½, cement:sharp sand, and punch it into the hole with a reinforcing bar or similar tool, packing the hole out in layers. The

Plate 11.21   Washing away laitance at a construction joint.

Plate 11.22   Making good honeycombed areas.

surface of the hole should be finished in the same way as the honeycombed areas.

PROPRIETARY WALLING SYSTEMS

There are many proprietary walling systems on the market—mainly steel walls for grain, timber walls for potatoes and concrete walls for silage, with exceptions, of course. There is little real logic in this choice. Timber can be used for almost anything, concrete similarly and steel too. Because of the risk of corrosion steel should not be used in silos.

It is essential to weigh up the pros and cons and make sure like is being compared with like when the costs of walling systems are being considered. For example, regardless of whether timber, steel or concrete is used for a potato store, plenty of insulation is still needed. Sometimes this is put outside the wall (in the case of steel) and sometimes on the inside (in the case of concrete). For timber silo walls an extra 1 m wide strip of concrete may be needed outside the walls compared with a precast concrete wall; the cost of this extra concrete must be taken into account. In a concrete version, however, extra concrete may be needed beneath the heel of the wall in some cases.

When deciding whether to use steel grain

walls in a building (Plate 11.23) its possible future change of use from a grain store to cattle housing should be taken into consideration. In view of the likelihood of manure coming into contact with the walls, concrete block walls may be more versatile.

It is not the aim of this book to make recommendations on the type of wall to choose, although it would not be prudent if some guidance was not given on which of the various types the authors felt most suitable for do-it-yourself construction. This should be kept in mind when making a choice. As has already been mentioned, in almost every case it is advisable to give plenty of time for thought.

If erecting a timber silo wall the position and type of fixing used to anchor the wall into place is vital. Rag bolts (Figure 11.35) undoubtedly give a first-class fix into concrete (as long as the

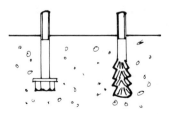

Figure 11.35   Rag bolts.

Plate 11.23   Steel grain walls.

(a) Bad practice   (b) Good practice.

Plate 11.24   Rocking a concrete drill produces a weak fix for anchor bolts.

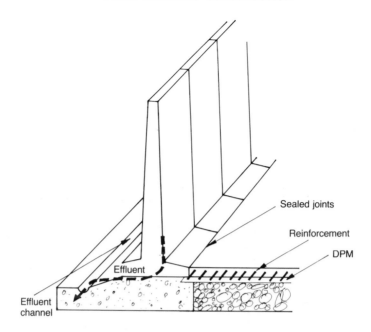

Figure 11.36   Silo wall/foundation designed for effluent collection.

quality of the concrete is correct), but locating them in the precise position they are required is difficult and bent rag bolts will not go into vertical holes in a timber rail. It may be safer, therefore, to drill the holes once the unit has been offered into position and the precise spot for the fixing into the concrete can be marked.

If it is decided to fix the timber in this way, an old drill bit or one that is undersized must not be used. If the drill itself has to be rocked to make the anchor bolt fit, then the anchorage in this imperfect shaped hole will be very second rate (Plates 11.24a and 11.24b). No fixings should be missed out either; more than one silage wall has suffered uplift because of inadequate fixings.

With concrete walls there are other risks. In a silo the joints may be sealed between the wall units effectively when the wall is new, but no sealant lasts for ever, and eventually it will harden or soften and the joint may leak. In this age of anti-pollution legislation it may well be forward thinking to cast a high-quality concrete footing on the underside of the precast unit so that leakage can be contained, collected and discharged safely (Figure 11.36). Many designs do not have regard for this risk.

If it is decided to tackle the installation of any of these proprietary prefabricated walling systems, ensure that the manufacturers supply sufficiently detailed instructions to enable the work to be undertaken. Also check that they have supplied the other ancillary items required. This could include sealants, fixings, bituminous paint or other protective materials.

Chapter 12

RENDERING

A RENDERING on a wall can provide protection against moisture penetration, whether from the outside as rain or from the inside as washing water and can be used to improve the appearance of a building. In Scotland in particular it is used extensively to achieve both these things. It can also be used to extend the life of a wall—crumbling brickwork or walls mainly of lime-mortar or clay with large stones or flints cast in (cob walls) still occur in many old buildings but are no longer suitable for modern farming methods. Applying a rendering to improve the internal surface of such walls where animals or crops are likely to come into contact with them is ideal. Renderings can also be used to provide a background for protective paints, as well as paints used to improve the appearance of a building.

In all these situations the durability of rendering itself depends on the bond between wall and rendering, the mix, the standard of workmanship, detailing and finish. Even the texture chosen can have a significant effect—smooth surfaces are generally less satisfactory than rough ones; smooth surfaces tend to develop a pattern of fine cracks, termed crazing, and often show the effects of weathering more readily than rough surfaces.

In common with most crafts, there is widespread use of jargon relating to renderings; some terms are local or regional and may have different meanings in different areas. Before describing how to achieve a good, durable rendering it is important to know what these terms mean.

Some Rendering Terms Defined

Background (backing) The material or combination of materials to which the first coat of rendering is applied.

Butter coat The soft final coat to which the aggregate is applied in dry dashing.

Comb A tool used for scratching the surface of partially set rendering to provide a key for the following coat. It has a wooden handle with a row of protruding nails or wires.

Compo A cement–lime–sand mortar.

Darby A wooden, steel or alloy tool, consisting of a flat blade about 1.2 m long with two handles, used for straightening and floating.

Dry dash or pebble dash A finish in which suitably mixed aggregate of natural or manufactured materials is thrown onto a freshly applied coat of mortar, and left exposed.

Dubbing out The process of filling in hollow places on a solid background before the main body of rendering is applied. May also be employed where projections or extra thicknesses are required, e.g. for very small breaks or panels.

Final coat The final continuous coat of rendering material; in dry dash finishes, it is the coat onto which the dash is thrown while the coat is still soft; in roughcast or Tyrolean finishes, it is the last coat thrown on to complete the finish.

Grading Particle size distribution. The proportions by weight of particles of different sizes in a granular material. Well-graded sands have just the right amount of very fine, fine and coarse particles.

Harling See roughcast.

Hawk A tool for holding mortar for application by a trowel. It usually consists of a smooth flat piece of wood or aluminium about 300 mm square, with a small handle attached to the centre of the underside.

113

Key (mechanical key) Localised inequalities, sometimes specially produced, in the surface of a background or undercoat, providing a mechanical bond for the applied mix.

Lime A material which may be either quicklime or hydrated lime.

Masonry cement A cement made from ordinary Portland cement and other materials, which will produce a mortar of high plasticity with a strength suitable for masonry and brickwork.

Pricking-up coat The first coat applied on metal lathing.

Ready-mixed mortar Mortar (usually lime and sand) mixed before delivery to the site.

Rendering A mix based on cement and/or lime with the addition of sand or other aggregates, which is applied while plastic to building surfaces and which hardens after application.

Roughcast (wet dash; harling) A finish produced when the final coat, containing a proportion of fairly coarse aggregate, is thrown on as a wet mix and is left in the rough condition. The texture is regulated by the size of the coarse aggregate.

Sand, sharp Coarse sand, the particles of which are of angular shape.

Spatterdash A mix of cement and fairly coarse sand, prepared as a thick slurry. It is thrown on as an initial coating to provide a key on dense backgrounds having poor suction, or to reduce or even-out suction of other types of background.

Stipple A textured finish produced by dabbing the surface with a brush.

Suction The property of a background which determines its rate of absorption of water.

Tyrolean finish A spattered type of rendering, the final coat being applied by a hand-operated machine.

Backgrounds

Before deciding which mix to use, the quality and type of background needs to be assessed. The surface must also provide a good key to support the rendering.

On brick walls and open-textured blocks rake out the joints, give a preliminary brushing down and spray with water.

On hard, dense material such as dense blocks, engineering brick or in-situ concrete a stipple coat will need to be applied. This consists of 1 part of cement and 1½ parts of fine sand (by volume) with water and a bonding agent, such as styrene butadiene (SBR). The proportions recommended by the manufacturer should be used to achieve a thick creamy consistency.

The mix should be brushed well into the surface, using a firm bristle hand brush. More material should be put on the brush and the coated area stippled over with the brush to give a good key (Plate 12.1). About 0.25 m² should be covered at a time. In calm weather, the wall can be covered with a sheet of polythene to allow the coating to cure, or sprayed regularly with water for two days. No further work should be done until this coating has hardened, waiting seven days if possible.

On disintegrating surfaces or painted surfaces a separate support may have to be provided for the rendering *either* by fixing galvanised wire mesh or expanded metal of 12 mm mesh to the background with rust-resistant masonry nails, *or* by fixing vertical, rot-proof, timber support battens (50 mm × 25 mm) to the background at

Plate 12.1   A stipple coat being applied.

450 mm centres and attaching the wire mesh to these battens.

Ingredients

The ingredients for rendering are sand, cement, water and sometimes lime. The sand must be clean, sharp and well-graded. The do-it-yourself builder may have difficulty in recognising the ideal sand. A coarse, gritty sand with lots of very small stones in it is not ideal, nor indeed is a sand with a predominance of very fine silty material in it, or one with only one size particle (typical sea shore material). A 'plastering' or 'rendering' sand (often called soft sand) as distinct from a building or a concreting sand (often called sharp sand) is the one to go for. Sharp sand will generally be more durable than soft sand but is more difficult to render with. The cement can be ordinary Portland cement or masonry cement. Masonry cements are made to produce a smooth, workable mix without the use of lime (see Table 12.1). Lime is used in conjunction with ordinary Portland cement to give a workable, cohesive mix.

The mix to be used is determined by the background onto which the rendering is being applied, and by the purpose of the rendering. On 'weak' backgrounds, such as aerated concrete blocks, use Mix A (see Table 12.1) for the backing or first coat and Mix A for the second, final coat. On most other backgrounds, the first coat should be of Mix B. Externally, the second coat should also be of Mix B. In farm buildings where high durability is required—against pressure washers and/or acid attack—the second coat should be of Mix C.

While the amount of cement is determined by the mix proportions, the amount of water is largely determined by the sand. With poorly graded sands the amount of mixing water needed becomes excessive and produces a poor-quality mortar which is liable to excessive shrinkage. Most cracking in renderings is attributable to the use of too much water in the mix—the direct result of using very fine or poorly graded sands.

Admixtures

Admixtures are sometimes added in rendering mixes to improve the working properties of the material or to modify their properties in the finished job.

- Plasticisers may be used to improve the workability of a mortar without the need to increase the water content unduly.
- Integral waterproofing admixtures may be used to make a rendering less absorbent to rainwater.

The admixture manufacturer's recommendations regarding quantities, method of mixing and use should be followed carefully.

Mixing the Mortar

Small quantities of mortar can be mixed by hand. The materials should be measured out in the requisite proportions by volume and mixed together in their dry state until a uniform colour is produced. Then enough water is added to give a workable consistency. When using a mixer, most of the water and all the sand should be put in, adding the cement a little at a time, and finally enough water to reach the required

Plate 12.2   Mortar of the right consistency hangs on the hawk.

Table 12.1   Approximate quantities of materials needed to cover 100 m². Cement comes in 50 kg bags, lime (at half the density of cement) in 25 kg bags. Plasticiser is added to manufacturer's instructions.

Mix	Proportions (by volume)	Materials	Quantities		
			Thickness of rendering		
			6 mm	10 mm	12 mm
A	1	cement	2 bags	3½ bags	4 bags
	2	lime	4 bags	7 bags	8 bags
	9	sand	0.6 m³	1.0 m³	1.2 m³
	or				
	1	masonry cement	3 bags	5 bags	6 bags
	6	sand	0.6 m³	1.0 m³	1.2 m³
	or				
	1	cement	2½ bags	4 bags	5 bags
	8	sand + plasticiser	0.6 m³	1.0 m³	1.2 m³
B	1	cement	3 bags	5 bags	6 bags
	1	lime	3 bags	5 bags	6 bags
	6	sand	0.6 m³	1.0 m³	1.2 m³
	or				
	1	masonry cement	3½ bags	6 bags	7 bags
	5	sand	0.6 m³	1.0 m³	1.2 m³
	or				
	1	cement	3 bags	5 bags	6 bags
	6	sand + plasticiser	0.6 m³	1.0 m³	1.2 m³
C	1	cement	6 bags	10 bags	12 bags
	¼	lime	1½ bags	2½ bags	3 bags
	3	sand	0.6 m³	1.0 m³	1.2 m³
	or				
	1	masonry cement	6 bags	10 bags	12 bags
	3	sand	0.6 m³	1.0 m³	1.2 m³
	or				
	1	cement	6 bags	10 bags	12 bags
	3	sand + plasticiser	0.6 m³	1.0 m³	1.2 m³

consistency.

When it is mixed the mortar should be placed on a table top—many plasterers use a 1 m square top. The mortar is then transferred from the table to the hawk. If it 'hangs' on the hawk when it is held upside down for a few seconds it is of the right consistency (Plate 12.2). Some of the mortar is then transferred from the hawk to the trowel, tilting the mortar on the hawk and sliding off a small amount of mortar onto the trowel from what is now the top end of the

hawk, and returning the hawk instantly to the horizontal.

If the mortar can be transferred to the trowel in this way the rest is relatively easy! If this proves difficult then put the hawk, loaded with mortar, up against the wall. A small amount of mortar can be pushed from the hawk onto the wall with the trowel. As pressure is applied to the trowel it should be moved up the wall, keeping the lower edge about 10 mm from the wall.

Applying the Mortar

Having completed the preparatory work two coats of rendering are usually applied, since a single coat will permit the joints in the brickwork or blockwork to show through. Before the first coat is applied the background should be dampened (but not saturated) to provide uniform suction and prevent the rapid absorption of water from the rendering.

The first coat should be applied using firm pressure on the trowel (Plate 12.3), at a maximum thickness of 10–12 mm. When applying the rendering over expanded metal or wire mesh, the first coat should be thick enough to enclose the metal completely and applied with sufficient pressure to push the mortar through the mesh.

A uniform thickness of rendering can be obtained by fixing 10 mm thick battens temporarily to the wall and screeding off the first coat with a straightedge (Plate 12.4). Any low spots can be dubbed out with small dabs of mortar placed onto the surface with a wood float. Then the entire surface of the first coat should be smoothed over using the wood float rather like a carpenter's plane. This levels the

Plate 12.4   Screeding off the first coat with a straightedge.

Plate 12.3   Applying the first coat; usually applied in two layers.

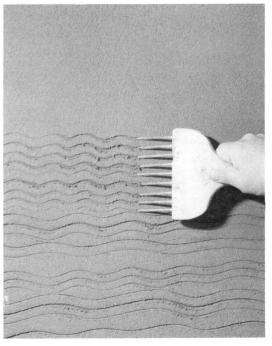

Plate 12.5   Combing the first coat to give a key for the second.

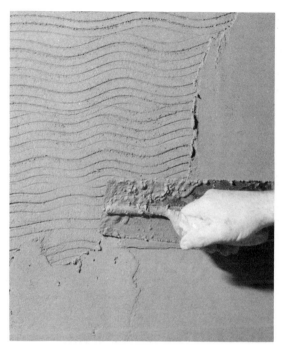

Plate 12.6   Applying the second coat.

surface and compresses the mortar. This should then be combed horizontally to provide a key for the second coat (see Plate 12.5).

The surface should be allowed to dry for as long as possible—not less than 48 hours and preferably for seven days—before the second coat is applied. Thorough drying permits shrinkage to take place, thereby reducing the risk of cracking in the second coat. After seven days the first coat should be dampened and then the second coat applied, 6 mm thick (Plate 12.6).

To reduce the risk of cracking, the rendering should be divided into panels by joints at not more than 5 m centres. The position of the joints should be chosen to suit the appearance of the building. A joint is formed by making a V-shaped cut in the rendering (Plate 12.7). If it is necessary to ensure that moisture does not penetrate the joint, a mastic sealant may be applied in the cut when the rendering is mature and dry.

Finishing

The final coat can have a number of different finishes. Externally, the sandy gritty surface left

Plate 12.7   Cutting the mortar to form a joint.

Plate 12.8   A wood float finish is suitable for external work.

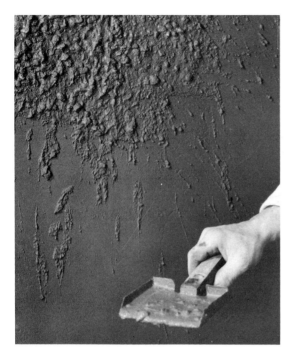

Plate 12.9   The roughcast finish.

by a wood float may be satisfactory (Plate 12.8). Internally a smooth dense finish which is easy to clean can be produced with a steel trowel.

To obtain a roughcast finish an undercoat of 1 part cement, ½ part lime and 4½ parts sand should be applied. The mix for the roughcast top coat should consist of 1 part cement, ½ part lime with 3 parts sand and 1½ parts shingle or crushed stone. The maximum size of the shingle or crushed stone may vary from 5 mm to 15 mm. Sufficient water should be added to obtain a wet, plastic mix which can be thrown onto the wall from a bucket using a hand scoop (Plate 12.9). In order to distribute the mix evenly and give a uniform texture, great care should be taken to obtain a wide, even spread.

For dry dash a 1:½:4½ mix to which a waterproofing admixture has been added is used for the first coat. The aggregate for the finish may be, for example, calcined flint, spar or pea shingle, graded from 15 mm to 5 mm in size according to choice. The stone should be well washed and drained prior to its application.

The second coat, termed the 'butter coat', which is to receive the aggregate, should consist of 1 part cement, 1 part lime and 5 parts sand,

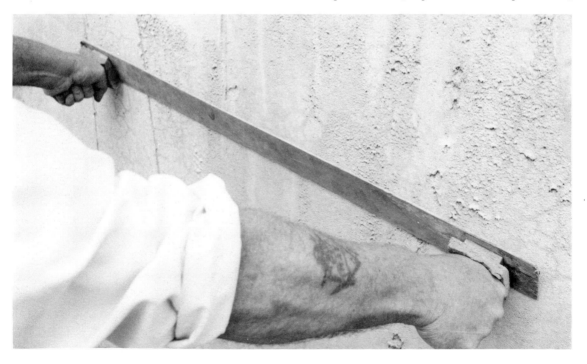

Plate 12.10   Regulating the surface with a 'darby'.

Plate 12.11   Applying a dry of pebble dash.

applied approximately 10 mm thick. A straight-edge or 'darby' should be drawn over the face to obtain a regular surface while the mortar is still soft (Plate 12.10). The selected aggregate can be scooped from a bucket and thrown onto the surface (Plate 12.11). As with roughcast, great care should be taken to obtain a wide and even spread, in order to distribute the aggregate and give a uniform appearance. The aggregate

Plate 12.12   Tamping pebble dash to achieve good bond.

should then be lightly tamped into the butter coat with the face of a wooden float to ensure that a good bond is obtained (Plate 12.12).

Rub and Fill

In many cases, such as piggery partition walls, internal silo walls or external grain walls which are to receive a protective paint, it is not necessary to apply a rendering. The surface of the blocks can be sealed with a rub and fill (or 'bagging') coat.

A mix of 1 part of cement and 1½ parts of fine sand should be used adding water to reach a rich creamy consistency. This is applied to the wall with a soft-haired brush (Plate 12.13). The mix is worked into the wall with a ball of hessian or a wooden float with sponge rubber fixed to its face and any excess removed (Plate 12.14). This should be allowed to harden for three days.

Painting

It may be necessary to apply a decorative finish or chemical-resistant paint. A wide range of special paints is available but, as concrete is

Plate 12.13   Applying a rub-and-fill mix to the wall.

Plate 12.14 Working the rub-and-fill mix into the face
of the blocks.

alkaline, only alkali-resistant paints should be used—unless the surface has been given a special alkali-resistant priming coat. The following paints may be applied directly to concrete or cement rendering:

Cement-based paints These seal up porous surfaces and provide a hard durable finish which resists the penetration of water. They are made in white and in a range of light colours, and reflect light and heat well. The paint comes in powder form and is mixed with water to the manufacturer's instructions before application.

Chlorinated rubber-based paints These are highly resistant to chemical attack. Their use is usually restricted to such places as dairies, milking parlours and areas where there is a serious danger of chemical attack (in silos for instance). Manufacturer's instructions should be followed.

Other paints Chemical-resistant synthetic, resin-based paints are also available and can be applied to renderings.

Chapter 13

FLOORS

LAYING A floor in a farm building is the one job that everybody tackles at some time or another. Perhaps they think it is the easiest building job. 'Anybody can lay a bit of concrete, can't they?' It is true, any able-bodied person can lay a bit of concrete, and in almost every case concrete will be the material chosen for the floor of a farm building.

If good, hard-earned money is being spent on the materials, then it makes good sense to get the maximum possible benefit from them. Thus a clear understanding of what is to be achieved, thoughtful planning of the job and a thorough investigation into costs are needed. All the tools and specialist materials should be on hand in advance.

This chapter will look at many different types of floor—grain store floors, insulated floors, heated floors, parlour floors, workshop floors, silo floors, etc. They all have their own specific requirements. Some will only carry animals and the men that look after them. Others will have to carry very heavy loads indeed. Some will be subject to severe abrasion, others will be subject to chemical attack; some need to be 'watertight', some oil resistant. There are a different set of objectives in each building. So it is not just a matter of 'laying a bit of concrete'.

We have already defined some of the terms used in the building world. Floor laying has its own jargon words which need explaining.

Some Floor Laying Terms Defined

Admixtures (additives)   Chemicals which can be put into concrete to modify its properties in some way.

'All-in' (ballast)   Sand and stones mixed together to which cement is added to make concrete.

Base or (preferably) sub-base   The layer of material immediately beneath the concrete or other wearing course.

Blinding   Sand or other fine material used on top of the sub-base to produce a smooth surface.

Coarse aggregate   Gravel or crushed stone more than 6 mm across.

Damp-proof membrane (dpm)   A thin layer of waterproof material (polythene, bitumen) spread under the concrete to prevent upward movement of water to the surface of the floor.

Fine aggregate   Sand or crushed stone, 5 mm across or less.

Forms, formwork or side-forms   Timber or metal beams used to contain the concrete and stop it from spreading when it is still in a semi-liquid state.

Grano   A layer of concrete usually less than 75 mm thick used as a wearing surface which contains granite chippings, 6–10 mm across.

Grout   A mix of cement and water (sometimes the water has other things added to it) made up to a thick creamy consistency.

Hardcore   Normally large pieces of brick, stone or concrete from old, demolished buildings.

Laitance   Fine sand, cement and water which sometimes forms a slurry-like layer on top of newly laid concrete.

Lightweight aggregate   Manufactured or selected material, much lighter in weight than ordinary stone, with a honeycomb-like internal structure.

Oversite concrete   Concrete laid as a 'working platform' during building which is covered

122

towards the end of the 'contract' with a proper floor.

No-fines concrete Concrete made with cement and stones only. No sand is included in the mix.

Screed A hand-compacted regulating or levelling layer of a cement:sand mix of moist consistency not normally used as a wearing course.

Stop end A piece of wood placed vertically, which is used to define the limit to a section or area of concrete. It is normally removed at a later date.

Topping Fully compacted, specially specified layer which forms a wearing course.

Water bar Proprietary, pre-formed rubber, neoprene-rubber or metal strips which can be built into joints to prevent leakage of liquids.

Loading

It is easy to understand that a wheel carrying a 4 tonne load will do more damage to a floor than one carrying only 1 tonne. To avoid damaging the floor it is necessary to spread the 4 tonne load over a greater area of the ground beneath it. To achieve this spreading effect it is necessary to increase either the thickness of the sub-base layer (often called the hardcore) or the structural material in the floor, usually concrete.

It would seem logical to assume that a 4 tonne wheel would do twice as much damage as a 2 tonne wheel. Unfortunately it is not as simple as that; the damaging effect increases dramatically as can be seen in Table 13.1.

Table 13.1 Comparative 'damaging power' of different axle loads

Axle load (tonnes)	Damaging power
1.8	0.0025
3.6	0.03
4.5	0.09
6.3	0.35
8.0	1.0
10.0	2.3
12.7	5.8

Tests in the United States many years ago made it possible to classify wheel or axle loads according to their damaging power. Some typical loads are shown in Figure 13.1. The figures in Table 13.1, together with many years of accumulated experience, allow the specification of certain thicknesses of concrete and certain thicknesses of sub-base layers beneath the concrete for a whole range of farming situations. These are set out in Tables 13.2 and 13.3.

Similar figures can be used for the thicknesses required for roads and other paved areas around the farm. These are also included in Tables 13.2 and 13.3 in this chapter although they relate specifically to the design of roads in Chapter 17.

Table 13.2 A classification of sub-grades for concrete and the minimum thickness of sub-base required

Type of sub-grade (soil)	Definition	min. thickness of sub-base required (mm)
Weak	Heavy clay, silt and peat	150
Normal	Sub-grades other than those defined by other categories	75
Very stable	Sands and gravel soils. This category includes undisturbed foundations of old roads, etc.	0

Sub-base

The sub-base layer in a floor or road does a number of jobs. It carries construction traffic, forms a flat surface onto which the true structural material is laid and, most importantly, it helps to spread the loads to be carried by the floor or road. Many people call the layer immediately beneath the concrete the 'hardcore', but the proper term for this layer is the 'sub-base'. Hardcore is usually regarded as broken brick, broken concrete or crushed stones. It may be cheap to obtain but unless it is a 'graded' material—that means it has large, medium-sized, small pieces and dust in it—then it should not really be used as a sub-base material. A floor or road is only as good as its foundation and this is what a sub-base is.

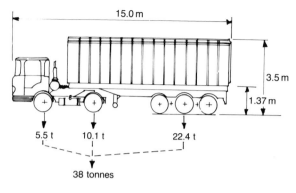

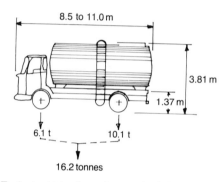

Figure 13.1   Typical vehicle dimensions and axle loads.

can squeeze up into.

Crushed, as distinct from broken, brick, concrete and crushed stone will make good sub-base material but ensure that these materials *do* contain a mixture of large (50 mm), medium (20 mm), small (10 mm) and fine (dusty) material. The other main requirement for a good sub-base material is that it is free of chemicals. In particular it should be free of sulphates which may attack concrete. All that can be done to check this is to ask the person supplying it! Likely suitable materials include hoggin, quarry waste, 'crusher run', iron stone, ash or shale (as long as they are sulphate free), shellit or scalpings.

One of the best sub-base materials is a material called 'lean concrete'. This is a mixture of cement, sand and stones, as in normal concrete, but with a very low cement content and almost no added water. This mix is laid and compacted in the same way as other sub-base materials, but, being a concrete, it sets hard and rigid. It is perhaps the best sub-base material, but compared with other materials, it is likely to be more expensive. Any ready-mixed concrete supplier will give a quote. With all these materials it must be ensured that there is good compaction— use a vibrating roller for preference, a vibrating plate compactor as second choice and a tractor as a poor third.

The technique called 'cut and fill' has been dealt with in Chapter 6. On many sites this will be necessary to achieve good siting in relation to other buildings and the correct falls. It must be ensured that the fill materials have really settled and have been properly compacted in layers. No

The sub-base must be well compacted, rolled down, and only a graded material will respond to this compaction. A material which is made up of large pieces only cannot be compacted. Imagine trying to compact ball bearings, there will always be spaces left, spaces which concrete can flow down into and spaces which, under pressure, soil

Table 13.3   Suggested thickness (mm) of concrete for different sub-grades and different applications

Type of loading	Sub-grade type					
	Very stable		Weak		Normal	
	unrein. conc.	rein. conc.	unrein. conc.	rein. conc.	unrein. conc.	rein. conc.
Cattle, light tractors and trailers (3 tonne maximum axle load)	100	100	150	125	100	100
All other types of vehicles	125–150	125	175	150	150	125

amount of sub-base or concrete can disguise problems in this area. As already mentioned the sub-base helps to spread the loads. The thickness of sub-base material is therefore determined by the type of soil underneath it—different soils have different load-carrying capacities, and Table 13.2 sets out the requirements. In most cases it will be found that more than the minimum thickness suggested will be needed just to bring the levels of the finished floor up high enough. If it is decided that 125 mm of concrete is required but 300 mm of soil has had to be excavated in order to remove all the organic material, then 200 mm of sub-base will be needed to bring the surface of the floor up to the right level, even if 75 mm was all that was required for load spreading.

When the sub-base is being laid, over-filling should be avoided. It is a lot easier to add material than to remove it. If 150 mm of finished thickness is required a compacted level just below this should be aimed for. Unless a very fine sub-base material is being used the surface should be blinded with sand. A 10 mm thickness is ideal, and the sand should be compacted as well. This forms an ideal surface on which to lay the damp-proof material if it is required.

Damp-proof Membranes

With most floors it is worth while including a damp-proof membrane (dpm) under the concrete. It only increases the overall cost of the floor by a few pence a square metre and will allow more flexibility of use for the building. Even an implement shed may serve as a temporary holding area for grain at some time and the dpm will then pay dividends.

For load-bearing floors the best place to put the dpm is underneath the concrete and that is where the sand blinding is of benefit. A 250–300 μm polythene sheet should be used, spread right across the strip of concrete to be laid and held down by the formwork. It will of course be punctured by the pins holding the forms, so when the concrete has been laid and the forms are removed the next piece of polythene must be lapped over the first and, ideally, the joints should be taped. This operation must not be skimped; at least the two pieces of polythene should be rolled together to form a good seal.

The Concrete

The mix

For most purposes an RC35/40 or ST5 mix is the one to use for floors (see Chapter 2), but where chemicals are encountered, or where a particularly abrasion-resistant surface is required, an RC45 mix or even an RC50 would be worth while. The higher the number in the specification, the more cement the mix contains and the stronger and more durable it will be for any given workability.

Concrete gets its strength from the chemical reaction between the cement and the water. But the more water put in the concrete (although it may make placing easier), the weaker the concrete will be. There must be enough water to make the concrete handleable and compactable using the tools available, but it must not be too sloppy, as sloppy concrete is generally weak concrete, although there are exceptions.

Admixtures

In addition to the normal sand and stones that go into concrete mixes other materials can be used to modify the properties of the concrete for floors. These chemicals, called admixtures, may be helpful in some circumstances so a passing knowledge is worth while.

If it is really necessary to use sloppy concrete, a chemical called a superplasticiser can be added to the mix. This makes a normal, relatively stiff concrete into a flowing liquid, so much so that it must not be laid on slopes greater than 1 in 100 or it will flow over the formwork at the low end. The flowing characteristic will last for about an hour, after that the concrete stiffens up and behaves normally again. Whilst it is in the liquid state of course it can be levelled but requires no compaction.

Two other chemicals may also be of benefit on occasions. One accelerates the hardening process—the concrete can be put into service earlier; the other retards the stiffening process—it allows for more time to get the concrete into position and to work on it. This retardation only lasts an hour or so, after that the concrete will harden at the normal rate.

Accelerators are not advised for reinforced concrete but can be useful in un-reinforced concrete in cold weather. When concrete hardens it gives off heat. Accelerated concrete gives off even more heat. If this heat can be kept in the concrete with an insulating mat of straw it is less likely to be damaged by frost early in its life.

Materials called 'waterproofers' are also available. It would be unwise to use these in place of a dpm in a grain store, for instance. The waterproofer certainly helps to make inherently quite permeable mixes such as a rendering more waterproof, but in concrete floors the chemical waterproofer is no replacement for a dpm.

On-farm Mixing

Ready-mixed concrete will usually be most convenient for floors but farm-mixed concrete must also be considered. For small jobs in areas where access is difficult, where the material has to be transported some distance (50–100 m) and only small quantities can be handled at once, tractor-mounted mixers are useful. For bigger jobs the self-propelled, self-loading mixers capable of delivering 1–3 m³ concrete at a time are also available, often on hire. Quite high rates of work can be achieved with these latter units on organised sites, but unless care is exercised with the batching and loading, the consistency and mix proportions may vary from load to load. It is better to use sand and stones from separate stock piles too, than to use 'all-in' material.

Reconstituted 'all-in', when the supplier batches and mixes the sand and stones, is a fairly rare commodity. If available it should be used in preference to 'as-raised' material. The latter contains a varying proportion of sand and stones which makes batching difficult and a uniform quality almost impossible to achieve. It may be worthwhile considering costs before 'all-in' material is used.

Table 2.2 on page 20 indicates that 300 kg of cement is needed in each cubic metre of an ST4 mix, for every 1,860 kg of sand and stones. The 'all-in' material should have 35–40 per cent of sand in it—40 per cent of 1,860 kg is 740 kg. This is mixed with the 300 kg of cement and produces a mortar, in the concrete, of about 1:2½ (300 kg:740 kg).

If the sand is sieved out from a sample of the 'all-in' material (all the sand should pass through a 5 mm sieve) and it is found that about 60 per cent of the material has been removed, and this would be quite common, then this will result in

weaker mortar—60 per cent of 1,860 kg is 1,120 kg. When this is mixed with the 300 kg cement it gives a 1:3½ mortar (300 kg:1,110 kg). To achieve the same quality of mortar as produced with just 40 per cent sand (1:2½), more cement will have to be added—up to three bags more in each cubic metre of concrete. The extra three bags (150 kg), with the original 300 kg gives a mortar of 1:2½—450 kg:1110 kg.

If cement costs £3 per bag the additional cost of the cement required to make up the quality of this all-in material with 60 per cent sand will result in a cost per cubic metre in excess of that for ready-mixed concrete. If the sand is not sieved out to assess the quality of the 'all-in' material and the same quantity of cement is used, this will result in a floor with either poor performance or a shorter life, or even both.

It is much safer and better to buy sand and stones separately.

Ready-mixed Concrete

If ready-mixed concrete is being used and tamping is by hand, the order should be for a 125 mm slump—that is a measure of the work-

Plate 13.1 The workability of a concrete mix is measured by its 'slump'. A cone is filled in a standard way.

Plate 13.2   The cone is removed and the amount the cone slumps down is measured. The wetter the concrete the higher the slump.

Plate 13.3   Use the chute on the ready-mixed concrete mixer to advantage.

ability, or sloppiness of the mix (Plates 13.1 and 13.2). For compaction with a vibrating beam, a 75 mm slump should be specified. It may take the beam a little longer to compact it but it will result in a better quality floor because less water is used in the mix.

The slump test requires equipment that will not be available on the farm, but the ready-mixed concrete supplier may be prepared to send a technical representative, on occasions, to test the concrete for you. A 50 mm slump concrete is a stiff mix, and it will stand up in a cone-shaped heap as it leaves the chute of the truck. A 75 mm slump concrete will flow away from the chute but will need shovelling or raking into position. If the concrete flows away from the chute with little or no work and virtually finds its own level then the slump is likely to be 150 mm or more. Always use the chute on the truck to advantage, the concrete can be virtually spread, unaided by hand, with skilful use of the chute. Most ready-mixed truck drivers are happy to co-operate because it means they will be unloaded and away from the farm more quickly (Plate 13.3 and Figure 13.2).

Laying the Concrete

Whether a hand tamper or vibrating beam is used, the concrete should be spread uniformly between the forms and slightly proud of them. A surcharge batten (Figure 13.3) can be used to achieve this. A 10 mm surcharge is adequate for hand tamping the 125 mm slump concrete, 15 mm is better for the 75 mm slump concrete. Two small pieces of wood should be fixed to the underside of a 100 mm × 50 mm timber so that they rest on the forms—one on either side. As the timber is dragged forward it leaves a regular surcharge of concrete standing above the side forms (Plate 13.4).

This 10–15 mm of extra concrete is compacted down into the rest of the concrete with either a hand tamper (Plate 13.5) or the vibrating beam. Two passes of the hand tamper will be required for compaction, raising and dropping it onto the concrete and moving it forwards half its width (40 mm) each time. If excess concrete remains after two passes strike this off with a sawing motion of the tamper. The excess can be removed with a shovel during the process, and any low spots can be made up by sprinkling extra

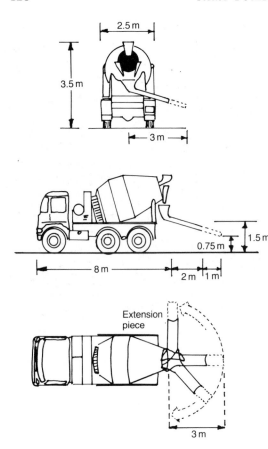

Figure 13.2   Use the chute on the ready-mixed concrete mixer.

Plate 13.4   Small timber packers rest on forms as the timber is moved forwards.

concrete onto the surface and either recompacting or punning it with the back of a shovel.

The vibrating beam will move forward along the forms by the action of the motor-driven vibrator. A slight pull on the ropes encourages it forwards—a small 'roll' of concrete being kept in front of each beam. A single pass with the vibrating beam gives good compaction (Plate 13.6).

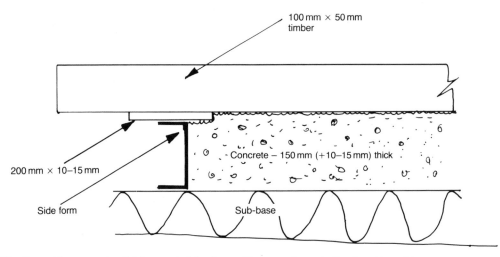

Figure 13.3   Spread the concrete slightly proud of the forms. Use a surcharge batten to achieve this.

Reinforcement

Reinforcement is sometimes used in floors to increase the space between joints—in silos and slurry stores it has to be used to comply with the Pollution Control Regulations. It may also help to strengthen the concrete in the floor but it is not there primarily for strengthening. The reinforcing mesh should be positioned 40 mm below the surface of the concrete. In this position it performs the job of keeping cracks to a minimum and ensuring that they are very narrow indeed.

Cracks may form in the surface of concrete due to a shortening of the material as a result of a fall in temperature or moisture loss. The reinforcement controls these cracks. The steel should be carefully and accurately positioned on 'chairs' of steel bars holding the mesh up from the base or hoops of mesh formed by cutting strips from the edges of the main reinforcing mat and bending the projecting tie wires up at right angles to form a toe (Plate 13.7).

The sheets must be lapped at their ends by 450 mm but not at their edges except in silo

Plate 13.5 A hand tamper in use.

Plate 13.6 A double vibrating beam. Keep a 'roll' of concrete in front of each beam.

Plate 13.7   Reinforcing mesh being laid onto hoops of steel cut from mesh. These support the sheets 50 mm below the surface of the concrete in a 150 mm thick slab.

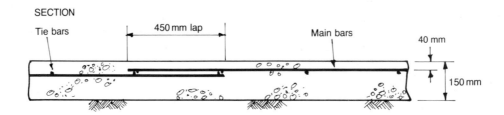

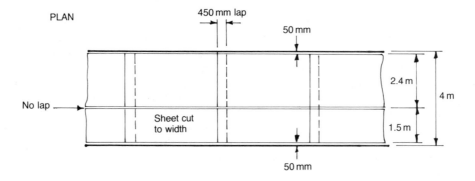

Figure 13.4   Lapping reinforcing mesh for roads—invert every other sheet.

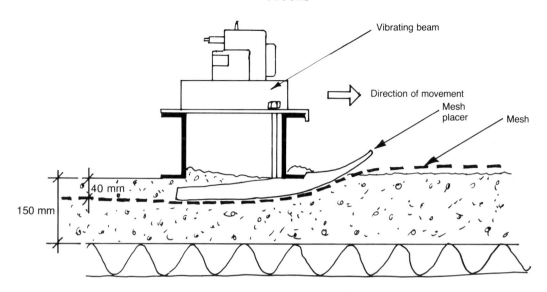

Figure 13.5 Mesh 'placers' or 'feeders' fixed to the leading edge of a double vibrating beam.

and slurry stores when edge lapping by 450 mm is also required. The steel should extend to within 50 mm of the edges of the strip (Figure 13.4).

If a significant quantity of concrete has to be laid with reinforcement in it, then it would be worth while fixing metal 'feeders' onto the leading edge of the vibrating beam as illustrated in Figure 13.5. In this case the reinforcement is laid on top of the uncompacted concrete after the surcharge has been formed and the feeders push the mesh 40 mm into the concrete as the vibrating beam moves forward over the mesh and the concrete.

Joints

It is important to know the names of all the different forms of joints and what their functions are. These are listed below:

Butt joints When a 'new' area of concrete is laid up to and touching a previously laid area of concrete a butt joint is formed between the old and the new. No jointing material is used in this type of joint.

Longitudinal joints When new concrete is laid over a whole floor it will normally be laid in strips the full length of the building—one strip being laid, the next missed, the next laid and so on across the width of the building. After a few days the intermediate strips can be filled in. The joint which runs the full length of the building between the first strip and the first infill strip is called a longitudinal joint (or a construction joint). It is in fact another form of butt joint. New concrete is being laid against old concrete although in this case the old concrete may only be a few days old. In a longitudinal joint no jointing material is used except in silos and slurry stores.

Construction or day work joints When work stops for lunch, at the end of the day, for a breakdown or at the end of a load of ready-mixed concrete, unless work will start again within an hour, a construction joint should be formed by fixing a piece of timber in position across the work. This timber, which is called a 'stop end', should be the full depth of the concrete and the width of the bay—normally a 150 mm × 50 mm length of timber is used. It should never be less than 1.5 m from another form of joint. Concrete areas less than 1.5 m wide or long are likely to crack under load. In silos and slurry stores these joints should be sealed and have waterstops in them.

Contraction joints Except in very cold weather wet concrete, freshly mixed and placed, will

Table 13.4   Fabric reinforcement for floor and road slabs of various thickness (not silos and slurry stores)*

Thickness of slab	BS standard mesh fabric to be used for maximum effective length of slab between free joints		
(mm)	15 m	30 m	45 m
125	A142	C283	C283/C385
150	A142	C283	C283/C385

* For 150–200 mm thick slabs of silo and slurry store floors use A393 fabric with joints at 5–15 m centres.

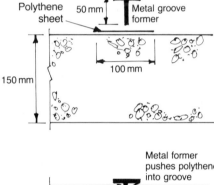

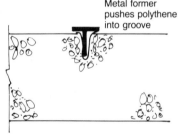

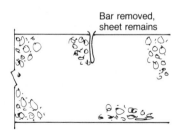

Figure 13.6   Unsealed contraction joint. Lay a 100 mm strip of polythene across the concrete. Press it into the surface with a metal bar. Remove the bar. Leave the polythene in position. The concrete will crack beneath the polythene. No cracks should appear on the surface.

always be larger in volume and therefore, when placed in a floor, longer in length than at any time in its future life. Because it shrinks as it hardens, contraction joints have to be formed to accommodate this shrinkage. In unreinforced concrete they need to be at 5 m centres. In reinforced concrete the spacing between contraction joints can be increased significantly (see Table 13.4). In silos and slurry stores these must be sealed and have waterstops under them (Figure 13.8).

Expansion joints   If concrete is laid in very cold weather it may expand to a length greater than its original wet length. If very long sections of concrete are laid (over 90 m), then expansion joints should be formed. These accommodate any expansion that may take place under these rather special circumstances. Expansion joints are filled with a compressible material which allows the concrete to expand into it. This compressible material should extend the full depth and the full width of the slab. Again in silos and slurry stores they must be sealed and have waterstops under them.

Plate 13.8   The polythene in position.

Plate 13.9   Pushing in the polythene with the bar.

Plate 13.10   Unsealed expansion joint. A compressible fibre board is placed full depth and full width in the concrete. This is supported by timber and the concrete placed around it on both sides.

Sealed joints   Construction joints, contraction joints and expansion joints on most farm jobs are not sealed. However, they can be sealed to prevent water and other liquids, and indeed grit and debris, from entering them. This is not standard practice, but all joints have to be sealed in silos and water or other liquid-retaining structures.

Joints are normally formed as concreting proceeds. In unreinforced concrete, which will be the majority of the work being done, they will be required every 5 m, and in reinforced work at the spacings shown in Table 13.4. The precise distance between contraction joints in reinforced concrete is best determined by the size of the sheets of mesh being used. These are usually 2.4 m wide and 4.8 m long. Having lapped them by 450 mm at each end, the joints will not occur at the 15 m precisely as set out in Table 13.4 but at a slightly shorter spacing than that. Various joints and the methods used to form and seal them are illustrated in Plates 13.8 to 13.23 and Figures 13.6 to 13.8.

Plate 13.11   The concrete is compacted up to the filler board. The timber is removed leaving the board in position. The space left by the removal of the timber is filled with concrete and the compaction process continued.

Plate 13.12   Sealed contraction joint—Method 1.
A groove is made in the concrete with the metal joint
forming bar.

Plate 13.13   A proprietary, plastic contraction joint
former is immediately pushed into the groove.

Plate 13.14   Two examples of contraction joint formers.
They are available in lengths up to 5 m and are a two-
part strip. The upper section can be removed when the
concrete has hardened; the lower section remains in the
concrete.

Plate 13.15   The concrete is made good around the
plastic former using a skip float.

Plate 13.16   When the concrete has hardened the top section of the former is removed.

Plate 13.17   A compressible, neoprene rubber sealing strip is pushed into the groove left. This can be done about 7 days after laying the concrete.

Plate 13.18   Sealed contraction joint—Method 2. A 100 mm wide polythene strip is pushed into the wet concrete with a thickened metal joint forming bar. This is left in position for an hour. A flat bar is not suitable; it must be 'thickened'.

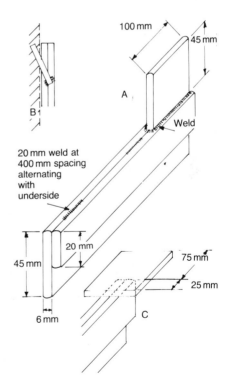

Figure 13.7   The 'thickened' metal joint forming bar. A and B are suitable for forming longitudial joints. C is suitable for contraction joints.

Plate 13.19   After about 7 days remove the polythene and if an accurately shaped groove is left push in the compressible neoprene rubber sealing strip.

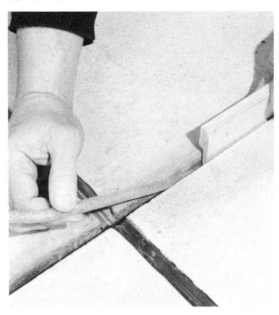

Plate 13.20   If a ragged edge is revealed when the polythene is removed partly fill the groove with a special 'debonding' material available from joint sealant manufacturers. Push this expanded foamed polythene 'rope' about 12–15 mm down into the groove.

Plate 13.21   Prime the concrete edges of the joint with a liquid supplied by the manufacturers of the sealant.

Plate 13.22   Seal the joint with a mastic—bitumen is used in roads but polysulphide or polyurethane sealants are used in silos.

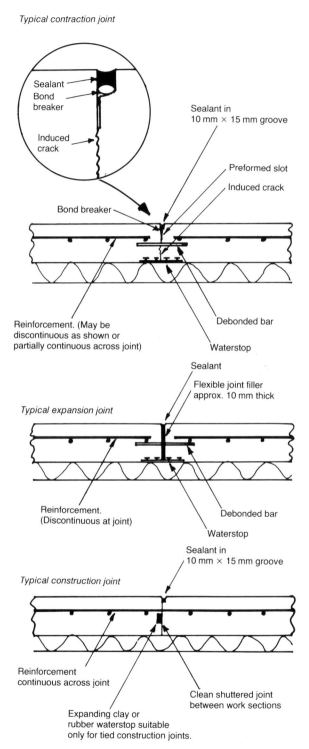

Typical contraction joint

Sealant
Bond breaker
Induced crack

Sealant in 10 mm × 15 mm groove

Preformed slot
Induced crack

Bond breaker

Reinforcement. (May be discontinuous as shown or partially continuous across joint)

Debonded bar

Waterstop

Sealant
Flexible joint filler approx. 10 mm thick

Typical expansion joint

Reinforcement. (Discontinuous at joint)

Debonded bar
Waterstop

Sealant in 10 mm × 15 mm groove

Typical construction joint

Reinforcement continuous across joint

Clean shuttered joint between work sections

Expanding clay or rubber waterstop suitable only for tied construction joints.

Figure 13.8 Sealed longitudinal joints. In silos it may be necessary to seal the surface of these joints.

Plate 13.23 Sealed longitudinal joints. In this case trowel away the concrete to enable either the shaped metal joint-forming bar (Figure 13.7) or the top section from the two-part contraction joint former (Plate 13.14) to be pushed in. Make good around these formers and remove them after an hour or so. Seal the joint as in Plate 13.22.

(Below) A well-constructed floor with sealed joints.

Table 13.3 compares the thickness of concrete for reinforced and unreinforced work. The extra 25 mm thickness needed for unreinforced concrete is always cheaper and easier to lay than reinforced concrete in the thinner slab. But in some jobs the fact that a slab can be laid with reinforcement in it with far fewer joints and less risk of cracks may be important. It has already been mentioned that in silos and in other water or slurry tanks leaks must be avoided. It may be decided to construct a silo that has a floor which is to be leakproof. Legislation on pollution is now more onerous than ever before and if the building is to be on permeable soils the National Rivers Authority will insist on sealed joints. In these circumstances to build a reinforced concrete floor may be a wise decision. The fewer the joints the better and the fewer the cracks the better.

It is not easy to form and seal joints to make them leakproof. The cracks are even more difficult to deal with. By including reinforcement both the number of joints, and hopefully of cracks, can be reduced significantly and this also may reduce the cost of the floor too. Again the cost needs to be looked into carefully.

A Comparison of Sealed Joints in Reinforced and Unreinforced Floors

If £40 is paid for a cubic metre of concrete and it is laid 100 mm thick it will cost £4 per square metre for the concrete. A cubic metre is really a square metre of concrete laid 1 m thick. If it is laid 125 mm thick it will cover 8 square metres and cost £5 per square metre. At 150 mm thickness it will cover 6.7 square metres and will cost £6 per square metre.

By including reinforcement and reducing the thickness of the slab by 25 mm the cost of the concrete can be reduced by £1 per square metre. The difference in the cost of labour for laying the extra 25 mm can be discounted but the cost of labour for putting in the reinforcement, unless the feeder bars (Figure 13.5) are used, cannot be discounted, although it may not be too time-consuming.

If the joints do not have to be sealed they can be formed at very little cost. Sealing joints is expensive, however. A good quality sealant to last ten years may cost over £1 per metre run of joint.

The cost of joints

When the cost of constructing a 3.7 m wide strip of concrete with sealed joints in unreinforced (150 mm thick) and reinforced concrete (125 mm thick) is compared, it is found that the extra concrete in an unreinforced slab costs £1 per square metre, whereas the reinforcement may cost £1.50 per square metre.

In the unreinforced slab joints are at 5 m centres, the joint is 3.7 m long and costs £1 per metre run—a total cost of £3.70 for each joint. This cost can be spread over a 5 m long × 3.7 m wide area and amounts to 20p per square metre of concrete—£1 per square metre extra for the concrete and 20p per square metre for the joint—a total of £1.20.

If joints in reinforced work are formed at 22.3 m centres (5 sheets of mesh) the £3.70 cost for the sealant is spread over an area 22.3 m × 3.7 m—less than 5p per square metre of concrete. However, because the reinforcement costs £1.50 per square metre it is still cheaper to lay unreinforced concrete with sealed joints than reinforced concrete with sealed joints.

Costs may not be the only criterion however. By reducing the number of joints the risk of leakage and therefore of pollution and possibly of prosecution may also be reduced.

Joint Spacing in Practice

Expansion joints as such are unlikely to be necessary in buildings unless the concrete is being laid in very cold weather. But provision for small amounts of movement can be made by including a bitumen-impregnated fibre board, which is the normal expansion jointing material, around the perimeter of the buildings where the floor abuts the wall. The same should be done around fixed parts of the structure (e.g. columns) in the middle of the floor. When it has been decided where the joints are going to be and at what centres and whether or not they are to be sealed, it then has to be decided how to form them. The ideal position for joints in both reinforced and unreinforced floors has already been considered, but the influence on all this of meal times, milking times, size of load of concrete, etc., must be remembered.

If a 6 cubic metre load of concrete is ordered and laid 125 mm thick and 3.7 m wide it will cover a 13 m length of floor. In a reinforced floor joints may be formed at 13 m centres; this would be a construction joint. The mesh would need to be cut to suit this dimension and the stop end pegged across the bay at the end of a load of concrete.

If a full 22.3 m run of floor needed to be laid before forming a joint, five full sheets of reinforcement, lapped by 450 mm at its ends and terminating 50 mm from each joint would be needed, and a full 6 cubic metre load plus a further 4.3 cubic metres of concrete would be required. The concrete at the end of the first load should not be allowed to set before the next load arrives. If this seems likely a construction joint must be formed and the mesh cut.

If an unreinforced floor is being laid the width of the bay is more flexible—the mesh size is not a controlling factor. But a width of 3.7 m is the optimum for minimum steel cutting and minimum waste ideal for both hand and machine compaction. A bay width of 4.9 m to 5.0 m is too wide for efficient hand tamping and on the limit for most vibrating beams.

A 6 cubic metre load laid 150 mm thick and 3.7 m wide would cover a 10.8 m long section of the floor and a contraction joint should be formed at the midpoint of this strip. At the end of the load a construction joint would be formed.

It is obviously desirable to select the bay width to suit all the equipment on hand. A 3.7 m width can be used for all floors but for concrete roads a narrower width is more economical.

Plate 13.24   The commonest texture found on farms is the tamped finish. This tamper has the ends of the beam notched out so that the timber bites deeper into the concrete. It is suitable for roads and cattle.

Texturing and Finishing

The texture or surface finish selected will depend on the predominant use of the floor. A workshop floor has a very different requirement from a cubicle passageway for instance. Many of the tools illustrated can be made quite easily in a farm workshop and time spent in thought and preparation is well repaid. Those that cannot be made can be purchased or hired, the quantity of work to be undertaken and the length of the 'contract' period will influence this decision. Long-handled brushes, texturing tampers, grooving tools, hand tools and even skip floats always 'come in handy' but power floats and power trowels, although superior in performance to hand trowels, can only be justified, even on hire, if the job being tackled is a large-scale floor, and

Plate 13.25   The range of brush finishes. The nylon yard broom (centre) gives good grip for vehicles. All are too abrasive for stock. Use a 3–4 m long handle on them to reach across the bay.

Plate 13.26   The wood float is suitable for cubicles and for areas used by sows and boars.

Plate 13.27   A light steel trowelling after a wood float is ideal for young pigs. Apply more pressure on the trowel and use it when the concrete is nearly firm for really smooth floors.

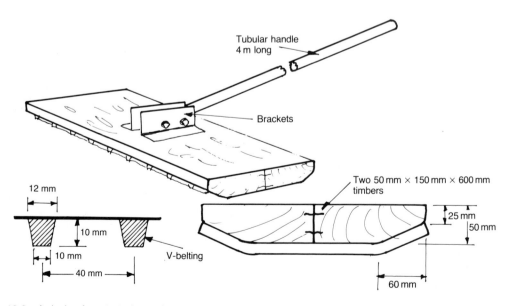

Figure 13.9   A design for a texturing tool to produce a grooved finish; ideal for cattle.

Plate 13.28   The texture produced by the grooving tool.

tighten it. After a further waiting period the trowels are used on the surface to give an even smoother finish and to give more compaction. The final trowelling may have to be left for up to six hours after initial finishing was carried out with a skip float. The sequence therefore, after tamping, is to use a skip float then to wait until the concrete can be walked on, to use the power float followed later by the power trowel. The machines are used by swinging them in a wide arc in front of you. An area 3 m or so wide can be covered with the machine moving slowly forwards with each successive arc.

This form of finishing is recommended for the floors of packing sheds, grain and potato stores, workshops, silos (unless self-feeding) and slurry stores. For workshops use an RC40 mix to give an even harder surface to the concrete.

Curing

After texturing or trowelling, the surface should be cured. This process is designed to slow down the rate of evaporation of moisture from the

concrete laying is being planned as a systematic and regular job for a period of days.

The tools required for most finishes are illustrated. The timing of the finishing and texturing operation is not too critical with brushes and the tamper—if the concrete is too workable some of the texture will be lost as the concrete will flow and the texture will 'settle'.

It is more important to catch the concrete right with the other tools illustrated. This is really a matter of trial and error, as the precise timing will depend on many factors—the original work-ability of the concrete, sand content and mix, the weather and other factors. The temperature at the time of placing and the amount of wind as well as the absorbency of the aggregate and whether or not admixtures have been used will all influence the timing of these operations. The particular tool may have to be tried a number of times until the time is right.

The use of mechanical finishing tools also has to be timed carefully. A power float should not be used until the surface of the concrete can be walked across leaving footprints no deeper than 3 mm. The machine is used initially with a full disc-shaped blade to flatten the surface and to

Plate 13.29   A skip float with a 3.6 m long handle and 1 m wide aluminium blade can be pushed and pulled across the surface to level and flatten it. Ideal for grain, potato and other storage areas and as preparation for power floating. This can be made up on the farm.

Plate 13.30   A power float can be hired and produces a dense, abrasion-resistant surface. This can be used when the surface can be walked on. It has a circular disc blade.

concrete. Spraying the concrete with water every few hours would achieve this but it is very time consuming and much less efficient than other methods.

The surface can be covered with a polythene sheet for instance, well weighted down at the edges. Alternatively the surface can be sprayed with a special curing liquid which seals in the water. This curing liquid is available from builders' merchants and is called a 'concrete curing compound'—usually a resin in a spirit solvent. Most of the proprietary names end in '. . . cure'. A thin film of the liquid is sprayed onto the surface with either a knapsack sprayer or a garden pesticide sprayer. After use the equipment should be cleaned thoroughly with diesel or petrol, or the resin will block the nozzle and the pump mechanism.

The curing membrane should be applied as soon as surface water has evaporated from the concrete. In warm, windy weather put it onto the surface almost immediately after finishing. If there is any delay, diagonal surface cracks may appear within minutes of laying the concrete in some instances. Curing should prevent this. (These cracks, called plastic cracks, usually only

Plate 13.31   The power trowel, the trowels replacing the disc, is used after power floating to give the final 'polish'.

Plate 13.32   Curing the concrete by covering with polythene sheet.

Plate 13.33 Applying a resin curing compound.

penetrate about 40 mm into the surface and are best filled with dry cement.)

At other times when drying conditions are less severe an hour or two may be needed before the surface water has evaporated. Polythene should not be put onto a watery surface, as this will cause glazing; and the resin should not be sprayed onto a wet surface either as it will not be nearly as effective as a curing agent (Plates 13.32 and 13.33).

Surface Hardeners

These chemicals can be used to advantage on some floors—piggeries, silos, workshops, etc. The chemicals react with the lime in the hydrated cement and have a secondary cementing action, filling pores and reducing the risk of dusting. If it is decided to use one of the proprietary forms—usually sodium silicate or magnesium-silico-fluoride—then the concrete should be cured by covering with polythene. The liquid curing compound will prevent the hardener from penetrating the surface when it is subsequently applied.

The hardener may of course be used on old,

dusting floors as well, to reduce the dusting problem—a problem which usually stems from highly workable mixes which have not been properly cured. Normally, however, the hardeners are used to reduce the permeability of freshly laid concrete and are applied about two to three weeks after laying the concrete itself.

Frost Protection

Concrete hardens and gains strength at a rate which is proportional to temperature. In cold weather it gains strength very slowly. If the water in the concrete freezes before the concrete has sufficient strength to resist the bursting action that the freezing produces, then the concrete will never harden properly. Freezing must be prevented when the concrete has just been laid.

If concrete has to be laid when frost is imminent then the freshly laid material should be covered with a 75 mm thick layer of loose straw. Ideally the straw should be sandwiched between two layers of polythene to keep it dry, as it is a much better insulant when dry than when wet.

Concrete should not be laid on frozen ground, as the bottom layer will freeze. If an area is prepared and the weather turns cold then it should be covered with straw to prevent it from being frozen. Just before laying concrete the straw should be cleared away; then once the concrete is laid, cover it with the straw again.

Opening for Use

The new concrete should not be used too soon. The longer it is left between laying and using it the better. Two weeks is ideal, but light vehicles can be put over it after four days in the summer and after seven days in the winter, as long as it has not been very cold, at or near freezing point, for those seven days. It should be left at least ten days before putting it into full service in the summer and two weeks at other times.

VENTILATED FLOORS

If ducts are to be formed in the floor for drying or conditioning crops such as grain, seeds, potatoes or onions, the building sequence needs to be planned carefully to simplify concrete and other material handling problems. All the levels must be carefully set out and from then on there are a number of different options available.

The first option is to lay a 150 mm thick floor on a damp-proof membrane to the required falls all over the building, using an RC35 or an ST5 mix, and to build up the duct walls in 150 mm thick concrete blocks on this floor.

As a second option, a dpm can be laid on the blinded base material and then 100 mm thick strips of concrete across the building to act as the duct floor and foundation for the walls, then the duct walls can be built up in blockwork. The dpm should be covered between strips with plenty of sand to avoid damaging it during the rest of the building operation.

When the walls are strong enough, the hollows in the blocks can be filled with a 1:3:2 concrete of cement:sharp sand:10 mm maximum-sized aggregate, and 200 mm long pieces of 12 mm reinforcing rod are pushed 100 mm vertically down into this concrete—one per block. Then the spaces between the ducts are filled in with a dry lean concrete mix or a granular material which is compacted in layers with a plate

vibrator. The dry lean concrete will be a more expensive material than the alternatives but it is less likely to cause settlement problems, and because it is delivered in a ready-mixed truck, placing the material is much simplified. A 1:16 mix should be ordered from the ready-mixed concrete supplier. The plate vibrator should not be put too close to the walls otherwise they may be pushed over!

In order to cast the floor with the necessary lips in it to carry the duct covers, reusable, collapsible formwork will need to be made up to strut against the walls (Figure 13.10). Care must be taken when driving in the folding wedges or again the walls will be pushed over.

The quality of the lip is very important. To ensure that full compaction is achieved in this difficult area, the concrete should be compacted all along the top edge with a poker vibrator. Also ensure that the formwork is clean and well-oiled between uses. A vibrating beam can be used for the concrete in the floor, forming contraction joints in these strips as work proceeds. Unless the strips are reinforced the joints should not be more than 5 m apart.

If possible the surface should be finished with a power float and power trowel and then cured.

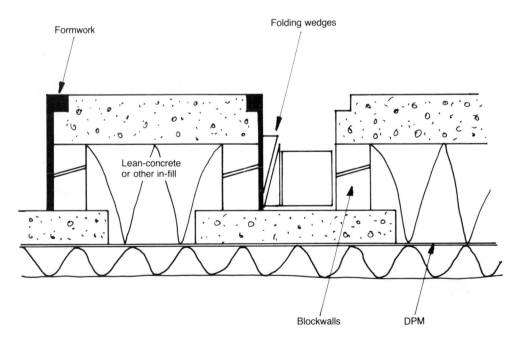

Figure 13.10   Concrete block duct walls in ventilated floor store.

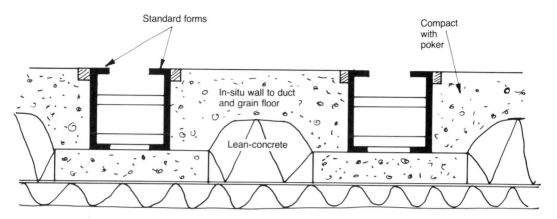

Figure 13.11   In-situ concrete duct walls and floor.

The formwork can be removed the next day, cleaned and re-oiled. The 'sequence summary' shows the various stages in the work.

A third option is to cast the walls of the ducts in concrete. For this robust reusable formwork will again need to be constructed and the job planned carefully (Figure 13.11).

A number of proprietary systems of ventilated floors are available, some in-situ concrete, some timber over a concrete sub-floor, others precast concrete over a concrete sub-floor, and finally a brick floor can be used. With all these systems the manufacturer's instructions must be followed to the letter. Details will not be given here. In each case careful setting out is imperative. For those that require a concrete sub-floor, the accuracy of laying this and the tolerances in levels achieved will be reflected directly at the surface of the ventilated floor itself. Great care must be taken (Plates 13.34–13.38).

Plate 13.34   Precast concrete ventilated floor storage system by Mid-Norfolk Concrete Company Ltd.

Plate 13.35   Precast concrete units on timber boards on in-situ concrete floor by Ventec Limited.

Plate 13.36   A timber ventilated floor system by Challow Products Agricultural Ltd.

Plate 13.37   Proprietary in-situ concrete floor system by GFT Limited with inflatable duct formers, subsequently removed.

Plate 13.38   The finished floor by GFT Limited.

Sequence Summary for Ventilated Floors

If possible the building sequence should be planned with a ready-mixed concrete truck's chute in mind (Figure 13.2). In all options excavate or fill, place and compact the sub-base and blind with sand.

Option 1

Stage 1 Cast floor on a dpm.
Stage 2 Build up perimeter walls for base of main duct in concrete blocks.
Stage 3 Build up walls for first one or two lateral ducts. Fill hollows in blocks with concrete, place steel bars.
Stage 4 Place and compact infill.
Stage 5 Fix edge forms for floor.
Stage 6 Cast concrete floor.
Repeat stages 3 to 6.

Option 2

Stage 1 Cast foundations for perimeter walls and main duct walls on a dpm.
Stage 2 Lay sub-base and dpm for first one/two lateral ducts.
Stage 3 Cast duct bases.
Stage 4 Blind dpm with plenty of sand.
Stage 5 Build up walls for first one/two lateral ducts. Fill hollows with concrete, place steel bars.
Stage 6 Place and compact infill.
Stage 7 Fix edge forms for floor.
Stage 8 Cast concrete floor.
Stage 9 Repeat from stage 2.

Option 3

Stage 1 Cast complete floor over dpm as in Option 1 or 2.
Stage 2 Place and compact 'hills' of lean concrete. Compaction is important but difficult.
Stage 3 Set up formwork.
Stage 4 Cast walls of ducts and storage floor in one.
Stage 5 Remove formwork.
Stage 6 Repeat stages 2–5.

MILKING PARLOURS AND MILK ROOMS

For parlour floors acid resistance, slip resistance and cleanability are needed; acid resistance to counteract the lactic acid which forms rapidly in spilt milk, slip resistance for both herdsmen/women and cattle in the constantly wet conditions, and cleanability, or smoothness, to allow quick and easy cleaning.

Unfortunately cleanability and slip resistance are almost incompatible. To get good grip the floor needs to be rough and yet rough surfaces are difficult to clean. There is one possible compromise, however, and that is to use an abrasive, hard-wearing 'grit' at the very surface of the floor. The grit most commonly used is carborundum or aluminium oxide which can be trowelled into the top skin of the floor.

The method of construction used for parlour floors in particular, is determined by the parlour equipment manufacturer's method of installing his fittings. If they are suspended from wall and roof the floor can be compacted and finished in one operation. But if the fittings are mounted on posts let into the floor then it will be necessary to provide a 65 mm topping layer over the base concrete.

In the first instance a 100 mm thick, RC45 or RC50 mix, is placed, compacted and trowelled—usually by hand because of the limited areas involved. The concrete should be allowed to stiffen, or tighten up before trowelling it for the first time, and allowed to tighten up even more before trowelling it a second time. The interval between first and second trowellings may be several hours—in warm weather perhaps two hours and in cold weather up to four hours. Just before the second trowelling the carborundum or aluminium oxide particles should be sprinkled uniformly over the surface. About 1.5 kg per square metre of graded 1.70 mm–600 μm particles should be used. The timing of this operation is vital; if done too early the particles will sink in and be ineffective, if done too late they will remain on top of the concrete and will be brushed away or worn away by the cows' feet. The concrete should be cured after this trowelling-in operation.

If a topping layer has to be used, the first layer, 100 mm thick, should be laid using an RC35 or an ST5 mix, left with a rough finish and covered with polythene to cure. The next day the surface should be pressure washed to remove the top skin of cement and expose the stones on the surface without dislodging them. The polythene should then be replaced. When the parlour equipment has been installed, pressure wash the floor again to remove all dust and debris and leave the floor wet.

The floor should be left overnight and then all the excess water brushed away. A cement and water grout of creamy consistency is then mixed up and applied in a thin film with a soft, long-handled brush to the surface, working it well into the aggregate. Before this grout has dried a 65 mm thick topping of an RC45 or RC50 mix should be laid using a 10 mm maximum-sized aggregate, compacting it thoroughly. The concrete should be allowed to stiffen before trowelling for the first time, and as in the previous method the concrete must be allowed to stiffen before applying the grit, trowelling it in and finally curing the surface.

INSULATED FLOORS

The Objective

In the chapter on walls the need for insulation to control heat loss in buildings was mentioned. This helps to provide the correct environment and healthy living conditions for the animals. It is also important to include insulation in the floor of the house. Pigs spend much of their life lying down and the lower critical temperature—the temperature at which the animals feel cold and uncomfortable and convert body fat or food to heat to keep themselves warm—is as much as 7°C lower on insulated floors than on uninsulated floors.

The insulation should be confined to the pigs' living areas, as its construction makes it unsuitable for very heavy loads. If well designed and constructed it will keep the volume of concrete the animals must warm up when they first lie down to a minimum, as well as cutting heat flow from the animal's body to the floor, while the animal is lying down. It will have a waterproof topping to keep the insulation dry, be hard wearing and durable and have a suitable non-slip surface.

Research at the Scottish Farm Buildings Investigation Unit in Aberdeen has shown that the best insulated floor is one which has a very thin topping over the insulation layer. With traditional cement:sand mixes it is not possible to lay a topping less than 20 mm thick. However, new materials have become available which can be laid between 3 mm and 5 mm thick to give adequate load-carrying capacity, good wear and chemical resistance at reasonable cost. For dry sows, farrowing sows and baby pigs the additional cost can be justified. For fattening pigs, over 50 kg, the traditional materials are quite satisfactory.

Insulation is sometimes used in cubicle beds for dairy cows. In this case the insulation is confined to the area of the bed beneath the cow's udder. This will be mentioned again in the section on cubicle beds.

If an insulation layer made of special manufactured lightweight aggregate is used, such as Glic, Leca, Lytag and others, mixed with cement, then a damp-proof membrane is not necessary. Any moisture drawn up to the bottom of the lightweight concrete layer will remain there as there is no capillary action between the particles to draw moisture to the top surface.

Construction

If expanded polystyrene boards are to be used as the insulation material, they should be laid on a trowelled layer of oversite concrete; more care will be needed when laying that concrete in these circumstances than if lightweight concrete is the insulation. A thin topping layer cannot be used over the polystyrene as the cement:sand material will not bond to it. A topping of at least 50 mm thick will be needed.

If the lightweight aggregate can be bought readily, either direct from the manufacturer or from a local concrete block manufacturer, a 10 mm particle size should be ordered if the thin topping is going to be used, and a 20 mm size particle for the normal cement:sand topping.

A mix of 6 parts of aggregate to 1 part of cement by volume should be used (Plate 13.39). Some manufacturers suggest pre-wetting the aggregate to improve workability. No sand or other fine aggregate should be used in the mix. It may be possible to buy this material ready-mixed, but it may be necessary to mix it on-site.

The quantity of water put in the mix is important. If too much is put in then when the

Plate 13.39 The mix for a no-fines, lightweight aggregate concrete insulating layer.

mixer is tipped up to discharge its contents, all the cement and water will run out first and all the aggregate later. To avoid this a thick grout should be made in the mixer to start with then all the aggregate can be added and finally the rest of the water, a little at a time, until all the particles of aggregate are coated with cement. When the mix is tipped out of the drum a small amount of aggregate should remain sticking to the inside walls of the drum.

If a package deal pig building is being erected, much of the work below damp course level can be done by farm staff—setting out, excavations, slurry channels, floors and dwarf walls. This section will only be dealing with floors and with package deal buildings it is likely that the floors are being laid over the oversite concrete.

If it is not a package deal job and the complete building is being erected by farm staff, including all the walls and the roof, then it may be decided to clear the site and excavate channels and foundations and then put up the blockwork. In this case it will be cheaper to leave the floors till later. A saving will be made on oversite concrete at the very least because a no-fines lightweight

aggregate concrete insulation layer can be laid directly onto the blinded sub-base.

To construct the floor the area to be concreted will need to be excavated, the organic soil removed and the levels fixed, including all the falls. Then a 100 mm thick sub-base layer of granular material such as hoggin should be placed, and compacted until the top surface is closely knit, checking the levels. This is then covered with 10 mm of sand as a blinding layer and well compacted. Side forms 150 mm high should be fixed as necessary, to define the top levels of the finished floor.

Lightweight concrete
The lightweight aggregate should be mixed, placed between the formwork and screeded off to a level either 3 mm or 20 mm below the level of the top of the forms depending on what topping mix is being used, tamping it lightly. If the 3 mm thick topping is used, press the lightweight material into position with a steel trowel to leave a smooth, close knit finish. This should be covered with polythene and left for 24 hours. If a traditional topping, 20 mm thick is used, before the lightweight concrete has set the

Plate 13.40 Lay strips of lightweight material about 1 m long and cover immediately with the 1:2½, cement:sharp sand mix.

cement:sand mix should be spread over it (Plate 13.40). A 1:2½ mix of cement:sharp concreting sand should be used, accurately measured, and the mix should be semi-dry. A handful of the mix squeezed in the hand should stay as a ball. If the ball falls apart then there is insufficient water in it. If it squeezes out between your fingers then it is too wet.

The choice of sand is important. Most sharp sands have quite a lot of 5 mm particles in them. If the floor begins to wear, for whatever reason, then sharp particles will be exposed on the surface and will be abrasive to the pigs' feet. There is a natural limestone sand available in the north of Wiltshire near the village of Summerford Keynes which will wear away at the same rate as the rest of the floor and will not become abrasive. It may be worth while fetching a load of this material if a lot of floors have to be laid.

When mixing a cement:sand flooring mix most of the water required for a batch should be put into the drum, then add half the cement, then all the sand, then the rest of the cement and finally, water as required, until the mix is of the right consistency. If it tends to ball up in the mixer two or three bricks can be thrown in as well, to break down the balls. The bricks can be easily taken out of the barrow afterwards and used again.

The lightweight concrete should be laid in strips about 1 m long. The 20 mm thick wearing surface of cement:sand should be laid immediately on top of the fresh lightweight concrete to the level of the side forms and compacted fully with a tamper. A wood float can be used like a plane to take off the high spots and reveal the low ones (Plate 13.41). Extra sand:cement mix should be added and patted into position with the float. This should be repeated as necessary until a perfectly smooth surface is produced.

If a gritty non-slip surface is required the wood float should be used to finish the top surface. For a smoother surface, a steel trowel can be drawn very lightly across the surface produced by the wood float. The surface should be kept thoroughly damp for seven days by covering with a polythene sheet to ensure proper curing.

After two weeks, and before the pigs are put in, the hardness can be improved and the permeability of this cement-sand floor can be reduced by applying a magnesium-silico-fluoride-

Plate 13.41   Use a wood float like a plane.

based concrete surface hardener. This is available from builders' merchants. It is essential to get the right type—magnesium-silico-fluoride—and that it is applied according to the manufacturers' instructions.

Rubber latex toppings
If a 3–5 mm thick topping is being used a special fine sand will need to be purchased. This is sold by some garden centres as silver sand. The particle size suggested is that which passes through a 300 μm sieve but is almost completely retained on a 150 μm sieve. It is also available dry and bagged from suppliers of industrial sands.

A mix of 1 part of cement with 2 parts of the fine sand, together with a special rubber latex—a styrene butadiene rubber (SBR)—gives a very good wearing surface which has improved chemical resistance compared with ordinary cement:sand materials. If any wear does take place, because the surface is made up of fine particles the floor will never become as abrasive as a conventional cement:sand mix would.

Two coats of the SBR mortar may be required. The first coat consists of a 1:2 mix of cement:dry sand by volume mixed with a 50/50 solution of SBR and water, or at dilution rates recommended by the manufacturers, to form a stiff but workable mortar. This is trowelled into the surface of the lightweight aggregate concrete which is tamped lightly and then trowelled flat (Plates 13.42 and 13.43). The 1:2 mortar mixed with latex (Plate 13.44) is finished smooth and provides a covering about 3 mm thick to the no fines aggregate (Plate 13.45). If a trowelled finish is required and the surface has not 'dragged' at all giving fine hair cracks, it can be left in this form. If a coarser texture is required brush the surface to provide a key for the second coat (Plate 13.47), allowing the first coat 24 hours to harden.

For the second coat a 1:1 mix of cement to dry sand is used with neat SBR or a diluted solution recommended by the manufacturers. This is mixed in a deep straight-sided container. The best tool for mixing is a perforated plate welded across the end of a suitable length of tube (Plate 13.46). This is used flat onto the bottom of the container with a pressing and twisting action, dispersing the solids which are added gradually to form a thick creamy grout when fully mixed. A fine soft-bristled brush is used to apply the grout about 1 mm thick and to work it

Plate 13.43   Trowel it to produce a smooth, flat surface.

Plate 13.42   Tamp the lightweight material to receive the thin surfacing.

Plate 13.44   Apply the latex mortar to the insulating layer just 3 mm thick above the uppermost particle of lightweight aggregate.

Plate 13.45 Finish the surface with the trowel or 'apply' a brush texture to receive a second coat.

into the surface. Finally the brush, with more grout on it, is drawn across the still workable surface so that the marks settle to a regular miniature corrugation of rounded appearance (Plate 13.47). This should be kept damp for a minimum of two days to allow the cement to gain strength and the floor should be left to dry slowly for a further five days. All equipment should be washed thoroughly and regularly as work proceeds. Approximately 5 litres of SBR, 25 kg of cement and 50 kg of sand will be needed for each 8 to 10 square metres of floor laid 3 mm thick. The floor should be laid within the individual pens in the livestock house. If the area to be laid within each pen is more than 13 square metres or if the length is more than 1½ times the width, the floor should be divided into bays.

The joints should be formed using a temporary timber stop end to support strips of formica or similar material which penetrate the full depth of the lightweight aggregate. The lightweight aggregate is laid up to and beyond the stop end, the stop end is removed and the gap filled with more of the mix. The formica sheets form a permanent joint in the floor thus

Plate 13.46 Some of the ingredients and equipment needed to produce the latex surfacing mortar.

Plate 13.47 Applying the second coat with a fine bristle brush.

allowing shrinkage. Joints should lie parallel in the floor as far as possible and should be kept to a minimum since water may penetrate at these points.

If laying the extruded expanded polystyrene-type of insulation material, the oversite concrete must be smooth and true. It is laid between forms, compacted and must be finished carefully. Then the extruded polystyrene boards can be laid either close-butted or tongued and grooved and then the 50 mm cement:sand topping. Care must be taken not to damage the polystyrene with the barrow, shovels or even boots. Scaffold boards laid over the surface will help. In this type of floor at least 50 mm of topping will be needed to give it sufficient strength and self-weight to reduce the risk of curling and the resultant tendency to crack. The thermal performance of such a floor is not high though and the other methods of construction may be preferred for this reason.

Repairs to Insulated Floors

The thermal performance of a floor is important when specifying and building new floors but it is also important when carrying out repairs. A repair method is needed which does not significantly increase the thickness of the topping and yet is durable, not too expensive, can be textured as required but which covers the old, worn and often cracked and abrasive surface.

Preparation
A new surface cannot be stuck to old, dirty concrete or old, dirty cement and sand toppings. Pressure washing on its own is unlikely to produce a surface which is clean enough to achieve a good bond. Most old, abrasive, worn floors are likely to have a very thin coating of fat or body oils and may have ingrained skin, hair and other body tissues. Detergents in hot water, steam or, preferably, degreasants will be needed to remove this type of material so the first job in any repair operation must be to clean the floor thoroughly and completely (Plate 13.48). First pressure wash and then degrease.

Industrial degreasants are available from many sources. After using them, pressure wash the floor again. In most cases the clean floor will need a further stage in its preparation before applying the repair material. Even though the floor has worn and become abrasive it is unlikely to have been eroded to the same extent

Plate 13.48 Use a degreasant to clean the floor thoroughly.

everywhere. The areas adjacent to the trough, particularly if you wet feed and even more so if you feed skim or whey, are likely to be the worst affected. If you feed dry on the floor then the areas where the feed is dropped will be the worst. In the corners of the pen the floor may still be in a reasonable condition, perhaps still smooth.

It is much more difficult to bond the repair material to smooth surfaces than it is to rough. It may well be necessary to provide some key to these smooth areas to achieve a good bond. This can be done by brushing an acid cleaning or etching solution over these areas and leaving it for fifteen minutes (Plate 13.49). It will eat into the smooth surface to expose sand grains and give an improved key. Manufacturers of degreasants can usually supply these acid materials as well. It is important to pressure wash away all traces of these acids (Plate 13.50). Preparation is now complete and resurfacing itself can get under way—the new surface can be applied.

The same SBR latex mortar can be used as that used for new floors—the 1:2 mix of cement:fine sand. A normal building sand should not be used as it is almost certain to contain silt as well as coarse particles and is not suitable.

Plate 13.50   Wash away all traces of acid.

Plate 13.49   Etch all smooth areas with acid.

Plate 13.51   Brush the latex grout into the surface as a bonding coat.

Before applying the mortar, any washing water should be brushed away and the surface allowed to become damp dry. Then a bonding coat of cement: neat SBR latex grout can be applied. This is mixed to a thick creamy consistency and brushed over the floor (Plate 13.51). Small areas should be done at a time and it should be brushed out as far as possible, leaving a thin film only. Before this has dried, in other words while it is still tacky, the SBR latex mortar should be applied with a steel trowel in as thin a layer as possible. A layer of no more than a 3 mm thickness above the top of the protruding stones or sand grains should be aimed for. The objective is not to increase the total thickness of the topping over the insulation by a significant amount, but merely to replace the eroded mortar (Plate 13.52).

The trowelled surface may well have a suitable texture in itself. A more skid-resistant texture can be produced by drawing a fine bristled brush across the finished work. If this is too abrasive a compromise can be achieved by using a second coat of SBR latex mortar (the 1:1 mix of cement: fine sand) on the next day.

Plate 13.52 Applying a thin trowel coat to complete the repair.

Other Repairs

There are many forms of proprietary materials available for repairing floors. Some are based on the same SBR latex already mentioned, others are based on some form of resin material—acrylics, polyurethanes or epoxy resins. Many of these are suitable for repairing pig floors. Some of the manufacturers of SBR latex also supply pre-packed material systems. Consult the manufacturers before using these materials to find out if they are suitable and use them in accordance with the manufacturer's instructions.

It is also possible to use these resin materials as well as the SBR latex, cement and fine sand mortars for repairing feed troughs. Use the same cleaning and application techniques. Some resin based materials may require a dry background. The instructions should always be consulted.

If the joints between the salt-glazed pipe-based troughs are eroding, then special acid-resistant, resin-based jointing materials should be used. Ordinary cement-based mortars are not ideal in these areas where acid concentrations are high. The SBR latex mortars are more acid resistant than mortars without the addition of latex and will therefore stand up well to less concentrated exposure in a floor, but in a trough joint where quantities are small, the more expensive specialist materials can be justified.

Smoothing and Roughening

If the floors were originally laid with crushed limestone fines instead of silica sand or even with a natural limestone sand from the south Midlands it may well be possible to grind down the protruding particles of sand with either a small, hand-held, floor grinder which employs carborundum stones, or with the larger industrial floor grinders. Specialist plant hire companies and contractors have this equipment. Floors laid with normal sharp sand or granite fines are not normally suitable for treatment in this way.

In scraped passages it is quite possible that the surface of the floors will have become too slippery and may need to be roughened. Small-scale equipment to form grooves in the concrete or to scale off the whole top skin of the concrete is becoming more widely available (Plates 13.53 and 13.54). Alternatively, a compressed air driven scabbler or other special shot scaling

Plate 13.53 Equipment to form grooves or to scale off the surface of concrete is now available.

Plate 13.54 The tungsten carbide tipped flails which do the work.

Plate 13.55 Compressed air driven scabbler at work.

Plate 13.56 The tipped hammer heads of the scabbler chip away the concrete.

equipment can be used and these are available from plant hire and other companies which do the work under contract (Plates 13.55 and 13.56).

Silo Floors

The Pollution Control Regulations require silos and slurry stores to resist corrosion and remain impermeable for a minimum of 20 years with routine maintenance. BS 5502: Part 50 deals with slurry stores in great detail and calls up BS 8007 (mentioned again in Chapter 18) to achieve impermeable structures. Similar standards of design and construction are required for silos.

Great care is necessary when selecting a site for a silo. Consideration must be given to its relationship with other buildings which house stock likely to consume the silage, and the method of filling and emptying. It is also necessary to prevent leakage of effluent into the ground to avoid the pollution of drains and streams. Effluent must be collected, stored and disposed of in a controlled manner. It is necessary to consult with the National Rivers Authority when design and siting are under consideration.

The bearing pressure that the walls exert on the ground may also be a significant factor. In many designs bearing pressures do not exceed 50 kN/m² and the soils listed below are likely to provide adequate strength.

- Firm or stiff clay (not soft clay)
- Sandy clay
- Boulder clay
- Shale clay
- Compact sand (not loose sand) or sandy gravel

If there is any doubt the advice of a chartered engineer must be sought for this and other design information.

For larger silos some excavation will almost always be necessary. Exposed rock can involve major expense to remove so that should be avoided if possible. Soft, organic clays may also be a problem; they must be replaced with consolidated fill to form a load-bearing surface. In general, areas of fill should be avoided. Excavated areas provide much better and more uniform support.

Before starting work on the floor (or walls) make a thorough investigation of the site for drains of any kind. Field drains must be exposed and diverted to ensure effluent does not enter them. This may well necessitate flexible sealed joints between the pipes. They must not be surrounded with concrete. Field drains which cross the silo site should be removed.

Surface water from aprons around the silo must be diverted from the effluent pit. If the silo is roofed, roof water must also be disposed of separately.

Mixes

Concrete is an alkali and as such is attacked by acids. The richer the mix and the lower its water content, assuming it is still workable enough to be properly compacted, the more durable will be the concrete. An RC45 mix using ordinary Portland cement, 20 mm maximum-sized aggregate and medium workability is the minimum grade that should be used. The higher the grade of concrete used the longer the life of the silo. Even richer mixes with 400 kg of cement/m³ of concrete, with a water/cement ratio of 0.5 and incorporating silica fume and a plasticizer should not be ruled out.

Design

As heavy (8 tonne) tractors are used to compact the silage and even for filling, the silo should have a 150 mm thick floor. For 10 tonne machinery a 200 mm thickness may be necessary.

Sealable, watertight joints incorporating waterstops are needed if the silo is to comply with current pollution regulations. The previous sections on frequency of joints and the influence of reinforcement on frequency must be taken into account.

Where there is any risk of pollution it will be wise to incorporate reinforcement to reduce the number of joints, to seal them and to waterproof them with waterstops (Plate 13.57).

In these circumstances the concrete should be at least 150 mm thick. Waterstops laid under the joints on the base material with the concrete compacted around them are preferred for expansion and contraction joints. In construction joints waterstops which are fixed half-way up the vertical face of a joint, and expand when wetted, perform well. (Figure 13.8.)

Plate 13.57   Surface water bar being laid under a longitudinal joint in a silo.

Construction

After excavation to the required falls, 1 in 80, both as a crossfall and longitudinally, the sub-base material can be placed and compacted. This should then be blinded with sand, making provision in this sub-base for any drainage channels and depressions which are to be formed in the slab. Then 250 µm (1000 gauge) polythene sheet should be laid over the sand blinding to further reduce the risk of effluent presenting a pollution hazard. It should be laid so that any effluent which seeps through to this level tends to drain towards the effluent collecting tank. Floor laying can then proceed as before.

As the Pollution Control Regulations require silo floors to be impermeable they should really be built to BS 8007 standards. This implies the use of a GEN1 concrete blinding beneath the floor. In most silos, being constructed in 'alternative strips', this is impractical and the sub-base described above is to be preferred. For further information on joints see pages 131–139.

Joint sealants

For silos, joints should be sealed with either a two-part pouring grade polysulphide, poly-urethane or similar effluent-resistant sealant.

It must be remembered that many sealants should only be used when the concrete is at least two weeks old, and dry, as the bond of sealant to concrete may be affected by surface moisture.

Drainage channels

Acid attack is likely to be most noticeable in the drainage channel which should be provided outside the walls and elsewhere in the silo where the effluent collects in quantity and then flows towards the effluent tank. Special protective measures are justified in this area and even then regular maintenance will be necessary.

To protect the channels after the concrete has been cured and allowed to dry out, apply an effluent resistant sealer. Discuss this with the manufacturers who advertise in the farming press and other agricultural journals. The channels must all fall towards the effluent collection tank and the polythene underlay beneath the slab should do the same. Leakage can then be kept to a minimum. The level of effluent in the tank must be checked frequently during the eight weeks after filling, and the tank emptied as necessary. Concrete aprons surrounding the silo must not be drained towards this tank and silage should not be made on the apron.

Repairs to Silo Floors

The two most satisfactory methods of repairing a silo floor are to overlay it with concrete or hot rolled asphalt. Concrete: isolate the old concrete by a blinding layer of sand; cover this with a polythene sheet, and overlay with a further 100 mm thick concrete slab—levels permitting, using the RC45 mix.

Hot rolled asphalt: use a 40–50 mm thickness of compacted hot rolled asphalt (HRA). The mix should comply with BS 594: 1985 Table 4 schedule 1A or 1B, but contractors may be able to advise on alternative mix proportions which may also perform satisfactorily.

To accommodate temperature differences the bitumen binder should be Schedule 1A, south of a line drawn from Liverpool to the Wash, and Schedule 1B north of that line.

The grade of bitumen used should be chosen by the contractor but he must have the correct equipment for laying the selected HRA mix. More flexible mixes with a low stone content may suffer surface scuffing from loaders but this damage can be made good with bitumen or heating and recompaction.

HRA is best laid using a Blaw Knox or Barber Green machine, but in small silos hand laying may be necessary and a mix with a higher pen grade bitumen or smaller aggregate size will be required. In all cases an asphalt contractor must be employed to obtain a satisfactory job. A list of member firms is available from British Aggregate Construction Materials Industries (BACMI).

The finished surface should be dense and have a close knit texture.

HRA should not be confused with Tarmac or Bitmac, both of which are likely to fail following exposure to the dung or urine from cattle. The large aggregate in Tarmac or Bitmac is only coated in the binder, whereas in HRA the mix composition is similar to concrete with a higher proportion of binder and filler (fine aggregate).

The method of application and surface preparation is as follows:

- Steam clean or high pressure wash the concrete surface to remove all traces of loose material.
- Cut a chase at least 50 mm deep × 500 mm wide at the open end of the silo to give a smooth change in surface levels to the new topping. Feathered edges are liable to mechanical damage.
- All existing joints and cracks should be cleaned out and enlarged where necessary. These are then filled using hot poured bitumen, pitch epoxy sealant or similar material.
- Brush apply bitumen emulsion to surfaces of holes and depressions, fill with HRA and compact.
- Apply a bitumen tack coat to floor area.

- Compact HRA with at least an 8 tonne roller or equivalent vibratory roller. Adequate compaction must be achieved at wall junctions and corners by vibratory plate or pneumatic rammer.
- HRA will compact to a denser mix if it is laid between walls or kerbs. Under normal circumstances the tack coat provides an adequate seal between floors and existing walls, but where large movements are likely, e.g. between a sleeper wall and concrete floor, a bituminous or epoxy sealant should be poured into the joints.

Other methods

If self-feeding silage is practised and the floor has become very abrasive to the feet of animals due to the erosion of the cement mortar away from the stone leaving them standing proud, this harshness can be reduced by chipping away the top of the stone and any weakened concrete with a multi-headed, compressed air-driven scabbler. This can be hired from most plant hire firms; the compressor will have to be hired as well (Plates 13.55 and 13.56).

If there are joints which have been sealed and need to be cleaned out and resealed, or cracks which need to be routed out and sealed, equipment can be hired specially for the purpose from specialist plant hire firms (Plate 13.58).

Isolated patches in the silo floor can be repaired using SBR mortars. This repair technique is described in the section headed 'Patching floors' which follows later on in this chapter.

Slurry Store Floors

The floors to all slurry stores and tanks should be built to a similar standard to silo floors in

40–50 mm HRA topping   50 mm deep × 500 mm wide chase in existing floor slab

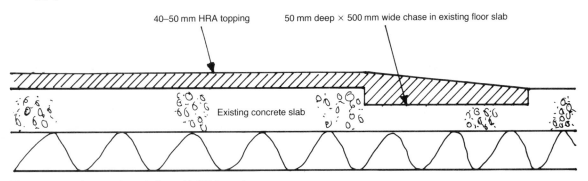

Figure 13.12   Section through floor with HRA repair.

Plate 13.58　A crack router being used to enlarge and prepare cracks for subsequent scaling.

order to comply with the Pollution Control Regulations. They must be impermeable. The concrete for a slurry or weeping wall store may be of a slightly lower quality than that for a silo. Slurry will not attack the concrete. It will not be necessary to use an RC45 mix. The British Standard BS8007 specifies a C35A mix which is equivalent to an RC40—see Table 2.1 on page 19.

Cubicle Floors

In an attempt to reduce mastitis and to produce fewer injuries to animals there is still a demand for better and more effective cubicle bed maintenance and litter management. A concrete floor in its various forms is probably the easiest rigid form of floor for the do-it-yourself builder to lay. In addition:

- It keeps its shape and thus eliminates floor maintenance.
- It allows cleaning at the rear of the cubicle to be carried out easily and regularly.
- It can be textured to assist the retention of litter.
- If sand is used as bedding the concrete can be formed into a lip at the back of the cubicle.

- It provides the ideal base for mats if these are considered desirable (Plate 13.59).
- It can be insulated if this is thought to be necessary.

Cows, in themselves, are able to tolerate a wide range of ambient temperatures, and in well-ventilated, draught-free buildings where bedding is provided to keep the cows clean and comfortable, the amount of heat lost to the floor is not critical. In view of this, uninsulated cubicle beds have been laid in the majority of buildings.

If cubicles are not re-littered regularly, the bedding becomes trodden, soiled and wet—the state which will encourage bacterial multiplication and is thus undesirable. Heat losses can be reduced and a degree of comfort retained using small quantities of bedding if some form of insulation other than bedding is incorporated. It is important, however, to clear off the rear of the cubicle base, remove soiled bedding and re-litter daily. A cubicle base with no lip to the kerb aids this procedure.

Unlipped bases retain litter less easily but aid cleaning and drainage. The litter stays drier, thus reducing the rate of bacterial multiplication. The surface texture of the cubicle base will

Plate 13.59　An 'Enkamat' carpet in a concrete based cubicle.

influence litter retention too, but must not decrease cow comfort.

For lipped cubicles where sand is used for bedding, a 50 mm lip should be provided; a smooth finish should be used with rounded edges to the lip. Figures 13.13 and 13.14 show the construction profile of the back of a lipped and unlipped cubicle. If insulation is to be used it is only necessary in that area of the cubicle which will be in contact with the cow's udder. The topping, or wearing surface, laid over the insulation should be as thin as possible and yet be adequate to carry the weight of the animal. The front of the cubicle should be of normal dense concrete, 100 mm thick using RC35 or ST5 mix.

Plain concrete

A good surface on which to spread the bedding is provided by 100 mm of RC35 or ST5 concrete laid over a damp-proof membrane on a 75 mm thick layer of compacted sub-base (Plate 13.60).

Plate 13.60   Cubicle with wood shavings as bedding.

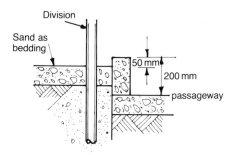

Figure 13.13   Lipped cubicle for use where sand is the bedding material.

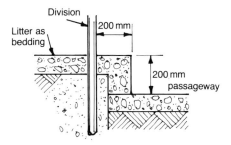

Figure 13.14   Unlipped cubicle for straw or other bedding material.

No-fines dense aggregate concrete

In the late 1970s many farmers laid no-fines dense aggregate concrete in cubicles in an attempt to provide a free-draining insulated floor to which litter would cling. Experience has shown that the litter, while clinging to the surface, rapidly blocks the pores of the material, reducing the permeability almost to that of plain concrete. The insulation value is also very limited. If it is decided to lay this type of floor a 150 mm thick layer of no-fines concrete should be used made with normal dense aggregate, graded from 20 mm to 10 mm in a 6:1 mix with cement but no sand. This mix is more difficult to lay successfully than normal concrete with sand in it, and the water content is critical too if good bond, stone to stone, and a durable surface are to be achieved (Plate 13.61).

No-fines lightweight aggregate concrete

Figure 13.15 shows a suggested cross-section of a floor using this type of material. It has been described in the sections on piggery floors in some detail. For cattle, a topping layer over

Plate 13.61   No-fines cubicle bed—no longer permeable.

the insulation of one of the following types is suitable:

- 25 mm to 30 mm of RC35 or an ST5 type mix, medium workability using ordinary Portland cement and 10 mm maximum-sized aggregate
- A semi-dry well compacted cement:sand mix (1:2½) of the same thickness
- To gain full benefit from insulation, a 10 mm thick mix of 1 part cement and 2 parts sharp (concreting) sand mixed with a 50/50 mixture of water/styrene butadiene rubber latex.

Other materials

Compacted chalk and other similar, semi-rigid, permanent materials tend to deform with perpetual use and provide an uncomfortable lying surface even when littered. They are also more difficult to clean than concrete. If it is decided to use them make sure that the compaction is of a very high standard, using a vibrating plate compactor at the very least. Cement-grouted, no-fines bitumen has been used in cubicle beds with some success, but this material is more expensive than concrete and has to be laid by a specialist contractor. It has a density very similar to that of concrete, so despite its warmer 'feel' (due to heat being absorbed on its black surface) the amount of heat transmitted through the material is similar to that through concrete.

Other black bituminous materials also have a warmer 'feel' than concrete but have a similar density and thus similar heat-transmittance properties. They are generally less durable than concrete and will require maintenance. They are not really suitable for laying by farm labour particularly with the high density materials.

Texture

Special textures on the surface of the concrete in a cubicle bed are not necessary to make it skid resistant. Dry concrete is not slippery. Texture can help to retain litter but it may affect drainage if not carried out judiciously.

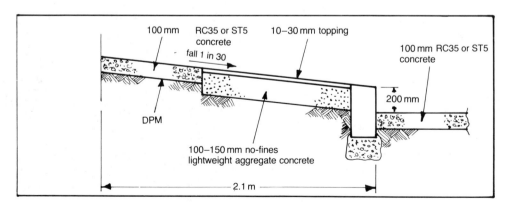

Figure 13.15   Section of insulated cubicle bed.

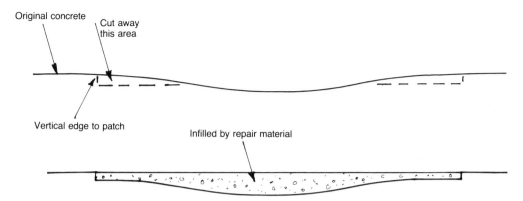

Figure 13.16   Repairing a 'patch'.

A ribbed or tamped finish is sometimes preferred at the front of the cubicle. The ribs or tamp marks should run across the cubicle. At the rear they should be parallel to the length of the cubicle to facilitate drainage. As an alternative a wood float finish can be used or a brush texture may be chosen for the rear of the cubicle to improve the litter retention on unlipped beds. The lines produced by the bristles should again be parallel to the length of the cubicle.

Patching Floors

Well-laid floors and toppings will last a long time, but there are some conditions which are encountered from time to time on the farm which are extremely aggressive and patching may be necessary. This can be done quite successfully but if the new material is to stay put, then good preparation is essential. For holes less than 10 mm deep proprietary patching material which is advertised in many farming journals can be used. For 10 mm to 40 mm deep holes a 'concrete' mix can be used in a concrete floor and a bituminous material in bituminous floors.

Preparing floors for repair
Any damaged, weak or unsound material must always be removed in the area to be patched. In a concrete floor if the concrete is sound but nonetheless has been worn away, resulting in depressions in the surface, the concrete will have to be cut back so that a clean vertical edge is formed around the perimeter of the area to be patched (Figure 13.16). This vertical edge will be necessary also where the concrete has been damaged by acid or when repairs are required

for any other reason. The same preparation is desirable for bituminous materials.

The removal of poor concrete, the roughening of the surface of the area to be patched and the cutting back to a vertical edge can best be carried out with the pneumatically-driven percussive tools such as a scabbler (Plate 13.62). The use of this type of machine has already been mentioned in the 'repairs to silo floors' section. They are available from some plant-hire companies. A compressor will also be needed to drive them of course so, unless there are several patches to do, the cost of this type of relatively

Plate 13.62   A scabbler which chips away the surface of the concrete.

large-scale equipment may rule it out. For small areas electrically driven tools, such as Kango hammers or Bosch can also be used. These are much slower than the scabbler but do the job perfectly well. Hand work with chisels is even slower but for just one or two small patches it may be all that is necessary.

Dust and grit should be removed from the area to be patched, preferably with a jet of air, the surface should then be brushed with a stiff broom to remove loose particles. This should be followed by further washing and brushing with water.

Priming
For twelve hours prior to laying the new concrete, the surface should be kept damp. Neat cement/water slurry is then worked into the surface and any excess removed. Care must be taken to ensure that the slurry does not have time to dry out before the new in-fill material is placed.

Filling the patch
The mix for filling the patch should consist of 1 part cement to 2½ parts sharp concreting sand or a 1:1:2 mix of cement to sharp sand to small stones (10 mm maximum-size). The depth of the hole determines which mix is used. If it is between 10 mm and 20 mm deep, the cement:sand mix should be used; if it is more than 20 mm deep then the 1:1:2 mix should be used. The amount of mixing water must be carefully controlled. A semi-dry mix is wanted that is just possible to compact but does not produce a wet layer of cement, fine sand and water on its surface (laitance), after compaction.

The filling material should be spread over the whole surface of the patch so that there is a small surcharge. Then it should be tamped or even vibrated into place and trowelled from the centre towards the edges of the patch to ensure that a good bond is achieved around the perimeter. It can then be textured as required and cured. It should be left for about four days as a minimum before putting vehicles or animals over it.

Alternative repair techniques
Many bonding aids are now available in proprietary forms. The use of the SBR latex which is commonly used as a bonding aid has already

been mentioned. But if very thin surfacings are required then the epoxy and other resins will be economic. They do have one big advantage over concrete in that they harden in a few hours. For repairs in parlours for instance this may be invaluable. They should all be used in accordance with the manufacturers' instructions.

Retexturing Concrete

A scabbler has already been considered for removing protruding stones in silos and for the preparation of areas to be patched but it is sometimes necessary to texture large areas of concrete simply because it has become too slippery. In areas which are regularly scraped with a tractor-mounted scraper polishing is quite common. Smooth polished, wet surfaces are very slippery indeed.

Mechanical methods
If large areas have to be tackled and the access to the site is good, one of the most effective techniques is to use the scabbler. A five headed unit requires about 3.4 cubic metres per minute of air (120 cfm) at 0.69 N/m² pressure (100 psi). Using this tool a rate of work of about 30 square metres per hour can be achieved. The tungsten carbide tipped hammer heads on the machine chip away the surface of the stones and surrounding mortar to leave a rough but not too abrasive surface.

If the machine and the compressor are working properly, once the air line to the scabbler is opened it will operate rather like a hover mower and will 'float' on the surface of the concrete. It just needs to be pushed backwards and forwards or swung from side to side until the required texture has been produced. If it is allowed to stop for a few seconds in one position a hole will be dug in the floor in that position and will cause puddles to form in the floor even after tractor scraping. Obviously this is to be avoided.

Alternatively a concrete scaling, or planing machine can be used (Plates 13.53 and 13.54). The flails on this machine can be set to produce a series of grooves in the surface—used in two directions this gives the familiar diamond pattern—or to remove more or less the entire surface of the concrete. They are driven by petrol or diesel engines, and these machines operate at 100 square metres per hour.

For small areas electrically driven percussive tools mentioned in the section on 'patching' can be used quite successfully. Rates of work are very slow with these machines—about 3 m² per hour—so they should only be used for small areas where operating space is limited. These and other small hand-held scaling hammers can also be used to chip away the surface of smooth concrete on old cattle slats. Only the centre strip of each slat should be roughened and you have to be careful not to break away the edges of the slats (Plate 13.63).

Acid etching

If the concrete is relatively new (less than one year old) it may be possible to increase the depth of texture very slightly by etching away the cement mortar from around the stones with an acid. This technique was mentioned when the repair of piggery floors was discussed. The acid used is a hydrochloric acid (available as spirits of salts from chemists). It should be diluted with water (1 part acid to 4 parts water is likely to be suitable) and applied to the surface at a rate of 0.35 litres per square metre.

Acids should be added to the water, never the other way around, using a plastic watering can and rubber gloves and wellington boots. The acid is brushed over the surface with a soft broom and left for about fifteen minutes until all effervescence stops. Then all traces of the acid should be washed away with plenty of water. The process can be repeated with a stronger solution if necessary (1 part acid to 2 parts water).

It does not pay to be too optimistic about what can be achieved with this technique. New concrete will be eroded, and relatively poor concrete may be eroded, but old, good quality concrete ought not to be affected too much even by the 33 per cent solution. In view of this, it would be wise to buy a small quantity of acid to start with and try it. If it works satisfactorily then the full quantity required for the job can be bought.

HEATED FLOORS

In Chapter 15 the importance of having electrical work, at the very least supervised by a qualified electrical engineer will be emphasised. This applies to electrical heating in floors just as much as any other electrical installation. However, the concreting work in this type of floor can be done and of course the preparation. Under-floor heating installations are used in pig buildings, in creeps and sometimes for weaners and give very low electrical running costs. Figure 13.17 shows typical cross-sections. This type of floor can be laid over an existing concrete floor or onto a properly compacted sub-base which has been blinded with sand.

In both cases it is necessary to prevent moisture movement up through the floor. Extruded polyurethane or extruded polystyrene sheets, 40 mm or 50 mm thick, should be laid as insulation. The 'tongued and grooved' variety of this insulation material is best as it ensures that the insulation material has no air spaces between the sheets.

There are a number of alternative forms of construction used from the insulation upwards.

Plate 13.63 Kango hammer with scaling head being used to roughen slats.

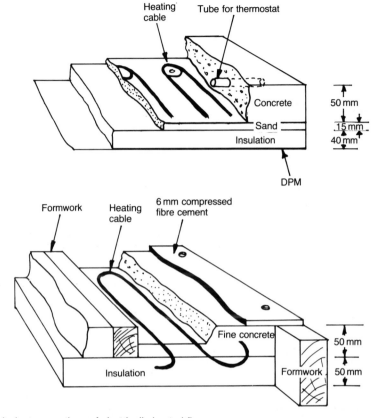

Figure 13.17   Typical cross-sections of electrically heated floors.

Two are illustrated in Figure 13.17. As a third alternative a 25 mm thick layer of a 1:3, cement:sharp sand mix can be laid over the insulation. This should be compacted and finished with a wood float. This is then allowed to harden for at least 24 hours. At this stage the assistance of an electrical engineer will be needed. He will position the cables ready for the top layer of concrete to be placed. It must not be forgotten that it is necessary to sub-divide this concrete into bays with joints in the same way as with every other sort of concrete.

In all cases the top layer of concrete should be laid with an 'over sanded' mix. This is to ensure that there are no air voids around the cables otherwise there is a danger of them overheating. A 1:2:2 low workability mix of cement to sharp sand to 10 mm maximum-sized aggregate, 60 mm thick, should be used and the concrete worked into position ensuring that the cables are not moved in the process. The surface should be finished in the same way as with any other pig floor and then left to cure. The heating cables should not be turned on in an attempt to reduce the 'drying time', as this may affect the quality of the concrete and may even cause cracking.

Ideally the cables should be turned on about six weeks after laying the concrete and even then they should only be left on for a few hours each day.

Before the installation is turned on at all it should be tested by the electrician for continuity, earthing, etc. The qualified electrical contractor or the Farm Energy Centre can give guidance on the electrical load that will be used in this form of heated floor. For creeps it will seldom exceed 300 watts per creep and if an insulated creep lid is used the load can be reduced to 150 or even 100 watts. For weaners heating loads will vary from 70 watts per square metre up to 250 watts per square metre, again depending on factors such as the degree of insulation, the volume per pig in the building and the weight of the animals.

Chapter 14

WATER SUPPLY

ARGUABLY the standard of clean or potable water supplied by the various water companies in this country is among the best in the world. There are many water byelaws and regulations to protect and maintain these standards, and users as well as suppliers now have increased responsibilities with legal penalties for those who fail. The byelaws and interpretation thereof are now unified throughout the industry with the main requirement being to prevent waste, misuse, undue consumption and contamination. Under new 1989 water byelaws greater emphasis is placed upon the problem of contamination and risk categorised into one of three areas. The risk of contamination may cause some difficulty for agriculture because often little regard for the regulations has been evident up to now. This situation may change abruptly because these regulations are retrospective and the water companies will progressively begin inspecting existing premises. Within farm buildings drinking troughs and bowls, chemical and pesticide mixing tanks, hose union taps and milking parlours pose potential risks and may need upgrading to the later regulation.

Examples of the three contamination risk areas might be as follows:

Class 3 Domestic situation where there is little risk of contamination to the water supply with any substance harmful to health.

Class 2 Probably most farm situations where harmful substances are infrequently present.

Class 1 Serious contamination by a substance likely to be harmful to health and continuously or frequently present, e.g. a milking parlour or spray mixing tank.

Back Syphoning

It may not be immediately apparent how easy it is to contaminate a water supply but it has

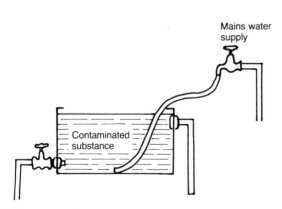

Figure 14.1 An unacceptable arrangement which is against regulations.

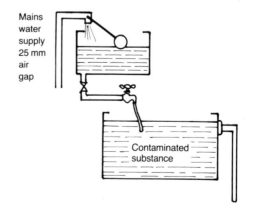

Figure 14.2 An acceptable method of supplying water to storage vessel containing unclean or contaminated water.

occurred from sheep dip solution and pesticides. How does this happen?

If a hose pipe is connected as in Figure 14.1 filling a spray tank directly off the main supply, then any drop in pressure in the main (caused perhaps by a burst) could result in water in the spray tank being drawn, or syphoned, back into the main. Upon resumption of the supply, this contaminated water could be widely distributed to other users in the area.

Whilst a burst water main is a fairly rare occurrence, other large drops in pressure causing back syphoning are not. An industrial user may suddenly draw off a large volume, the fire brigade may be testing hydrants or using them in earnest; or routine repairs and maintenance to the mains supply may cause a temporary drop in pressure. Therefore it is important to realise that the conditions for back syphoning are common and the consequence for negligence serious. An acceptable practice is to maintain an air gap (normally 25 mm is sufficient) between the supply pipe and the maximum level in the tank or cistern. (Figure 14.2). These particular drawings are taken from Severn Trent Water Company recommendations.

Water Regulations

Set out below are very broad interpretations of current water regulations applying particularly to agriculture. They are in no way comprehensive and are only included to illustrate the general reasoning behind the regulations and byelaws. Copies of actual regulations are available from the water companies. Some of the regulations are common sense; some are more involved.

- All water fittings must be serviceable and not produce waste, undue consumption or contamination.
- Fittings of dissimilar metals must not be used because of corrosion by electrolytic action. Generally only fittings manufactured to the relevant B.S. or Water Research Centre approval are acceptable for both new and repair works.
- No pipe or cistern can receive or convey water not supplied by the water company so there is no possibility of two supplies being intermixed. This includes any temporary cross connection arrangement (Figure 14.3). Figure 14.4 shows an acceptable arrangement.
- Every water fitting, whether inside or outside a building, must be placed and protected to minimise the risk of frost and mechanical damage.
- Pipes must be laid underground to a depth of at least 750 mm but not more than 1350 mm.
- Drinking troughs. Each supply to a drinking trough or bowl must be fitted with a ball valve or other effective device to control the flow of water and must be protected from damage and contamination. The supply pipe must be at least 25 mm above the top edge of the trough or bowl. The only alternative is to arrange a supply from a separate cistern with its own ball valve.
- Storage cistern. Each storage tank or cistern should be positioned so that it can easily be inspected and cleaned. Cisterns must be cov-

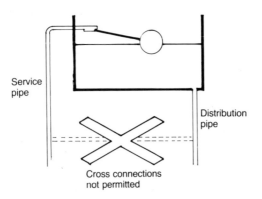

Figure 14.3 Temporary cross connections of water supplies are against regulations.

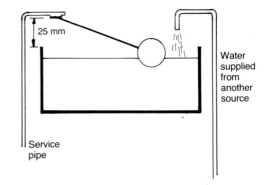

Figure 14.4 An acceptable arrangement.

ered to keep out light, insects, dust, rats, mice and birds, but not fitted with an airtight cover. The inlet pipe must be higher than the overflow pipe by at least the equivalent of twice the bore of the pipe, 25 mm being a practical minimum.

- Hose union tap. Any hose union tap connected directly off the main (with the advantage of mains water pressure) must have a double check valve (non return valve) fitted as close as possible to the tap. In addition permission to connect each such tap must be obtained in writing from the water company concerned. This is also a retrospective requirement. An example would be a wash down hose in a milking parlour pit where if the drainage gully blocked and the hose were left laying on the floor a risk of contamination occurs. Hence it is probably a Class 1 risk as noted above.
- Point of use. Under recent legislation water companies and users have responsibilities and Health and Safety obligations right up to point of use, and not just up to a storage tank or cistern. The particular regulations are too specific and detailed to include here, but are intended to ensure that no-one would inadvertently drink, or connect a water supply, from a cistern such as Figure 14.4 (or similar arrangement whereby water had been used for some other purpose and then returned to the cistern) assuming it was potable water.
- Notice. Five working days notice in writing to the water company concerned are required before commencement of any work involving laying underground water pipes or the installation of any tap, fitting or water using appliance.

Water company experts are always available to advise on the regulations and various installation details and their advice should be sought at an early stage. Farmers with their own well or borehole whilst not directly affected by these regulations will still have responsibilities under Health and Safety and COSHH requirements to ensure their supply is safe.

Plumbing

Plumbing systems on farms can be something of a nightmare. Some installations may be nearly a hundred years old with pipes of lead, cast iron,

asbestos cement, galvanised iron, copper and more recently polythene and rigid plastics with solvent welded joints. Moreover, it is possible to come across the complete range of materials and fittings on any one farm. However, recently the whole business has been rationalised and plumbing is now a relatively simple operation although to interface a new system with an old one can be difficult. There are many infuriating complications in fittings due to the change to metric.

Obsolete systems

Lead pipe with wiped soldered joints was undoubtedly the most successful over the years with its high resistance to corrosion and easy installation, although skill with jointing was necessary. Lead is now condemned, however, because of concern over high lead levels in water and should be replaced wherever possible.

There are many cast-iron systems still in existence although not too many are found on farms. Their main disadvantage is that of corrosion and poor tolerance of ground movement caused by frost or subsidence.

Some asbestos cement systems are in existence and give good service although in time the joint clamps corrode and fail, and the system leaks. They are also liable to fracture due to ground movement.

Galvanised iron

Galvanised iron was the predominant system until the advent of plastic systems. Galvanised iron has reasonable corrosion resistance and a large range of fittings is available. Whilst such pipes were used below ground they are now most frequently used above ground since the pipework is rigid enough to be largely self-supporting and livestock, particularly pigs, cannot chew it.

A galvanised system is time consuming to install, although modern motorised threading machines can be readily hired and greatly improve efficiency. Also care and thought is necessary when installing a system to ensure that various components can be removed for service without dismantling all the pipework. There is a range of standardised galvanised fittings with a British Standard Pipe thread for all sizes of pipes. A similar range of black iron fittings is available for oil, steam and chemical installations. Pipe fittings are sized on the nominal

inside diameter of the pipe. Common sizes are
½ in, ¾ in, 1 in, 1¼ in, 1½ in and 2 in upwards.
During fitting it is vital that all joints are
coated with PTFE tape or another non-setting
compound, or corrosion of the joints will prevent future disassembly.

Copper
Not much copper pipework is used on farms as it
is easily damaged by livestock and has a higher
cost. Nevertheless, for hot water systems it is
excellent and is often used in milking parlours
and the farmhouse. Modern copper systems are
useful as they are easy to install, require little
space and do not corrode. The system is built
largely round the domestic plumbing market and
common pipe diameters are now 10 mm, 15 mm,
22 mm, 28 mm and 35 mm. These sizes compare with ⅜ in, ½ in, ¾ in, 1 in and 1¼ in
prior to metrication. Fortunately the pipes and
fittings between metric and imperial are inter-
changeable except for ¾ in and 22 mm. Copper
pipes can be joined with either compression
fittings or soldered joints. Plate 14.1 shows a
compression fitting which works by compressing
a loose ring onto the pipe during initial tighten-
ing of the joint.

Solder joints
Where many joints are required, the use of
soldered joints is much cheaper and not much
more trouble. Plate 14.2 illustrates all that is

Plate 14.1   A compression joint on a copper pipe.

needed to produce efficient soldered joints.

Initially all surfaces must be thoroughly
cleaned with wire wool and/or a wire brush. The
surfaces are coated with a flux paste and heat is
applied. As soon as the components are hot
enough, solder from the reel is touched on the
joints and as it melts is drawn into the joint by
capillary action. It is a rapid and easy operation
and can be made simplicity itself by the use of
'Yorkshire' fittings which contain their own
solder within a circumferential groove as shown.
Just clean, flux and heat the components to form
the joint.

Polythene pipes
Underground pipes on farms will universally
be of polythene and various sizes and grades

Plate 14.2   Only simple
equipment is required to
produce soldered joints.

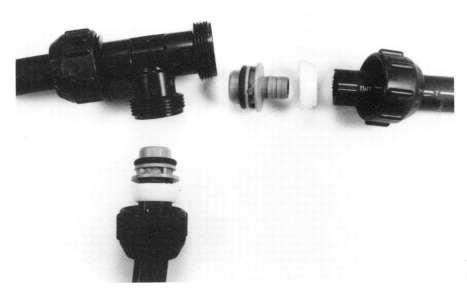

Plate 14.3 Plastic fittings for polythene pipes.

have previously been available. The requirements of all the water suppliers have been unified into one grade of pipe to metric dimension which has the now familiar blue colour. This is of great benefit during subsequent excavation enabling ready distinction between water and black PVC covered electricity cables. Unfortunately the blue pipe is U.V. degradable and must be shielded from direct sunlight if used above ground. A unified black pipe will soon be available for above ground use. In a curious departure from accepted practice the blue pipe is denoted by its outside diameter and not by the normal and more relevant inside diameter.

Underground fittings for polythene pipes must be of gunmetal or of a type resistant to dezincification. Dezincification is another complicated corrosion process and resistant fittings are marked D.R. (Figure 14.5). In some areas

D.R. fittings are required above ground because of the nature of the water supplied.

The water companies are now exclusively using plastic fittings on smaller supplies (Plate 14.3). We have found these Polygrip fittings (invented by a farmer) extremely successful and use them extensively. They can be connected to a range of obsolete pipes and sizes, including lead, with appropriate inserts, which is heaven sent when a digger breaks a pipe just before milking time. Whilst the fittings should be tightened with a spanner, they can be overtightened which cracks the body of the fitting.

Figure 14.5 Water fittings which are dezincification resistant are marked thus.

Plate 14.4 Copper pipe compression fittings are also used for polythene pipes just by changing the compression rings and placing an insert in the pipe.

Chapter 15

ELECTRICAL INSTALLATIONS

IN THIS chapter it is not intended to turn the DIY builder into an electrician, as electrical installations are not really DIY tasks. It is not advisable to attempt to install new or to extend or modify existing wiring installations on your own unless you really do have the required knowledge. An approved electrical contractor should be employed. In the section on electrically heated floors, Chapter 13, the need to use skilled and qualified contractors for that type of work was emphasised. All wiring in farm buildings should comply with the latest edition of the 'Regulations for Electrical Equipment of Buildings' published by the Institution of Electrical Engineers, so it is best to employ qualified contractors.

It does not pay to improvise or even to be unconventional when it comes to electrics. This may lead to fatal shocks, burns, injuries to stock and humans or cause fire. Stick to the rules and if there is any uncertainty call somebody in. Your local Electricity Company will be happy to help. They all have their own specialist 'Farm Electric' man available for consultation. The Farm Energy Centre also produces an excellent range of publications. 'The Essentials of Farm Lighting', Handbook 25, is quoted in this chapter.

Changing plugs, mending or replacing fuses, replacing flexible cable and checking miniature circuit breakers are jobs for the experienced layman. For the rest, extreme caution is recommended and even for these simple jobs care must be taken—always switch off at the local switch and in most cases switch off at the mains, remove the mains fuse and put it in your pocket while you are working.

Terminology

You may have decided already that this is one area of work which will not be tackled on a DIY basis. If it is decided to assist a skilled electrician then the following terms should be known:

- The flow of electricity through a cable or through an item of equipment is called the *current*. The rate of flow is measures in *amps (A)*. It is analogous to the flow of water through a pipe in litres per second—but this is only an analogy.
- The electrical pressure at which electricity is delivered is termed the *voltage*. This is measured in *volts (V)*. The analogy for this is newtons per square metre or, in imperial terms, pounds per square inch. This is really the pressure difference between two points. This causes the current to flow.
- The rate at which a piece of electrical equipment will take power from the electricity supply is the *electrical power* of that equipment. This is measured in *watts* or *kilowatts (W or kW)*. For a given machine it is the product of V × A. Machines will have their power ratings specified on a plate or at least the V and A should be! An electric light bulb, typically, has the power rating of 60 W, an electrical heater perhaps 5000 W or 5 kW and a large fan motor a rating of 30 kW. As a rule of thumb 1 hp = ¾ kW.
- The resistance of a conductor, a piece of copper wire for instance, is measured in *ohms*. Copper, a good conductor, has a low resistance. Nichrome, used for the elements in electric fires, is a poor conductor and has a very high resistance. For simple relationships

$$\frac{volts}{amps} = ohms.$$

- The electrical power of a piece of equipment (in kW) multiplied by the time in hours that it is operating, equals the consumption of electricity of that item in *Units* or *kilowatt hours*.

One possible way of economising on electricity consumption is to use what is known by most electricity companies as the 'Economy 7' tariff. This system enables the use of electricity for a 7 hour period between 12 midnight and 8 am at a reduced rate per unit. Standing charges and daytime rates are usually a little more expensive but overall a saving is likely. For further information contact your local Electricity company.

Supply

The electricity supply in the UK is based on a three-phase system—it is delivered along three live wires with one neutral wire (415/240 V). However, the supply to individual householders and many farms is only single phase. It is delivered along one line with one neutral wire. If it is considered that a three-phase supply is needed—and for the bigger items of equipment such as fans and motors, the three-phase model will usually have a significantly lower initial cost than its single-phase equivalent—this should be discussed with your Board. The cost of installing different cables, transformers, meters, etc., may not be justifiable in all cases.

For portable units, power tools and the like, a reduced voltage supply should be used—the 240 V mains supply is taken through a transformer to give a 110 V supply with a significantly reduced risk from shocks. In workshops and other buildings where portable lighting units may be required a built in step-down transformer should be considered. This should be installed at eaves level and then 110 V cable can be run to the special outlet sockets as required. These should be kept about 2 m above ground as well, so that they are not damaged by tractors or stock.

This low voltage supply is particularly valuable in farm buildings where the risk of damp and dust at the outlet socket is high. But the system must not be overloaded. In a workshop a 2.5 kW transformer will probably be needed. The length of each lead to appliances should be kept down to 6 m and if necessary a 110 V portable distribution unit can be used. The colour code for 110 V is yellow, and flexible leads with a yellow outer casing should be used for all 110 V cable runs.

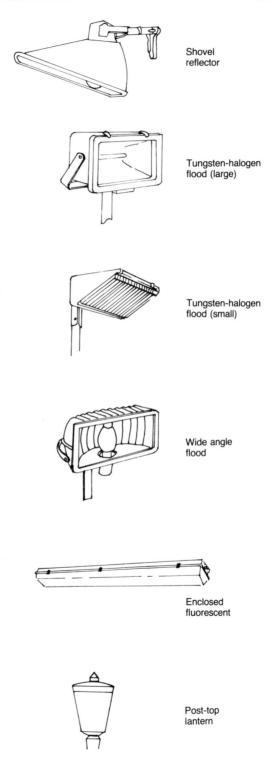

Shovel reflector

Tungsten-halogen flood (large)

Tungsten-halogen flood (small)

Wide angle flood

Enclosed fluorescent

Post-top lantern

Figure 15.1   Some examples of light fittings.

Lighting

The range of lighting equipment available is now immense. It would be wise to seek advice on selection for any given purpose. Dusty conditions such as are found in a mill/mixer unit, in a grain dryer or in conditioning areas and where hay or dried grass are handled, should all be subject to special care. The heat from a normal filament lamp could ignite dust which has settled on it and all the heat it produces is lost energy.

For the efficient use of energy, running costs, lamp replacement costs as well as installation costs must be considered. A 40p lamp with a 100 W rating and a 1000 hour life would have cost about £5.50 at the end of its life. From Table 15.1 a compact fluorescent lamp giving the same amount of light would consume just 25 per cent of the electricity and should last five times as long before replacement.

A good lighting system is also one which is safe and durable in the place of use—in dusty places, near grain installations for instance or damp ones such as milking parlours—distributes the light evenly, in the right quantity and without causing glare. This obviously needs careful thought.

Suspended light fittings should be avoided if possible. Rigid mountings are much safer. It must be ensured that they are high enough too, particularly if the building is to be used by vehicles and machines such as combines. Fittings should be mounted above eaves height or door height if possible and positioned where they can be cleaned and re-lamped. Regular maintenance is as important for lights and fittings as for any other equipment. Once a year they should be cleaned and all lamps replaced, either then or when they have reached the end of their normal lives (See Table 15.1).

It would be advisable to use miniature contact breakers (mcbs) to protect circuits rather than fuses if possible, ensuring that good sound earthings are available.

Table 15.1 shows some alternatives to the normal filament lamps and fluorescent tubes and also shows the vast range in efficiency of lighting products that are now available. For some tasks the ability of a lamp to show coloured objects in their natural and actual colour is important—for grading, sorting and packaging for example. In these circumstances choose a lamp with a 'Deluxe' colour rating.

For security lighting low pressure sodium is

Table 15.1   Lights and their relative performance

Lamp type	Luminous efficiency Lumens/Watt	Life (hours)	Colour rendering	Lumen range	Application
Filament	13	1000	Perfect	200–2200 (25W–150W)	General lighting
Compact fluorescent	52	5000	Deluxe	200–1400	Amenity lighting
Mercury fluorescent	52	7000	Fair	1700–110000	Grain dryers; cattle sheds; large enclosed areas
Metal halide	55	6000	Deluxe	13600–166000	Large enclosed areas; external area lighting
High pressure sodium	96	8000	Poor	3000–123000	Sheep buildings; workshops; area lighting
Low pressure sodium	200+	7000	None	1800–26000	Security and amenity lighting

Ruck, J., 'Lamps Can Lop Costs', *Farmers Weekly*, 12 April 1985.

the most efficient light source but colours are indistinguishable. An 18 W lamp gives as much light as a 150 W filament lamp and costs about 1p a night to run.

It is not efficient use of energy to have too much light, of course. Some discharge lamps such as high-pressure sodium are only available in powerful ratings and may be unnecessarily bright in some situations.

Before making your choice seek the advice of the Farm Energy Centre, or a major light manufacturer.

The choice of light fitting itself can also influence safety and efficiency. A fitting with a built-in reflector may result in 25 per cent more useful light being available. Fittings to suit normal dry atmospheres, dusty atmospheres, corrosive situations (ammonia from dung and urine is one of these corrosive materials) and flammable conditions are available. One which satisfies all these and is resistant to pressure washing may be a sound, long term investment in farming situations.

In the British Standard for Farm Buildings (BS 5502) the levels of local lighting recommended are as set out in Table 15.2.

The unit of measurement of light is called *lux* and is equal to one lumen per square metre. A typical 100 W filament bulb at 240 V has a lumen output of about 1250 lux; compared with, for example, bright sunlight at 80,000 lux, an office at 500 lux and moonlight at 0.2 lux.

Table 15.2 Levels of local lighting in workplaces (table from BS 5502: Section 3.5: 1978)

Task or location	Standard service illuminance	Notes
	lux	
Inspection lighting		
Inspection of farm produce where good colour rendering is needed	500	Careful choice of fluorescent tube types
Other inspection tasks where additional light is needed	300	Using local or portable lights
General lighting		
Farm workshop	100	
Milk premises	100	Where milk is handled or stored
Sick animal pen	50	Where frequent veterinary attention is given
		Veal units included in next item
Baby calf nursery	50	5% daylight factor is adequate
Other farm and horticultural buildings:		
1. Where adequate daylight is admitted	20	
2. All other buildings	50	(except as Note 4 below)

1. In animal buildings and other places (apart from those specified in the table) a lower illuminance may be employed for animal welfare purposes, and in horticultural buildings a higher illuminance may be required for crop production. However, when operators are present, lighting must be provided at least to the standard given in the table.
2. The standard service illuminance is that used for design purposes. A service illuminance is an average over the area throughout the life of the installation. The standard service illuminance is the recommended service illuminance for the application, and may apply to the whole area or only to the task areas. When measuring, values will be found that exceed the mean, with others below the mean. The illuminance at a point is measured by holding a lightmeter in the plane of the work at working plane height.
3. In any building where extra illuminance is needed temporarily to aid the performance of a task, a portable luminaire of suitable design should be used, or extra localised lighting brought into use. The portable lighting equipment should be capable of producing an illuminance of at least 300 lux on the task and its immediate background. It is recommended that the task lighting should be additional to the general lighting indicated in the table.
4. In farm buildings not provided with a 5 per cent daylight factor, a standard service illuminance of 50 lux is required, but where a windowless building is entered through a vestibule which excludes daylight, provided that the vestibule has a standard service illuminance of 50 lux, acting as a light/dark adaption zone, the main building may be lit to a standard service illuminance of 20 lux as required.

Chapter 16

VENTILATION AND INSULATION

VENTILATION

FOR MAXIMUM health and performance, livestock require a good environment. An efficient ventilation system removes excess moisture, some disease-causing organisms, dust, waste gases from the stock and will help to provide an environment which is acceptable to the stock, the stockmen and the building. As the moisture-laden stale air leaves the building so fresh air enters and this must be well distributed but not produce draughts. Even on still days there must be enough movement of air to remove the moisture generated per day—if not, condensation will occur. There may be as much as 10 litres of moisture per day to be removed from the building for each animal housed. If it is not removed condensation will certainly occur as well as stuffy, humid conditions in which bacteria thrive. There will also be damp bedding and permanently wet floors—all conditions which will result in poor animal performance.

Natural Ventilation

This chapter will concentrate on natural ventilation of cattle buildings and on the improvement of poorly ventilated buildings. Natural ventilation, a system which has no help from fans, is cheap to provide. Its sources of 'power' are the wind and the heat generated by the animals. This heat is sufficient to warm the incoming air which, now being lighter, will rise over the colder air and leave the building at the upper openings. This warm air is then replaced by cooler, heavier air from outside which, in turn, is warmed and begins to rise. This is termed the 'stack effect'. For the system to work two openings are needed in a building—the lower one for inlet and the upper one for outlet. The

openings must be large enough to allow sufficient air to enter even on calm days when only the stack effect produces air movement. In these circumstances a 2°C temperature difference between inside and outside is likely and this will be sufficient to cause the movement.

On windy days the air may enter and leave the building at the same level—entering on one side and leaving on the other—really as a result of pressure differences outside the building caused by the wind. In these circumstances the inside and outside temperatures may well be the same and the main requirement must be to prevent draughts caused by high-speed air movement.

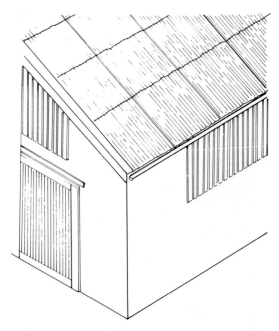

Figure 16.1 If ventilation is provided in gable ends as well as in the walls blank off both within 2 m of the corner.

176

Figure 16.2 (a)   Space boarding.

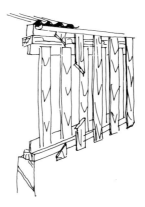

Figure 16.2 (b)   Adjustable space boarding.

Remember that air inlets produce the dominant effect on air distribution and if not correctly arranged can cause draughts.

The pressure differences really produce a 'sucking and blowing effect'. A wind pressure is normally produced on the weather side of the building or wall and a 'suction' is created on the 'lee' side and on the roof. To prevent draughts from occurring in these circumstances the inlet opening will need to be baffled in some way by space boarding, slotted steel sheeting or a nylon mesh material to reduce the wind speed as it passes through the windbreak or baffle into the building. If the end of the building is ventilated as well as the sides both should be blanked off within 2 m of the corner of each elevation. End ventilation should not be taken right up to the ridge as it might short-circuit the desired air flow

Plate 16.1   Space boarding for inlet ventilation. Crown cranked roof top outlets may be inadequate.

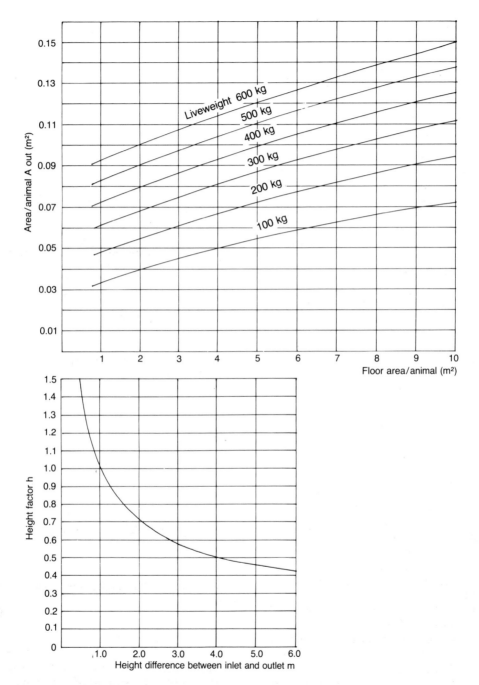

Figure 16.3   Ventilation areas for cattle buildings.
Top: outlet area for height difference of 1 m. Thus A out for 400 kg animal at 4 m²/head is 0.093 m²/head.
Bottom: height factor. For a height difference of 3 m height factor is 0.58. Outlet area required is thus
0.093 × 0.58 = 0.054 m²/head.
Inlet area is twice outlet area.

(Figure 16.1). Access openings should be fully covered by doors or sheeted gates to full height or flaps provided above them. Any proprietary materials should be accompanied by data indicating the equivalent voidage or openings the material provides. For space boarding (Figures 16.1, and 16.2 and Plate 16.1) the effective opening is:

$$\frac{\text{gap width}}{\text{board width + gap width.}}$$

Figure 16.3* shows how ventilation areas for cattle buildings can be calculated. However, many people are happy to accept standardised values—0.045 square metres per head as a minimum outlet area (inlet areas are always reckoned to be twice that of the outlet areas). It should not be forgotten that a building normally has inlet openings on both sides.

These standardised figures were recommended as long ago as 1891 but unfortunately very few people took much notice of this recommendation until about 1970. Consequently many livestock buildings are severely underventilated. Ideally a building should be orientated across the prevailing wind and thus its axis should usually be N/S in Britain. Gable end ventilation should be avoided if possible.

Outlet Design

Reviews of research and other studies by the Centre for Rural Building in Aberdeen have highlighted some interesting aspects of outlet design. In general terms an open ridge is the best way to provide outlet ventilation and the simpler the design of this the better. Upstands to the ridge may help to reduce the entry of rain and snow but ridge caps definitely increase the risk of entry of wind-driven snow in particular. On calm days they will reduce the entry of rain and snow (Figure 16.4).

In 1978 the SFBIU, now the Centre for Rural Building, suggested a method of producing a protected open ridge to reduce the entry of rain and snow.† Many farmers had felt, quite unjustifiably, that an open ridge would allow unacceptable quantities of water to enter the building and this had prevented the more widespread application of open ridge ventilation. The design suggested by the SFBIU is shown in Figure 16.5 and is now available as a stand-

*BRUCE, J. M., *Farm Building Progress* **42**, October 1975.

†BRUCE, J. M., *Farm Building Progress* **53**, July 1978.

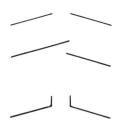

Figure 16.4   Three types of open ridge vent.

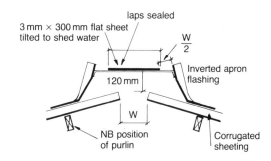

laps sealed

3 mm × 300 mm flat sheet tilted to shed water

$\frac{W}{2}$

120 mm

Inverted apron flashing

W

NB position of purlin

Corrugated sheeting

Figure 16.5 (a)   Protected open ridge design. W is not normally less than 150 mm.

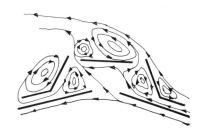

Figure 16.5 (b)   Airflow patterns shown by water table tests.

ard product from many roof sheeting manufacturers. The fibre cement sheeting manufacturers have a flat protective sheet which should be laid with a slight fall to one side so that rain or melting snow does not run along the bottom of the sheet and drip through the open ridge, but drips

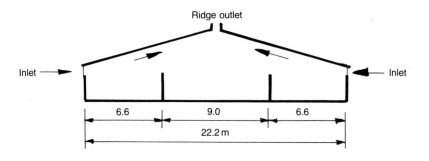

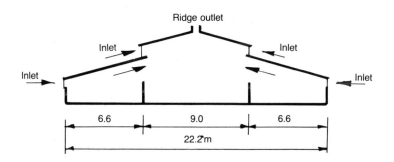

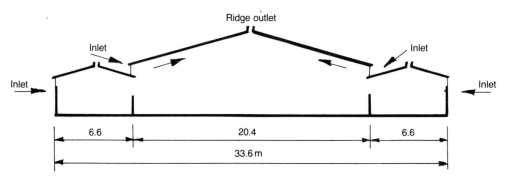

Figure 16.6   Ventilation of multispan buildings.

to one side onto the projecting roof sheets and runs down the corrugations beneath the flat surface of the apron flashing. This moulded unit is fixed on top of the corrugated sheets as shown in Figure 16.5.

The now traditional ventilation patterns for multi-span buildings are shown in Figure 16.6 but these may work less than satisfactorily if the horizontal distance between inlet and outlet is great or if the roof pitch is shallow (10° or less).

Improving Ventilation

In these circumstances in both old and new buildings the open ridge can be supplemented or even replaced by two other forms of outlet

Plate 16.2   Raised end laps in practice.

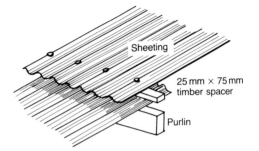

Figure 16.7   25 mm × 75 mm tanalised timber battens inserted between sheets at the lap.

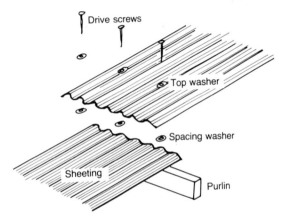

Figure 16.8   For short sheets spacing washers may be inserted between sheets at the lap.

ventilation—the raised roof sheet and the slotted roof.

The raised sheet method involves slackening off the hook bolts on the sheeting sufficiently to allow a 25 mm thick by 75 mm wide timber batten to be inserted between the sheets at the lap (Figures 16.7 and 16.8, Plate 16.2).* It may be necessary to replace the bolts with a longer version if the now common 'six inch' corrugated sheets are used. This method of improving ventilation is called the 'breathing roof' system. The gap produced is assumed to be equivalent to a 45 mm wide opening all along the roof if the information in Figure 16.3 is being used for design purposes.

In the slotted roof system the slots are provided in the opposite direction to the raised sheet method—they run from eaves to ridge. On an existing building the slots can be made by cutting along the crest of the corrugations either at the side laps, leaving the horizontal laps uncut, or down the centre of the sheets. Some additional fittings may be required in the sheets—in timber purlins the sheets can be drilled for additional drive screws and on steel purlins a small metal bridging piece used over the cut with the hook bolts being inserted through the slot.

For cutting slots a portable saw with a 9 in stone cutting disc should be used and this is clamped to a jig made up for the purpose (Figure 16.9).† It must be ensured that crawling ladders are used on the roof and that there is proper protection against the dust from the sheet with approved respiratory masks. The saw should be used with the cutting edge of the disc moving upwards towards the outside of the building to reduce the dust hazard. With this technique slots can be cut up to 20 mm wide (Plate 16.3).

On new buildings wider gaps can be produced with less risk of snow bridging by using corrugated sheeting laid upside down. With fibre cement sheeting 6 in corrugated sheets are laid 25 mm apart to form a continuous slot from eaves to ridge. Using this technique about 8 per cent will be saved on roofing material costs and

*BRUCE, J. M., Farm Building Progress 66, October 1981.

† Farm Building Progress 52, April 1978.

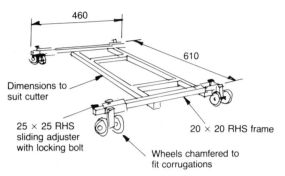

Figure 16.9   Roof slotting jig.
(Dimensions in millimetres)

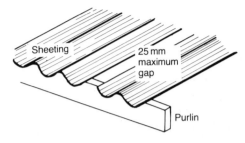

Figure 16.10   Laying corrugated sheets upside down for wider gaps.

the need to cut mitres on sheet corners will be avoided (Figure 16.10, Plates 16.4 and 16.5). Improved natural lighting will also have to be provided in the building and because the rougher side of a fibre cement sheet is now laid uppermost the sheet will gather lichen and moss more quickly and will 'tone in' with existing buildings and the countryside more rapidly. With 3 in fibre cement corrugated sheets one edge of the sheet will have to be sawn off to provide the necessary upturn on both sides of the sheet. With steel sheets many of the profiles

allow the sheets to be used upside down and provide the necessary upturn on the edges (Figure 16.11). Some suppliers reverse roll the sheets with the upturn edges to allow the sheets to be used the right way up.

Modifying Old Buildings

If the outlet ventilation needs to be improved in old buildings many of the techniques which have already been described are applicable—raised

Plate 16.3   Slotted sheets—sawn.

Plate 16.4   A new slotted roof with good gaps.

Plate 16.5   Slotted roof—new.

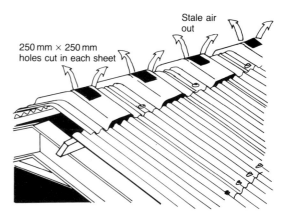

Figure 16.12   Increasing the ventilation on crown cranked ridge sheeting. Outlet area before modification 0.06 m²/run; after modification 0.13 m²/run. Protect rafters where applicable.

sheeting, slot cutting, spaced sheets, provision of open ridges, etc. Crown cranked ridge fittings along the ridge of the building seldom allow sufficient outlet area for cattle housing and will need to be improved. This can be achieved by cutting holes 250 mm × 250 mm in each raised section of the ridge sheeting. If there is a crown cranked unit on each sheet, when cut it will be equivalent to a 130 mm continuous opening at the ridge (Figure 16.12).

For old slate and tile roofed buildings some improvisation will be needed. The roofing material could be removed and replaced with short corrugated fibre cement sheets, with raised sheets, slots or open ridge (Figure 16.13) or

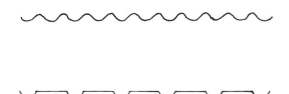

Figure 16.11   Upturned edges on two profiles of steel sheeting.

alternatively the ridge opened up completely. If the latter alternative is attempted, first the underfelt must be cut out and then a way of anchoring the top tiles or slates must be found, normally held by the ridge capping piece, and additional protection must be given to the timber roof members in the open section of the ridge.

To provide additional inlet area all that is needed is to knock a few holes in the wall! And that may not be as daft as it sounds. In many buildings additional inlet area will usually be provided at the eaves by breaking out the wall head between rafters. A stack effect needs to be achieved as a result of this and it must be ensured that the incoming air is not deflected by existing purlins to produce a down draught onto the animals that are standing or lying just inside the walls.

In some cases, of course, particularly in old portal-framed buildings, it may be possible to introduce space boarding as an alternative to existing sheet side cladding or block, brick or stone walls; or to use plastic netting as an alternative baffle. On timber buildings the 'net' should be fixed with 12 mm × 50 mm battens to the main building frame and to the walls. On steel and concrete buildings a frame of 50 mm × 50 mm timbers should be made up and the mesh fixed to this with the 12 mm × 50 mm battens;

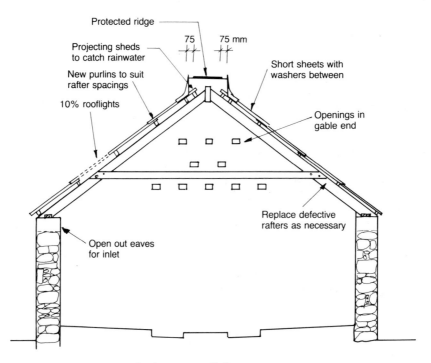

Protected ridge

75   75 mm

Projecting sheds
to catch rainwater

Short sheets with
washers between

New purlins to suit
rafter spacings

10% rooflights

Openings in
gable end

Replace defective
rafters as necessary

Open out eaves
for inlet

Figure 16.13   Modifications to old slate roof to improve ventilation.

this unit is then bolted to the frames. On
exposed sites caution is needed over the high
voidage area in some meshes—they are cheap
but may result in draughty conditions in the
building (Figure 16.14).

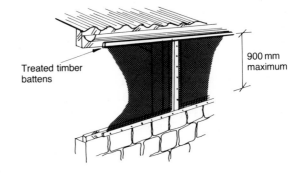

Treated timber
battens

900 mm
maximum

Figure 16.14   Mesh on a frame to replace sheeting and
provide more inlet ventilation.

INSULATION

Insulating materials will reduce the flow of heat
from the warm side of a roof, wall or floor to the
cold side. They will keep a building warmer or, if
necessary, keep it colder than a similar building
which does not incorporate insulation materials.
The benefits therefore include:

- less condensation
- protection from frost
- lower fuel costs either for heating or
  refrigeration equipment
- lower feed costs for stock
- less build-up of heat from the sun.

The insulation value of materials varies almost
directly in relationship to their densities. Low-
density or lightweight materials such as glass
fibre or expanded or extruded polystyrene have
a high insulation value—heat passes through
them very slowly; high-density or heavyweight
materials such as brick, concrete or steel have a
very low insulation value—heat passes through
them very much more quickly.

For the actual measurement of insulation
there are three commonly used terms:

- *Thermal conductivity* The insulation property of the material itself is called the K or λ value. This is really the measure of the ability of the material to transmit heat (W/m°C). The lower the K value the better the insulation.
- *Thermal resistance* This is the rate at which heat flows through a particular part of a building. This is determined by the thermal conductivity of the material and the thickness of that material (called the R value). The higher the R value the better (m² °C/W).
- *Thermal transmittance* This is the amount of heat that will flow through a square metre of the structure for each 1°C difference in the temperature from inside to outside (called the U value). The lower the U value the better the insulation.

Table 16.1 Some typical recommended U values for some farm buildings

Farm Building Type	U Value (W/m² °C)
Unheated piggeries	0.6
Heated piggeries	0.5
Poultry houses	0.5
Frost protection for crop storage	1.15
Protection from solar gain for crop stores	0.55
Refrigerated stores	0.4

Calculating Insulation Values

Most of the suppliers of insulation materials will also supply the information needed to achieve these U values. For instance, 50 mm of extruded polystyrene with a K value of 0.029 will provide a U value of 0.58. This can be worked out using

Table 16.2 Some typical K (λ) values (W/m² °C)

Materials etc.	K values
Bricks	0.84
Mortar (rendering)	0.50
Concrete	1.00
Aerated concrete	0.12–0.19
Extruded polystyrene	0.029
Glass or mineral wool	0.040
Timber	0.13
Polyurethane foam	0.023

Table 16.3 Some R values (m² °C/W)

Part of building	R values
Cavity	0.18
Internal surface	0.12
External surface	0.06

the following technique:

If the K or λ value of a material is known (the manufacturer's figure) then the R value can be determined by dividing the thickness (L), expressed in metres, by the K value.

Some typical K values are given in Table 16.2

If all the thermal resistances of the materials in a wall are added together including those for the internal and external surfaces of the wall itself this figure is inversely proportional to the U value:

$$U = \frac{1}{R_1 + R_2 + R_3}$$

Example: Potato box store (210 mm brick + 50 mm foam) and potato bulk store (200 mm reinforced aerated concrete panels)

λ or K values	bricks	0.84
	spray-on polyurethane foam	0.023
	aerated concrete	0.12
L thickness (m)	bricks	0.210
	spray-on polyurethane foam	0.05
	aerated concrete	0.2

R values	bricks	0.21/0.84	= 0.25
	foam	0.05/0.023	= 2.174
	aerated concrete	0.2/0.12	= 1.667
	outside surface		0.060
	inside surface		0.120

U value for 210 mm brick with + 50 mm spray foam

$$= \frac{1}{0.25 + 2.174 + 0.060 + 0.120} = \frac{1}{2.6} = 0.38$$

U value of aerated concrete panel wall (200 mm thick)

$$= \frac{1}{1.667 + 0.060 + 0.120} = \frac{1}{1.85} = 0.54$$

Both these figures are below those recommended for frost protection and protection against solar gain.

Plate 16.6 Sprayed foam being used to upgrade the insulation in a farm building.

The Applications

Some buildings which contain crops or stock can be insulated so that the heat given off by the contents keeps the building at the required temperature. The heat losses which occur by way of the ventilation should not be forgotten. It generally pays to over-insulate in these circumstances.

Ceilings in buildings can be effectively insulated with glass or mineral wool quilts or with extruded polystyrene boards. The quilts need vapour checks but the tongued and grooved polystyrene does not. Expanded polystyrene should only be used if it is part of a proprietary bonded composite board.

Sprayed polyurethane or polyisocyanurate foams are ideal materials for upgrading the insulation of farm buildings. The backgrounds must be clean and dry and the foams should always be sprayed afterwards with moisture-resistant and fire-proof paints. This form of insulation is normally carried out by specialist contractors however (Plate 16.6).

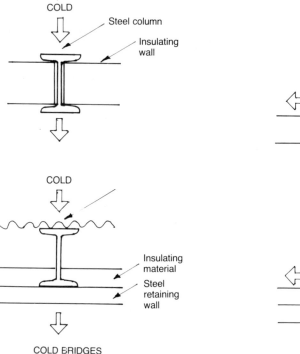

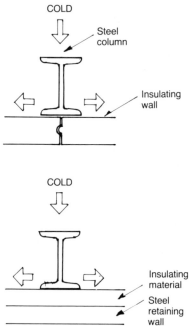

Figure 16.15 (*Left*) Walling systems which allow frost to penetrate into the building—thermal bridge. (*Right*) Walling systems which prevent frost from penetrating the building—thermal barriers.

For DIY work the addition of insulation boards or bonded panels is a more suitable method of upgrading the insulation value of buildings. A range of special fixing devices is now available for this work and these should be used if possible. Adequate protection must be installed against damage by impact from stock and machines.

Cold Bridges

It is most important in the design of insulation systems for buildings to eliminate what are called thermal or cold bridges (Figure 16.15). The insulation must be carried across the structural framework either on the inside or the outside. Some examples of how this can be achieved are illustrated in Figure 16.15.

Other buildings may need supplementary heating to maintain the correct temperature—pigs and poultry rearing buildings for example. In these cases the cost of insulation and its installation costs have to be weighed against the cost of heating fuel and the efficiency of the heating and control system. Once again it will usually pay to over-insulate.

For buildings where the inside temperature is more or less the same as the outside temperature insulation is not necessary. These include buildings for cattle, calves, sheep and some storage buildings.

Selection of Materials

For most applications the strength and impact resistance of the material, its fire resistance, its susceptibility to damage by pests (birds, rodents, insects, etc.) and moisture (some fibrous materials tend to collapse and thus decline in insulation value if permanently exposed to moisture) will need to be considered as well as its original insulation value and cost.

Condensation within the insulation material is

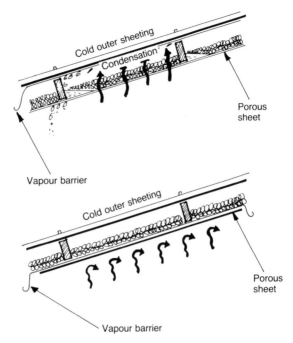

Figure 16.16 Use of barriers in roofs to prevent condensation within the roof structure.

one problem which may go unnoticed. It is good practice to attempt to eliminate it by installing a vapour check on the warm side of the insulation (Figure 16.16).* Tongued and grooved joints help to overcome the problem in 'board' materials. Taped joints are often a problem area. The surfaces to be taped must be completely clean, dust free, and dry. Aluminium foil, polythene sheeting or plastic paints can be used as a vapour check.

For walls, insulating blockwork is attractive, being easy to erect, unaffected by pests, with good fire-resistant properties. To achieve high U values cavity construction may be necessary, incorporating other insulating materials in the cavity (see Chapter 11).

---

*FORSYTHE, R. J. and SHEPHERD, C. S., 'Condensation Problems in Farm Buildings', West of Scotland College of Agriculture, 1977.

Chapter 17

ROADS AND PAVED AREAS

How DO YOU cost the benefits of a good farm road? Reliable access at all times of the year— that is difficult to cost! Higher speeds for all vehicles—the seconds saved in a 'Land-Rover' or similar vehicle, because they can travel at 30 mph rather than 10 mph is unlikely to be economic, but the reduced turnround of vehicles at silage time or grain harvest is likely to be much more beneficial. Nonetheless it is difficult to cost. Reduced wear and tear on machinery and implements are also difficult to cost.

It has been estimated that for every acre farmed at least 8 tonnes of material are handled every year. Compared with an unmade road, concrete paved roads result in an increase in transport speeds of over 50 per cent, a reduction in power requirement of up to 30 per cent and a reduction in fuel consumption of about 25 per cent.

It would be unwise to place too much value on this assessment but it would also be unwise to ignore it. It is certainly true that adequate roads are an essential of a farm's fixed equipment whether for vehicles or for stock. The aim of this book is not to make recommendations on design or choice of materials, but it concentrates on describing why things are done and how they are done. In this chapter the same principles apply. But bearing in mind the limitations of do-it-yourself and the influence of this on choice of materials, particularly in this chapter some discussion on the choice of materials is necessary.

Choice Of Materials

There is a wide range of 'blacktop' materials available to the road builder. These are sometimes termed 'flexible' materials. They are hard to the touch and indeed to the load from a wheel and thus transmit loads to the material beneath them in a similar way to a 'rigid' concrete road. But they will flex, with time. This means that foundation or sub-base settlement can be accommodated but will result in the formation of undulations rather than cracks in the surface.

The construction of a 'blacktop' road might appear to be a fairly straightforward process—the material is heated, spread and rolled. In reality it is far from simple. The materials recommended for use on a farm are high quality bitumen or asphalts and, apart from the control of heating, they must be laid while they are hot—there is no second chance at correcting a laying mistake. The material should be laid by machine at a single pass. A do-it-yourself approach to 'blacktop' farm road construction is not recommended. It is an operation best left to the experienced contractor. The only guidance which can be given is to ensure that the contractor undertaking the work is properly equipped and experienced.

The contractor should have a paver/finisher which receives the material, conveys it to a heated screed which not only controls thickness but also partially vibrates it. Compaction is completed by either a 10 tonne 'static' roller or a 5 tonne vibrating roller. If access is limited to a single lane in and out about 300–500 m by 3.6 m wide will be laid in a day. If livestock are to use the surface it must be ensured that the bonding material, the bitumen or asphalt, will stand up to dung and urine.

Technically the best road for farms probably is a concrete road, but this cannot always be justified economically. Certainly the same quality of road cannot be justified for the interior roads serving the fields as for that which connects the farmstead to the highway. The paved areas around the farmstead may also need to be of a different quality. But concrete is attractive as a DIY material, so if the farm's activities and the

Plate 17.1 (a)   A typical concrete farm road.

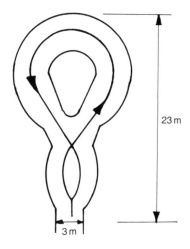

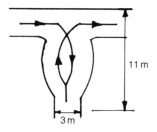

Figure 17.1 (a)   Special requirements of tractor and forage box (*from MAFF*).

greater reliance on forklifts and other mechanical handling equipment justify the construction of a properly paved road or yard, then concrete is the material to choose (Plate 17.1).

Having said this, it would be foolish to ignore costs altogether. Concrete may well cost twice or even three times as much initially as a road of local unbound material. For the farthest reaches of the farm network the cheaper alternatives must not be ignored.

Where to Build

In most instances the positions of roads and yards will have been determined many years ago. The necessity will be for the upgrading of existing areas rather than the construction of new. Where new buildings are being erected it is likely that internal paved areas will also be constructed and these could well be on 'new' ground. The position of the building itself will thus determine the location of the paving and this has already been discussed in Chapter 2.

On those rare occasions when new roads are being built, in addition to the choice of materials the following points must also be considered:

• The demand of the Local Authority on access to the highway.
• The need for cut and/or fill—both increase cost.
• Gradients and falls for drainage—must not exceed 1 in 4 or fall below 1 in 120 respectively (30 mm in 3.6 m).
• The special requirements of vehicles in and around farm buildings (Figure 17.1a).
• The extra width required at bends (Figure 17.1b.*)
• The location of passing bays—they should be located every 300 m to 400 m with visibility in mind (Figure 17.2).
• The need for culverts or bridges (Figure 17.3).
• The need for gates (which should open inwards) and livestock grids (Plate 17.2).
• Sight lines and farm entrances (Figure 17.4).
• Access to and from the road from fields and gateways at different levels—this should be avoided if possible.
• The risk from snow drifting or blown soil.

*Wiseman, J. *Farm Building Progress* 53, July 1978.

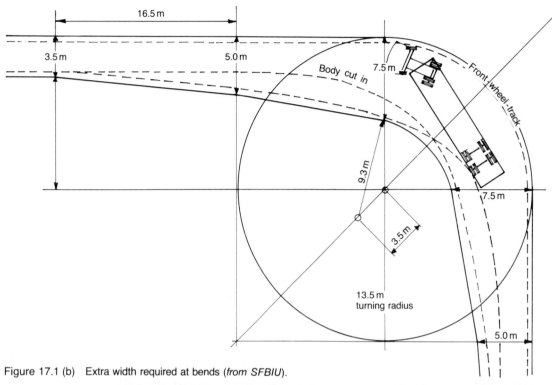

Figure 17.1 (b)   Extra width required at bends (*from SFBIU*).

Plate 17.1 (b)   The extra width is especially necessary at right-angle bends.

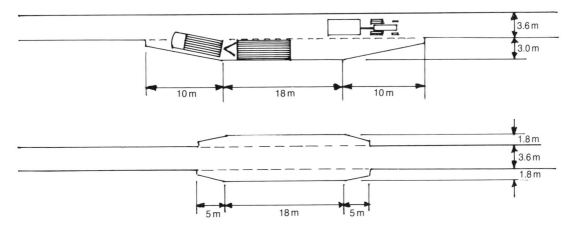

Figure 17.2   Passing bays.

Definitions

Sub-grade   The soil on which the road or yard rests.

Formation   The top surface of the sub-grade after 'earthworks' are complete.

Sub-base   A thickening or levelling layer which helps spread loads.

Base course   This spreads and transmits loads to the subgrade.

Surfacing or wearing course   This provides a smooth-running surface and protects the base; in concrete it also spreads load.

Plate 17.2   Consider the need for cattle grids.

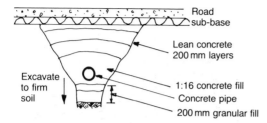

Figure 17.3   A typical culvert.

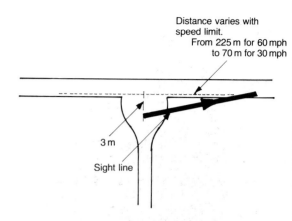

Figure 17.4   Find out what local authority sight line recommendations are.

Unbound Material (Macadam)

A Scottish engineer called Macadam published ideas on road making 250 years ago which still make sense today. In principle he stated that all roads rely upon the soil for their support and that if this could be kept dry the road would carry traffic. The thickness of material required to keep the soil dry determines the thickness of the road. He did not appreciate the load-spreading role of the road's structure.

In unbound Macadam the first step is to remove surface vegetation only. Wet spots should be dug out for refilling. It is a good idea to raise the road above the level of the surrounding ground in this form of construction.

The sub-base material should be hard, granular and permeable. Rubble, crushed stone or gravel are acceptable. It should be rolled in and finished to the required levels (falls). The maximum particle size for this course is 75 mm. The thickness of this course rarely exceeds 75 mm.

The base course should be of a smaller maximum size (50 mm) and should contain fine material to fill the voids between the large particles. Crushed stone, slag, quarry-waste, as-raised gravel and crushed rubble are suitable. The thickness of this course rarely exceeds 100 mm. It must be thoroughly compacted by rolling as well. The surface should be blinded with a layer of limestone dust, ash or similar fine material.

On stable ground, such as sand or gravelly soils, the total thickness of this form of 'paving' will not need to exceed 100 mm and all three layers may be combined as one. On less stable soils, particularly if the road is to carry heavy lorries in wet weather, a 250 mm thickness is required.

On peat soils, in the Fens, it is not unusual to find a 600 mm depth of material which has accumulated over the years. This is not the best form of road in these sort of conditions, however. Rigid pavements (concrete) which spread the load more effectively are to be preferred.

Waterbound Macadam

The only difference between this form of construction and unbound Macadam is that water is added to bond the stones together in the slurry of fine dust and clay. Unbound Macadams tend to turn into waterbound Macadams in the winter on most farms!

Tarmacadam

Tarmacadam is the layman's name for any 'black top' road. Currently tar is replaced by either bitumen or asphalt. The Macadams are produced using bitumen and crushed rock and they are available either open textured or, with more fines, as dense Macadam. Asphalt is more readily available in predominantly sand and gravel areas and uses more bitumen or a slightly harder grade than dense Macadam, with sand as the fine material. Hot rolled asphalt is the tough impervious layer used for major roads.

Soft bitumens, called 'cut back bitumens', are only suitable for patching (Plate 17.3). Hard bitumens (200 pen bitumen Tarmacadams and

Plate 17.3   A 'cold-rolled' material being compacted on a farm road.

Plate 17.4   A 'paver-finisher' being used to lay 'hot-rolled' material for a 'black-top' farm road.

50 or 100 pen asphalts) need the proper equipment for laying and should only be laid by experienced contractors as has already been stressed (Plate 17.4). Some producers have proprietary formulations which, although using softer bitumens, do provide hard, impermeable wearing courses.

CONCRETE ROADS

It has already been mentioned that concrete is the ideal material for the do-it-yourself road builder. However, it is the most expensive—initially. The temptation to economise must be resisted not only in the quality of the base work, the quality of the concrete and the thickness of the concrete, but also in its width. With an investment in this form of road, money should be spent wisely.

Before starting the work the exact place where the concrete will be needed must be known. ADAS have produced an excellent publication called 'Farm vehicle movement No. 2288' which provides all the information necessary to make this decision. The examples shown in Figures 2.1, 2.2 and 17.1a are three of many similar illustrations in this publication. It is important to put the concrete where it is needed, not where it is thought it might be needed.

For entrances to farms information published by the Road Haulage Association is most helpful (Figure 17.5). Table 17.1 is also taken from Road Haulage Association data. With this data an entrance can be designed which will satisfy all needs—the farmer's as well as the driver of the heaviest vehicle. It has to be supplemented of course with the 'sight lines' data in Figure 17.4, which has already been mentioned.

For paved areas around buildings attention must be paid to data concerning the vehicle

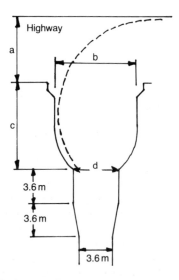

Figure 17.5   Layout of typical farm entrance from the Road Haulage Association.

dimensions, etc. Again the Ministry leaflet will provide this.

Drainage

Having decided where the concrete is to be laid, the next consideration is drainage of the area. If one inch of rain falls on one acre of concrete, in the region of 20,000 gallons of water will have to be accommodated. If it is allowed to run away over the edge of the concrete and do little else, it will soften, and subsequently cause failure of the sub-base, and indeed the concrete over this 'foundation'. The sub-base will no longer support the concrete properly and it will crack.

If there are no gulley pots or drains, then at least a 'french drain' should be provided on the low side of the concrete area. On roads the quantity of water is not really so much of a problem, but drainage should not be overlooked (Figure 17.6). The illustration shows a typical

Table 17.1   Dimensions of a farm entrance as recommended by the Road Haulage Association

Width of highway	a	3.0 m	6.1 m	9.2 m
Necessary dimensions of farm entrance	b	9.2 m	7.6 m	6.1 m
	c	9.2 m	7.6 m	6.1 m
	d	4.3 m	4.3 m	4.3 m

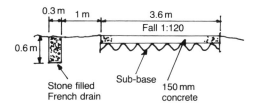

Figure 17.6 Typical fall and drainage provision on farm roads.

solution. It cannot be constructed at no cost though. If a trench is excavated 1 m deep having a 150 mm drain in the bottom and the trench is back filled with stone it will cost as much as the concrete (the material) per metre run of road. The type of drain illustrated is much cheaper than this course, and if the trench is excavated and backfilled with stone yourself, the material costs will be modest—perhaps £2 per metre run of drain. It should be remembered that this could save pounds in the long run. A good drainage system prevents sub-base softening and failure of the concrete from this cause.

Sub-base
Guidance on sub-base design and construction can be found in Chapter 13, pages 123–5.

The Concrete

The concrete mix recommended for all external paving for farms is shown in Chapter 2, Table 2.1. It contains a minimum of 300 kg of ordinary Portland cement per cubic metre of concrete, with 20 mm maximum-sized aggregate and is of medium workability. The concrete should contain an air-entraining agent to give a target air content of 5 per cent. This mix can be specified from any ready-mixed concrete supplier. A PAV1 mix from BS 5328 is equivalent to this and can be supplied by suppliers with an approved Quality Assurance Scheme (QSRMC).

Experience has shown that the combination of salt and frost on concrete can cause the suface to scale off. The mix suggested is intended to eliminate this problem. Provided there is an adequate cement content in the mix and not too much water, the air-entraining agent produces minute air bubbles in the concrete which act like pressure relief valves. They accommodate the stress developed in the surface of typically

saturated concrete when the water in the top layer freezes and expands in the winter time. Without the bubbles the pressures developed push the surface off the concrete—with the bubbles the problem is largely eliminated. Although salt is seldom used on farm roads it is frequently carried on to farm concrete on the underside of vehicles leaving the public highway.

The workability of the concrete is also affected by the water content of course. If possible, a vibrating beam should be used to compact the concrete. In this case the medium workability concrete should have a slump of about 50 mm. If the concrete is to be hand tamped ask for a 75 mm or even a 100 mm slump. Because of the extra water required for this higher workability the frost protection offered by the air-entraining agent may be impaired.

Preparation
If concrete is being laid over existing roads or yards, first ensure that any local soft spots are dug out, filled with a granular material and properly compacted—in layers if necessary. The high spots should be skimmed off with a tractor bucket and the levels set out. It is always easier to add material to achieve the falls required than to dig out old well-compacted hardcore. For yards where total areas and the dimensions are likely to be large, falls of 1 in 120 are sufficient. For roads 1 in 80 as a minimum should be aimed for. Provision must be made for drainage at the edge or with gulleys.

For new areas of paving, as for floors, vegetation and topsoil will need to be removed. Enough soil must be taken out to make room for the sub-base thickness plus the concrete thickness. If possible the top surface of the low side of the concrete should finish just above the surrounding ground level. The sub-base material is then placed and compacted leaving it just below its required finished level (20 mm). It should be made at least 150 mm wider on all sides than the concrete, as the solid foundation it provides makes it easier to place and fix the forms.

Side forms
Steel forms are quicker and easier to set up, as well as producing a more accurate job, than pieces of wood. Steel forms can usually be hired

but are a good investment if a lot of concrete is to be laid. For yards, square-edged forms produce the best result but for small jobs wooden forms are quite satisfactory. Steel pins, which are driven in to hold the forms in position, are also easier and quicker to use than wooden pegs. The steel pins fit through special housings on the outside of the steel forms. The housings also have wedges to anchor the forms onto the pins.

It is quicker to set up the forms to the required falls onto a base which is just below its finished level than to set them up accurately onto a base which is just a fraction too high. Small pieces of plywood or hardboard under the joints between the forms can be used to prop them up to their required level. Then more sub-base material should be pushed under the form with a shovel to provide full support.

The forms should be set to line using a string line and then brought to level using either boning rods or one of the simple but very efficient surveyor's levels—a 'Cowley' level is ideal (see Chapter 5). Fill up to the bottoms of the forms with the remainder of the sub-base material, or blind with sand as necessary. This is then compacted with a vibrating roller or vibrating plate compactor. To prevent the concrete from sticking to the forms spray them with either diesel oil or a proprietary mould release agent or mould oil from builders' merchants.

Other Materials and Equipment

The following must be planned in advance:

Slip membranes Polythene sheet (60 μm) laid over the base prevents moisture being sucked out of the lower layers of the concrete by a dry sub-base and also prevents moisture moving up from the base into the concrete if the sub-base is saturated. It also allows the concrete to contract and expand more readily.

Joints Contraction joints will be needed at 5 m centres in unreinforced concrete and at perhaps 22 m centres in reinforced bays. Expansion joints may be needed in long roads too. These are only necessary every 90 m and are only likely to be needed in roads as distinct from yards. Refer to Chapter 13, pages 131 and 133, for the joint-forming procedure.

Method of compaction See Chapter 13 for details.

Texturing See Chapter 13 for details.

Curing See Chapter 13 for details.

Concreting

It must also be decided in advance what is the easiest way to get the concrete into position. If ready-mixed concrete is being supplied the truck itself can be used to advantage. Unless there is an alternative means of access this will necessitate starting work at a point which is farthest away from the farm gate or highway and working outwards towards the gate. The base should be firm enough to carry the truck so that the driver can reverse up between the forms, using the truck chute to full advantage.

If mixing is to be done on site, self-driven mixers, tractor buckets or even hired dumper trucks will be required. Wheelbarrows are only economic for very small quantities of concrete (1–2 cubic metres).

If access is very difficult then it may be necessary to use a concrete pump. These are costly to hire and can only be justified for large quantities of concrete—almost always ready-mixed concrete. Some suppliers of ready-mixed concrete have concrete conveyors mounted onto their trucks to transport concrete into areas where access for the truck itself is impossible. Local depots should be asked about this service.

At least two men, and preferably three, are needed in the concreting gang. They should be able to lay at least 80 square metres of ready-mixed concrete in a day and fix the forms for the next day's work, assuming all the base preparation is done.

For other details such as surcharge, placing reinforcement, compaction, texturing, joint forming, and curing see Chapter 13.

Laying concrete on slopes
Special precautions need to be taken when laying concrete on a steep gradient. The mix should be stiffer than normal to reduce flow, yet should still be workable enough to be placed without difficulty. This problem can be discussed with the concrete supplier.

Individual circumstances will determine

whether to start at the bottom of the slope and work uphill or vice versa. This is normally determined by the accessibility of the area to be laid. If it is decided to start at the top and work downhill the concrete will flow in that direction and the surcharge may be lost; concrete may need to be moved to the high end to make up any low spots. An excess of concrete at the lower end when the work is finished should be removed after tamping. There may also be a tendency for the concrete to break away even after tamping is finished on very steep slopes, and this will encourage cracking.

If working uphill the surcharge may have to be reduced or even eliminated altogether and concrete may have to be moved from the low end after the concrete has been compacted to be placed above the vibrating beam or hand tamper.

On very steep slopes polythene should not be used under the slab. It must be ensured that the base is damp and stable. It may be necessary to go back over the surface to correct faults. On completion a stiff broom can be used to give the texture or alternatively finish with the grooving tool illustrated in Chapter 13, Figure 13.9. The grooves should not be made directly across the

direction of the fall otherwise they will trap water. They should be formed at an angle to the main slope.

Opening to traffic
Generally speaking the concrete road should not be open to traffic less than fourteen days after the completion of all concreting work, but light vehicles such as private cars and Land-Rovers could be allowed to use the road after seven days. In cold weather the hardening period should be extended for as many days as the temperature has been below freezing point. If rapid-hardening cement or an accelerator have been used in the mix the interval between finishing and opening to traffic can be reduced by half.

CONCRETE BLOCK PAVING

Concrete block paving consists of brick-sized concrete units (Plate 17.5) which can be picked up and laid with one hand. These are laid dry in an interlocking pattern (Plate 17.6) bedded in sand between permanent edge strips. Mechanical vibration is used to bed the blocks firmly with

Plate 17.5 Concrete paving blocks.

Plate 17.6 Paving blocks are laid 'dry' in an interlocking pattern.

sand in the fine joints between them (Plate 17.7). The combination of edge restraint, interlocking pattern and friction in the sand-filled joints locks the individual units snugly in place and prevents movement under traffic. The only special equipment required is a vibrating plate.

Block paving can be laid for short or long spells during periods when there is no other farm work, and it can be used for traffic as soon as it has been laid and vibrated. It is instantly usable concrete.

It may be necessary to traffic the partly paved area. If this has been the case remove the first 1.2 m or so of blockwork which will have been pushed down into the sand and the sub-base, then laying can be continued at any time in the future.

Block paving is ideal for farmyards but because of the relatively high cost of providing edge restraint it would be less economic than ordinary concrete for narrow strips of concrete such as farm roads. It is ideal for replacing other types of paving which have deteriorated through heavy use or inadequate initial construction, because it is instantly usable.

Plate 17.7 Mechanical vibration is used to bed the blocks into the bed of sand.

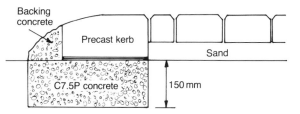

Figure 17.7 Precast kerbing as 'edge restraint' for paving blocks.

Materials Required

The sub-base will be laid as for a conventional road or yard and the material used will be as for other forms of construction. These have already been discussed.

The 'edge restraint' which must be provided all round the perimeter of the area to be laid in paving blocks must be established. If, in addition to buildings or the edges of existing concrete, either precast kerbing (Figure 17.7) or in-situ concrete (Plate 17.10) needs to be obtained arrangements must be made for the concrete to be provided. If the in-situ form of restraint is used then 200 mm long pieces of 12 mm diameter reinforcing bar will be needed to act as the dowels. These can be seen protruding from the surface of the footing concrete in Plate 17.6.

The blocks are laid on a screeded bed of sand, 65 mm thick. Hard, sharp sand is used for this course. It may be possible to use a screeding board resting on the kerb or existing concrete in some instances but normally temporary screeding rails will need to be provided. T-section metal strips are ideal for this purpose (Plate 17.8).

The final operation in the laying process is to sprinkle dry sand over the surface of the blocks and vibrate this down into the joints. The sharp sand can be used for this purpose as well.

Equipment

It is important to have the right vibrating plate for bedding the blocks; these can be hired from the larger plant-hire companies. The vibrator

Plate 17.8 T-section metal strips 'buried' in the sand used for screeding.

can also be used for compacting the concrete in the specially constructed edge restraint.

Ideally, for 80 mm thick blocks, the ones normally used in farmyards and paved areas, the vibrating plate should have a plate area of 0.25–0.5 square metres, a frequency of 75–100 Hz and a centrifugal force of 15–20 kN.

If there are large areas to construct it may also be worth hiring a block cutting machine (Plate 17.9). Small pieces of block are best chipped off with a bolster and hammer. These tools can also be used for cutting the blocks themselves although it is a time-consuming business unless it is mechanised.

For moving sand up to the laying face a hydraulically tipping tractor bucket is valuable and for moving blocks to the laying face from the stock pile a specially constructed tray which fits on to a sack barrow can be very useful. Blocks will normally be delivered by the manufacturer on pallets and a forklift to bring them up to the site is useful also.

Organising the Site

The block layer works from the surface he has

Plate 17.9 Cutting blocks to shape with a 'block-splitter'.

just laid and should be continually supplied with blocks so that he can always reach the next block to be laid without having to walk or stretch for it. Sand for the laying course is brought in from the other direction. It is bad practice to bring blocks across the sand and to take the laying course sand over the blocks which have just been laid to the area being screeded.

The minimum size of the laying team is two but three or four men can be kept busy, particularly if the laying pattern is organised so that two men can work on the face (see Figures 17.9 and 17.10).

Design

For areas close to the house which will take foot traffic and cars only, a 75 mm thick sub-base, a 65 mm thick course of sand and 60 or 65 mm thick blocks will be needed.

For areas which are to take normal farm traffic including the heaviest lorries the sub-base thickness should be at least 150 mm, the sand laying course 65 mm, but the block thickness should not be less than 80 mm.

Construction

The sub-base is prepared and compacted as for any other form of construction. It should be trimmed to the desired profile allowing for falls, etc. For the 80 mm thick blocks the surface of the sub-base should be 130 mm below the finished level of the paving. Any open textured areas should be blinded with sand to give a smooth, close-knit surface, using the plate vibrator to compact the area.

If no other form of edge restraint is available edge restraint should be prepared as illustrated in Plate 17.10.

The laying course of sand onto which the blocks will be bedded should be spread away from the starting point of block laying, starting from the edge restraint nearest the pile of blocks. The sand should be spread evenly with a rake between the edge restraints and screeded level with a straightedge. Where edges are bounded by walls or fences a temporary screeding rail should be used supported on piles of sand. When the main screeding is completed the temporary rail can be removed and the resulting groove filled with sand. For convenience, the

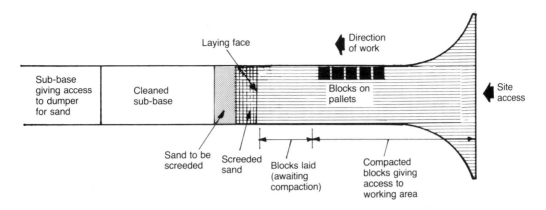

Figure 17.8 Organise the site for optimum performance.

sand should be spread and screeded about 2 m ahead of the block laying face at any one time. At no time during or after screeding must the sand be disturbed or walked on.

It is generally desirable to lay the blocks in a herringbone fashion as illustrated in Figures 17.9 and 17.10. To start with whole blocks should be used, laid against the edge restraint, fitting them snugly against each other. It is a good idea to run the barrow on planks when carrying supplies of blocks to the laying face. When a sufficiently large area of blocks has been laid complete the edges by cutting blocks to size and shape and fitting them into the spaces. Where edge footings with dowel pins have been prepared, blocks should not be laid closer than 175 mm from the line of pins. When 4 or 5 m of paving have been laid, they can be bedded into the sand with the plate vibrator. The blocks should be vibrated down to the required level;

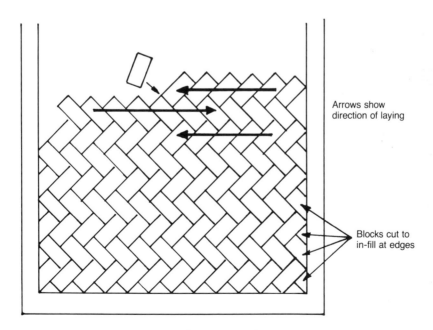

Figure 17.9 Herringbone pattern and method of laying for a one-man face.

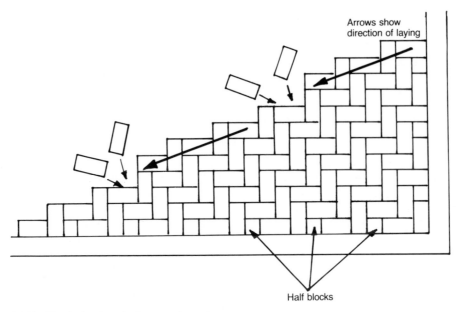

Figure 17.10   The laying face for two men to work on.

Plate 17.10   Compacting blocks and the in-situ edge restraint concrete at the same time.

this will normally take two or three passes of the vibrator covering the entire area with each pass so that the bed is even. The vibrator should be kept well back from the laying face—never closer than 1 m.

If the in-situ form of edging is being used carefully infill between formwork and the blocks with the mix specified on page 195 or a mix consisting of 1 bag of cement, 95 kg of sand and 175 kg of coarse aggregate. The mix should be on the dry side. If batching by volume, the proportions should be 3 parts cement, 4 parts damp sand and 7 parts coarse aggregate. The concrete should be tamped firmly into position and struck off to a level slightly proud of the blocks. The concrete is then compacted with a plate vibrator before or at the same time as the blocks are vibrated (see Plate 17.10).

To complete the bedding-in of the blocks, the sand is spread over the paving with a broom and a couple of further passes are made with the vibrator; one member of the team should constantly brush the sand in front of the vibrator as the work proceeds.

Opening to Traffic

Traffic can use the blocks as soon as the paving has been completed by vibrating the sand into the joints. If edge restraint has been constructed with either kerbs or in-situ concrete traffic must not cross these areas until the concrete has hardened properly—for at least seven days. If it is necessary for traffic to run over the uncompleted edges of the block paving area then the sand will need to be re-levelled, the first metre or so of blockwork removed and the edges relaid.

Removal and Reinstatement of Blocks

A major advantage of concrete block paving is that they can be removed and recovered for re-use in areas of local settlement or when services have been laid across the paved area. It may be necessary to break out three or four blocks in order to 'unzip' them but once these first few have been removed the remainder can be easily lifted. If services have to be installed or maintained the blocks can be lifted and reinstated afterwards.

The sides of the blocks will be encrusted with debris which must be removed before stacking the blocks for re-use. Unless the blocks are thoroughly cleaned it will not be possible to use them for reinstatement. After the blocks have been removed, the laying sand can be shovelled out and, if need be, stored for re-use.

When the sub-base has been reinstated or the services have been laid and the trench has been backfilled and fully compacted, the sand can be laid to level once again and the blocks replaced and vibrated into position.

Chapter 18

PITS AND TANKS

THIS CHAPTER is concerned with 'anything that is supposed to hold water'. There are numerous occasions on farms when there will be a need to build something to contain liquids—it may be a simple 300 mm footbath for cattle, or an even shallower one for the foot treatment of sheep, a rather deeper inspection pit in a workshop which needs to keep liquids out, or perhaps a full 3 m deep tank to contain silage effluent. In all cases it would be wise to attempt to make the pit, tank or channel as near watertight as possible, but current regulations for silos, slurry and dirty water stores and farm fuel stores make it an offence to cause pollution so leakage must be prevented whether from the inside outwards or vice versa.

Unless a prefabricated steel, glass fibre or glass-reinforced cement tank is to be used it is likely that building will be in concrete or possibly in masonry—blocks or bricks—in the least sensitive situations. To achieve a watertight concrete structure (that means one without cracks), it will almost always have to be reinforced.

The benefits obtained by including reinforcement have already been shown in the design and construction of silo walls and floors. In most pits and tanks the same benefits can be achieved, provided of course that sufficient steel of the right kind is used and is put in the right place.

Reinforcement

If an impermeable structure is to be constructed it will need to have been designed by a qualified person to comply with BS8007 code of practice for design of concrete structures for retaining aqueous liquids. In this chapter we have therefore confined our comments to principles and not made precise design recommendations. In all such cases, for example, it is easier to deal with reinforcing mesh than to have to fix a large number of individual reinforcing rods. For a foot treatment bath for instance (Figure 18.1) reinforced, in-situ concrete walls 11.2 m long would be the safest way to make a crack-free wall.

Figure 18.2 shows the number of sheets of mesh and the number and position of starter bars required. The 900 mm long bars should be pushed into the base for the wall as it is cast. The fine sand and cement should be brushed away from the top of the foundation concrete after compaction and then left to harden. Hang reinforcing mesh from these bars the next day and, having oiled the formwork, erect it on the concrete base. Standard, proprietary, formwork panels (Plate 18.1) will be suitable. The finished wall should be crack free.

The floor also needs to be reinforced in one long strip to prevent cracks. Ideally it should also have a sealed groove at the wall/floor junction on either side of the floor and a waterstop incorporated in the construction joint. A typical joint of this type is illustrated in Figure 13.8, p. 137.

Is this all necessary? For a footbath in the middle of a farm building complex, 100 m away from the stream, almost certainly it is not really necessary but these are the principles of construction for all below-ground, leak-free pits and tanks. If the principles outlined in this simple 'tank' are followed then such structures can be made in a similar way.

Figure 18.3 illustrates a design for a cattle foot wash bath. If the length is increased to 6.85 m the steel mesh only needs to be cut once.

The necessary design data must be known of course. For these narrow footbaths the loads are modest. For a silage effluent tank it is a very different matter—liquid is pushing the walls outwards when the tank is full and soil is pushing the walls inwards when the tank is empty. Both must be considered in the design of the wall if it is to remain crack free.

204

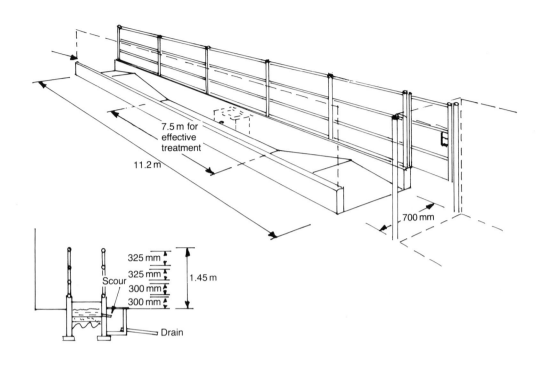

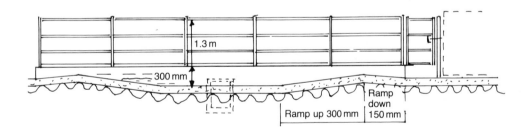

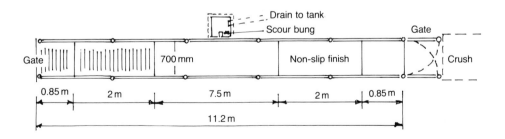

Figure 18.1 Foot treatment bath.

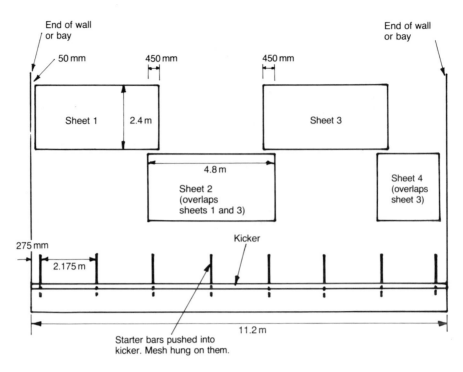

Figure 18.2 Layout of starter bars and mesh for reinforced walls and floors of pits and tanks.

Plate 18.1   Standard formwork panels.

This is the job of a civil or structural engineer or other qualified person and his advice or standard designs must be followed.

Excavation

For pits and tanks always excavate enough—initially. There may be a few isolated cases in clay soils where the excavated face of the hole can be used as the back shutter for concrete. In these circumstances it will be necessary to excavate to a precise dimension and trim manually. In most other cases however, space will be needed to work in the bottom of the excavation to set up forms, to apply waterproofing or protective coatings, or even to lay drains. It is easy to backfill either with gravel or spoil and to compact. Working in very confined spaces is tiresome and slow.

Before starting to dig ensure that the soil structure below the topsoil is known; for example, the likelihood of hitting rock. If this occurs it may pay to make a small sump and pump up to an above-ground holding tank or to lift the whole structure out of the ground. Trial pits will indicate what to expect.

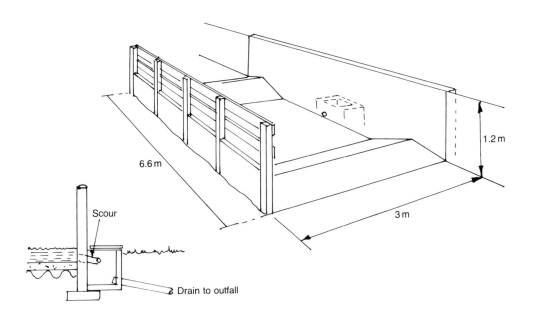

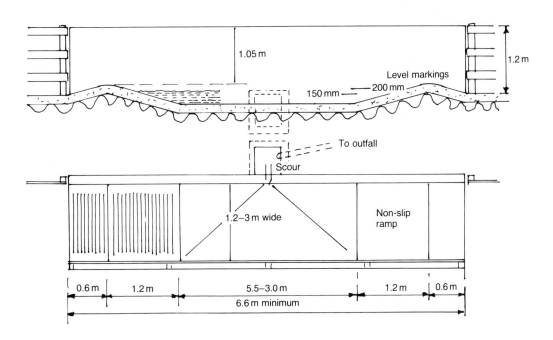

Figure 18.3   Cattle foot wash bath.

Table 18.1 Quantities and characteristics of slurry produced by livestock

Type of livestock	Body weight kg	Moisture content of excreta %	Volume of slurry litres per day	
			Range	Mean
1 dairy cow	450–560	87	32–54	41.0
1 beef bullock	200–450	90	19–28	27.0
1 dry sow	90–120	90	6.5–10	8.0
1 lactating sow + litter	90–120	90	9–14	12.0
1 pig—dry meal fed	45–75	90	3.5–6.5	4.0
1 pig—liquid fed (water:meal ratio, 2.5:1)	45–75	90	3.5–6.5	4.0
1 pig—liquid fed (water:meal ratio, 4:1)	45–75	94	5.5–10.0	7.0
1 pig—whey fed	45–75	98	9.0–15.0	14.0
1000 laying hens	2000	75	100–140	114.0
1000 broilers	2000	75	56–63	59.0
1 fattening lamb	45	89	1.8–2.4	2.2
1 sheep mature	60–80	89	3.4–5.0	4.0

An encounter with 'running sand' can be almost as expensive to deal with as rock! Strutting of the excavation is the least precaution to be taken in this case.

Dealing with the spoil can be a problem. Carting it away is expensive. It is best to try to spread it locally if possible. Some of it may be needed for backfill anyway so this should be given careful thought.

Sizes

The sizes of the channels and tanks that may be needed for the whole range of materials and enterprises will not be detailed here.

The effect of rainwater on the quantity of material to be stored should not be forgotten; 10 mm of rain falling on 10 m² of concrete will give 100 litres of water (0.1 m³). In some situations, for example an open silo or a midden, this is 'foul' water, capable of pollution and will need to be stored and spread rather than drained off.

Construction

Watertight joints between walls and floors in shallow channels, pits or tanks (1.0 m deep) can be formed in concrete by washing and brushing away laitance from the line of the wall/floor joint. For a depth in excess of this a waterstop may need to be used (Plate 18.2) and masonry

construction only is unsuitable—some forms of wall combine brick or blocks with in-situ concrete (Figure 18.4).*

In general terms blockwork and brickwork must not be expected to be completely watertight without added protection. The walls can be 'tanked' with asphalt, perhaps a polythene sheet or bituminous paint—a minimum of three coats—but mortar in itself is slightly permeable, as indeed are concrete blocks.

In effluent channels beneath slats in pig buildings, for instance, it has been unusual to include either reinforcement or joints, so inevitably the wall and the floor have cracks in them. These cracks seldom caused major prob-

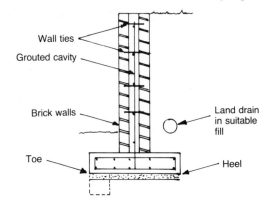

Figure 18.4 'Cavity' brickwork with concrete in-fill to form a reinforced wall.

*HASELTINE, B. A. and LUTT, J. N., 'Brickwork Retaining Walls', Brickwork Development Association, February 1979.

Plate 18.2   A water bar being used in a wall/floor joint in a grouted blockwork wall. A second inner leaf has yet to be built.

Plate 18.3   Prefabricated metal grain pit with concrete surround. (*Courtesy of P. Turney Ltd*).

lems because they became sealed with the fine organic material in the slurry if it began to seep through them.

However, with the introduction of new legislation in the 1991 Pollution Control Regulations (slurry, silage and farm fuel oil), it would be wise to include reinforcement either in proprietary form or as 6 mm mild steel bars in the joints, and to form dowelled and sealed movement joints in the walls and sealed joints in the floors of these channels. The methods of forming these have already been discussed in Chapters 11 and 13.

In most cases a 150 mm thick floor, with or without reinforcement, will be adequate. An ST5 mix can be used for all but the 'aggressive' substances. An RC45 mix is the minimum quality to use where silage effluent is in contact with the concrete.

It is strongly recommended that silage effluent is not pumped into or allowed to enter slurry channels or tanks as poisonous gases can be produced by the intermixing of these two materials.

Prefabricated Pits and Tanks

Grain intake and elevator pits

It is feasible to construct an in-situ concrete pit for these purposes using well compacted, high cement content, low water content, mixes with reinforcement. However, in the majority of cases a prefabricated steel tank is set into the ground for this purpose (Plate 18.3). It must be ensured that the tank is painted externally with bituminous paint before it is put into position and also that it has been provided with adequate holding-down provision. The hole will need to be backfilled with concrete, 'pokered' into position after the tank has been accurately located and levelled. This operation in itself or, subsequently, a high ground water level, can lift the tank out of the ground if adequate provision for holding it down has not been made.

Sheep dips and septic tanks

Glass fibre and glass reinforced cement tanks are now commonly used in these applications. Again it must be ensured that the hole excavated is large enough—do not economise. A layer of concrete should be placed under the tank. Level it and again ensure that the hole around the tank is backfilled with concrete pokered in behind the tank (Plate 18.4).

Proprietary Tanks for Silage and Other Effluents

Under the 1991 Control of Pollution Regulations there are several stringent requirements for effluent tanks, and foremost is the requirement that they are impermeable. Being factory made in one piece, proprietary tanks can be pressure tested before despatch which removes the joint sealing problems associated with precast and in situ concrete designs. It is also explicit that a below ground effluent tank should last for at least 20 years without any maintenance.

This clause recognises the extreme polluting and corrosive power of silage effluent together with the impracticality of attempting maintenance of such a tank. Because of various gasses produced it would be very dangerous to enter the tank without full breathing apparatus—seldom practical.

Types of tank

Proprietary 'one piece' tanks are commonly manufactured in glass reinforced plastic (GRP) with 'specials' for silage effluent with an acid resistant resin gel coat to the inside. Other materials include glass reinforced cement (GRC) and rotationally moulded medium density polyethylene. The regulations will allow steel and stainless steel (ex food processing industry) tanks to be used, even for silage effluent. A mild steel tank would corrode quickly

Plate 18.4   Prefabricated glass reinforced cement tank being let into excavated hole.

and therefore it would need to have a very heavy wall section to last 20 years, or to be internally lined or coated in some way. An engineer's report regarding the suitability of such a tank is likely to be necessary.

Steel and stainless steel tanks would be most applicable in above ground situations where for various reasons it was not possible to excavate for a GRP tank and the effluent was pumped from a small collection sump. Any low level outlets to such tanks must have two lockable valves or plugs in series.

If purchasing a proprietary tank for silage effluent a guarantee that it will last for 20 years should be sought from the manufacturer.

The size of the tank is based on the nominal volume of the silo at a rate of 20 litres per cubic metre of capacity. For larger silos above 1500 m³ the required rate drops to 6.7 litres per m³ recognising that the silo is unlikely to be completely filled at once.

Tank installation
The following comments apply particularly to GRP tanks, but are broadly applicable to any one piece tank.

GRP silage effluent tanks are available in the classic onion shape up to a capacity of 12,000 litres. Many silos will require larger capacity cylindrical tanks which are all about 2.75 m in diameter and up to 15 m long (Plate 18.5). The largest sizes are about 80,000 litres but it is possible to couple one or more tanks together.

It is necessary to excavate a hole to the nominal size of the tank plus 200 to 250 mm all round allowing for backfill material. The depth is the sum of tank diameter, invert/shaft length and an allowance for 200 to 250 mm concrete bedding; normally about 4 m in total. This is to the maximum effective depth that a wheeled digger can reach unless equipped with an extending dipper. In some circumstances a larger, more expensive 360 degree machine may be necessary. Few farmers will be knowledgeable about their ground conditions at such depths and rock, running sand and a high water table are likely to make installation very difficult. With a one piece tank there is little opportunity to compromise on depth of installation unlike a shuttered concrete tank perhaps.

In good stable ground conditions excava-

Plate 18.5   An 18,000 litre GRP silage effluent tank awaiting installation.

tion and installation may only take a few hours and it will be unnecessary for men to enter the excavation. This has important Health and Safety implications because an excavation of this depth would normally require full planking and strutting to the banks. If poor conditions are encountered, and even a minor cave-in can be serious if the excavator cannot reach back and clear it, then men may have to enter the excavation. Because any temporary support and strutting to the banks would prevent lowering in the tank the only other safe option is to batter the banks considerably and this will be 45 degrees as an absolute minimum requirement in some circumstances. Apart from considerable extra excavation there is extra expense with backfill material.

The proprietary manufacturers are meticulous in providing instructions for the installation of their tanks. Many of the points are common sense for what is a very fragile structure and will not be listed here. For most installations 200 to 250 mm of workable concrete is placed in the bottom of the excavation, the tank lowered into place, puddled into the wet concrete and set upright. Check the invert level if the tolerance is close. Immediately fill the tank with 500 mm of water to prevent movement and then proceed to backfill with concrete up to at least one third height. The water level in the tank must be kept 500 mm above the surrounding concrete or the tank will float which is a disaster. A workable concrete mix is desirable so that it will readily flow down under the tank because use of a vibrating poker may cause collapse of the tank.

With long, large capacity tanks longitudinal stress must be minimised and in this instance a bed of 100 to 130 mm of concrete is pre-laid to allow the tank to be accurately placed and supported before backfilling with concrete as above. Once the concrete is placed to one-third height in dry, well-drained ground the remaining backfill may simply be of pea gravel or other fine granular material. If the ground is not well drained the instructions will ask that the manufacturer's advice be sought. The manufacturer will then probably request that all the backfill is of concrete to resist the possibility of flotation; this is easy to place but expensive.

Taking a worst case situation and ignoring its self weight an 18,000 litre tank could exhibit an upward force of 18 tonnes in saturated

ground. The problem of flotation accompanies the installation of any below ground vessel. Concrete designs have an advantage in their greater self weight and the prospect of being able to extend the base concrete out into the surrounding subsoil to help anchor it. Unlike other aspects of life, there is no economy of scale when these problems have to be considered because the engineering difficulties tend to increase with increased size of tank. It may be better to install two or more smaller ones.

Concrete fill will give fair protection to a GRP tank should farm traffic stray over it in subsequent years, particularly the slurry tanker used to empty it. It is the writer's opinion that full concrete backfill will be advisable in most situations because such tanks are easily damaged before, during and after installation. For any routinely applied loading above the tank a reinforced concrete slab should be constructed spanning on to undisturbed ground.

Slurry Tanks

Precast concrete segmental tanks (Plate 18.6), large diameter concrete pipes up to 2.4 m in diameter, rectangular precast concrete box culvert sections and many other proprietary units are available for forming below-ground slurry tanks. Special care will need to be taken over jointing these units—particularly the wall/floor junctions—if a watertight structure is to be achieved. The manufacturer's instructions should be followed carefully.

For larger storage a butyl lined lagoon may well be the answer (Plate 18.7).

Lagoons

Slurry lagoons have always been the cheapest and easiest form of slurry containment. Merely dig a hole and push the slurry in. The fact that lagoons are not universally used stems from the considerable difficulty and sometimes expense in emptying them. In earlier days lagoons were often emptied using a dragline or large excavator working from the banks. Many lagoons now have a concrete floor and access ramp to enable normal farm machinery to cope with the annual emptying event. Others have been filled in.

Plate 18.6　Precast concrete sections being assembled for a slurry tank. (Whites Concrete Ltd)

Plate 18.7　Butyl sheet lining a slurry lagoon.

With the current legislative requirement to hold up to 4 months slurry and dirty water in storage unless a safe disposal option can be demonstrated, there is likely to be renewed interest in lagoons, at least for dirty water.

Unfortunately a slurry lagoon is no longer such a simple container to construct because the first and foremost requirement of the Control of Pollution Regulations is that it should be impermeable. That in turn suggests that an unlined lagoon can only be built on an impermeable clay base with impermeable clay banks. The impermeability the NRA may require is expressed as 10^{-9} m/sec which is the equivalent of about 1 mm in 12 days, or 1 m in 32 years. This is similar to the impermeability required for a landfill site. The clay content of any given subsoil needs to be in the range of 20 to 30% of volume. Lower than 20% the soil is likely to be permeable and above 30% will be difficult to compact and may shrink and crack upon drying, causing leaks.

Clay balance

Most lagoons will be 2.5 to 3 m deep with banks battered both sides to a gradient of about 1 in 2½ and a minimum width at the top of the bank of 2.5 to 3 m. It is important at an early stage to conduct a clay balance and ensure that, once the top soil is pushed away, the yield of clay from the proposed excavation is of sufficient volume to construct the banks. The requirement for 750 mm freeboard adds significantly to this volume. In some situations it may be worthwhile importing extra material from another site. Designs are possible whereby the central core to the bank is of impermeable material and backed up with permeable soil which makes for economic use of available clay.

Compaction

Proper compaction of material to the banks of any lagoon is paramount to its success. Material should be placed in layers 150 to 200 mm thick and compacted with a sheeps foot or vibrating roller; moisture content of the clay dictating which is the best machine to use. The compaction requirement and number of passes with the roller is similar to road industry standards.

An engineer

The above is just a glimpse of the important aspects of lagoon construction and at the time of writing it is hard to assimilate exactly what the NRA will require. Nevertheless the pollution caused by the failure of a large lagoon would be very serious and the design requirements are certain to be more stringent. A suitably qualified engineer is likely to be required to carry out a site investigation, assess the physical properties and impermeability of the soil and monitor the construction process so that he can certificate its compliance with the regulations upon completion. A far more detailed and time consuming operation than hitherto.

Lined lagoons (Plate 18.7)

In situations where permeable subsoils exist it is necessary to use some form of impermeable liner. In many respects the lagoon is constructed as above and lined with an impermeable imported clay layer such as bentonite or more usually lined with plastic or synthetic rubber sheet materials. The installation of sheet liners is usually carried out by, or under the supervision of, the suppliers, and specialist solvent or welding techniques are used to join the sheets together. The NRA will not necessarily be enthusiastic about a lined lagoon where the subsoil is very permeable because a sheet liner can be easily damaged and the resultant pollution may be undetected until a serious incident occurs. In such a situation a leakage detection system might be required whereby a drainage system is installed under the liner and connected to a monitoring point so that any failure of the liner is quickly found. Two separate sheet liners, one above the other, with a similar leakage detection system installed between them would be a safe but expensive option. These liners are usually tough enough to withstand a small tractor and rubber scraper to operate and clear out any residual sludge. Thicker slurry will be very difficult to remove without damage to the liner and their use for unseparated slurry probably inappropriate.

Safety fence

A stockproof and childproof fence is essential, consisting of wire netting with two strands of barbed wire above constructed to at least 1.3 m high. A form of escape from a lagoon is also advisable, which in its simplest form may consist of a few old tyres linked together to form an escape ladder.

List of Useful Organisations

East of Scotland College of Agriculture
Farm Buildings Unit
SCAE
Bush Estate
Penicuik
Midlothian EH26 0PH

North of Scotland College of Agriculture
Farm Buildings Department
Craibstone
Bucksburn
Aberdeen AB2 9TS

West of Scotland College of Agriculture
Farm Buildings Department
Auchincruive
Ayr KA6 5HW

British Cement Association
Century House
Telford Avenue
Crowthorne
Berks RG45 6YS

Ministry of Agriculture, Fisheries & Food
(MAFF)
Whitehall Place
London SW1A 2HH

Scottish Office
Agriculture and Fisheries Department
Pentland House
47 Robbs Loan
Edinburgh EH14 1TW

Department of Agriculture for Northern Ireland
Dundonald House
Upper Newtownards Road
Belfast BT4 4SB

Welsh Office
Department of Agriculture
Park Avenue
Aberystwyth
Dyfed SY23 1PQ

Centre for Rural Building
Craibstone
Bucksburn
Aberdeen AB2 9TS

Timber Research and Development Association
(TRADA)
Hughenden Valley
High Wycombe
Buckinghamshire HP14 4ND

Brick Development Association
Woodside House
Winkfield
Berkshire SL4 2DX

Farm Energy Centre
National Agricultural Centre
Stoneleigh
Kenilworth
Warwickshire

ADAS Headquarters
Oxford Spires Business Park
The Boulevard
Kidlington
Oxford OX5 1NZ

APPENDIX

Cattle: Floor area for cattle on solid floors

Weight of animal	Bedded area (excluding troughs)		Loafing/feeding area (excluding troughs)		Total area per head	
	Dairy	Beef	Dairy	Beef	Dairy	Beef
kg	m²	m²	m²	m²	m²	m²
200	2.00	2.00	1.0	1.0	3.00	3.00
300	2.75	2.40	1.2	1.0	3.95	3.40
400	3.50	2.60	1.4	1.2	4.90	3.80
500	4.25	3.00	1.6	1.2	5.85	4.20
600	5.00	3.40	1.8	1.2	6.80	4.60
700	5.75	3.60	2.0	1.4	7.75	5.00
800	6.50		2.2		8.70	

Cattle: Floor area for beef cattle* on fully slatted floors

Weight of animal	Area per head (excluding trough)
kg	m²
200	1.1
300	1.5
400	1.8
500	2.1
600	2.3
700	2.5

* Dairy cows should not be kept on fully slatted floors

Cattle: Width of feed face (trough length) for simultaneously feeding

Weight of animal	Width of feed face
kg	mm
200	400
300	500
400	550
500	600
600	650
700	700
800	700

In ad lib systems these widths may be reduced by 75%. Leave at least 1 m behind feeding animals for other animals to pass.

Pigs: Minimum floor areas for pigs loose housed in groups

| Weight of animal | Minimum area per pig (do not exceed by more than 25%) | | Total area |
| | Sleeping | Dunging | |
kg	m²	m²	m²
Up to 20	0.15	0.05	0.20
60	0.35	0.15	0.50
80	0.45	0.25	0.70
100	0.50	0.35	0.85

Pigs: Minimum trough length per pig for simultaneous feeding

| Weight of animal | Trough length |
kg	mm
Under 30	175
30 to 55	225
55 to 100	300

INDEX

218

FARMING PRESS BOOKS

Below is a sample of the wide range of agricultural and
veterinary books published by Farming Press.
For more information or for a free illustrated book list please contact:

Farming Press Books, Wharfedale Road
Ipswich IP1 4LG, United Kingdom
Telephone (01473) 241122

Farm Machinery BRIAN BELL

Gives a sound introduction to a wide
range of tractors and farm equipment.
Now revised, enlarged and incorporating
over 150 photographs.

Machinery for Horticulture
BRIAN BELL & STEWART COUSINS

A description of the basic functions and
uses of the diverse machinery used in all
aspects of horticulture.

Farm Woodland Management
BLYTH, EVANS, MUTCH & SIDWELL

Covers the full range of woodland size
from hedgerow to plantation with the
emphasis on economic benefits allied to
conservation.

Farm Workshop BRIAN BELL

A guide to establishing and running a
workshop, from planning the building and
selecting tools and materials to details of
workshop techniques.

Farm Office
MICHAEL HOSKEN & DOUGLAS BROWN

All aspects of farm office work from
choosing a filing cabinet to preparing
annual accounts.

Practical Accounting for Farm & Rural Business BEN BROWN

Covers the full range of accounting needs
from data collection through profit and
loss to analysis of results.

Farm Welding ANDREW PEARCE

A large-format, highly illustrated manual
for the workshop operative. Includes a
practical guide to MIG/MAG welding, arc
welding, gas welding/cutting and
soldering.

Farming and the Countryside
ERIC CARTER & MIKE SOPER

Traces the middle ground where farming
and conservation meet in cooperation
rather than confrontation.

Farming Press Books is part of the Morgan-Grampian
Farming Press Group which publishes a range of farming magazines:
Arable Farming, Dairy Farmer, Farming News,
Pig Farming, What's New in Farming.
For a specimen copy of any of these please contact the address above.